The Independence
of South Sudan

Studies in International Governance Series

Studies in International Governance is a research and policy analysis series that provides timely consideration of emerging trends and current challenges in the broad field of international governance. Representing diverse perspectives on important global issues, the series will be of interest to students and academics while serving also as a reference tool for policy-makers and experts engaged in policy discussion.

For more information, please contact:

Lisa Quinn
Acquisitions Editor
Wilfrid Laurier University Press
75 University Avenue West
Waterloo, ON N2L 3C5
Canada
Phone: 519-884-0710 ext. 2843
Fax: 519-725-1399
Email: quinn@press.wlu.ca

Walter C. Soderlund and E. Donald Briggs

The Independence of South Sudan

The Role of Mass Media in the Responsibility to Prevent

WILFRID LAURIER
UNIVERSITY PRESS

This book has been published with the help of a grant from the Canadian Federation for the Humanities and Social Sciences, through the Awards to Scholarly Publications Program, using funds provided by the Social Sciences and Humanities Research Council of Canada. Wilfrid Laurier University Press acknowledges the financial support of the Government of Canada through the Canada Book Fund for its publishing activities.

Library and Archives Canada Cataloguing in Publication

Soderlund, W. C. (Walter C.), author

    The independence of South Sudan : the role of mass media in the responsibility to prevent / Walter C. Soderlund and E. Donald Briggs.

(Studies in international governance)
Includes bibliographical references and index.
Issued in print and electronic formats.
ISBN 978-1-77112-117-0 (pbk.).—ISBN 978-1-77112-083-8 (pdf).—
ISBN 978-1-77112-084-5 (epub)

1. Mass media—Moral and ethical aspects—South Sudan. 2. Mass media—Social aspects—South Sudan. 3. South Sudan—History—Autonomy and independence movements—Press coverage—United States. 4. South Sudan—History—Autonomy and independence movements—Press coverage—Canada. 5. South Sudan—History—21st century. 6. Humanitarian intervention. 7. Mass media—United States. 8. Mass media—Canada. I. Briggs, E. Donald, author II. Title. III. Series: Studies in international governance

DT159.94.S63 2014   962.905'1   C2014-904145-4
                                                                                         C2014-904146-2

Cover design by Martyn Schmoll. Front cover image by Sven Torfinn/Panos. Text design by Angela Booth Malleau.

© 2014 Wilfrid Laurier University Press
Waterloo, Ontario, Canada
www.wlupress.wlu.ca

Every reasonable effort has been made to acquire permission for copyright material used in this text, and to acknowledge all such indebtedness accurately. Any errors and omissions called to the publisher's attention will be corrected in future printings.

No part of this publication may be reproduced, stored in a retrieval system, or transmitted, in any form or by any means, without the prior written consent of the publisher or a licence from the Canadian Copyright Licensing Agency (Access Copyright). For an Access Copyright licence, visit http://www.access copyright.ca or call toll free to 1-800-893-5777.

CONTENTS

	List of Maps and Tables	vii
	Preface and Acknowledgements	ix
Chapter 1	Sudan's North–South Divide	1
Chapter 2	International Intervention | From *Peacekeeping* to *Humanitarian Intervention* to the *Responsibility to Protect*	13
Chapter 3	The Responsibility to Prevent | Problems of Identification and Implementation	19
Chapter 4	Influencing Public Opinion and Foreign Policy Decision Making | The Role of Mass Media	43
Chapter 5	North American Press Coverage of the 2010 Sudanese Elections	53
Chapter 6	North American Press Coverage of the 2011 Referendum	65
Chapter 7	North American Press Coverage of the Declaration of Independence by the Republic of South Sudan	85
Chapter 8	Assessing the Effectiveness of the *Responsibility to Prevent* | The Impact of Press Framing on Policy Choices	107
Postscript	Developments since Independence	117
	Notes	127
	References	137
	The Authors	155
	Index	157

LIST OF MAPS AND TABLES

	Map of Africa	xiv
	Map of Sudan	xv
	Map of South Sudan	xvi
Table 8.1	South Sudan Coverage, by Newspaper	108
Table 8.2	South Sudan Coverage, by Type of Content	110

PREFACE AND ACKNOWLEDGEMENTS

Over the past half century southern Sudan has been one of the most conflict-prone areas of the world, having been embroiled in two civil wars lasting nearly forty years—the first from 1955 to 1972, and the second from 1983 to 2005. Estimates of deaths attributed to the latter alone stand at between two and two-and-a-half million, with an additional four million reported displaced from their homes. In assessing the severity of the situation, Sudan's heavy-handed response to the Darfur crisis and the consequent indictment of Sudanese President Omar al-Bashir by the International Criminal Court on charges of war crimes and genocide should also be borne in mind.

A Comprehensive Peace Agreement (CPA) ended the second civil war in 2005. That agreement provided for a referendum to be held in the south in 2011 to determine the region's future status vis-à-vis the north. One of the options in the referendum was independence for the region, which turned out to be the nearly unanimous choice (close to 99 percent) of those voting in January 2011. This result had been widely expected, as had large-scale violence to follow. Francis Deng, a prominent Sudanese diplomat and scholar, forecast over a decade ago that "self-determination for the South has been recognized as *a right that cannot be denied, wherever it leads*" (2002, 85; italics added), and, as the date of the referendum neared, US National Security Director Admiral Dennis Blair observed that "of all the countries at risk of experiencing a widespread massacre in the next five years, '*a new mass killing or genocide is most likely to occur in southern Sudan*'" (quoted in Sheridan, 2010a; italics added). It would have been difficult to find anyone who quarrelled with that assessment.

The relatively simple question that motivated this study, therefore, was what efforts were made by the international community to implement the "responsibility to prevent" doctrine identified by the 2001 report of the International Commission on Intervention and State Sovereignty (ICISS) as the first and best method of controlling serious conflict? The idea of prevention, along with the other components of the ICISS's *Responsibility to Protect* (that is, to react to failure to protect people at large, and to rebuild following serious conflict) appears at best to be a work in progress, as events in Libya, Mali, and perhaps Syria most of all, demonstrate. In other words, there is little consensus to date as to where and how these ambitious principles should govern state behaviour, or, as Frank Chalk and associates (2010) put it, there is obvious inconsistency in the *Will to Intervene* in serious conflict situations on humanitarian grounds. For those very reasons, examining the issue in the context of a case in which widespread bloodshed was thought to be virtually certain is important in terms of the development of international norms.

The specific focus of this study is the role the mass media played in interpreting and advocating the newly proclaimed (2005) prevention obligation. Precisely how much influence media have with respect to foreign policy decision making is still a matter of debate among communication and political scholars, but it seems clear that it lies somewhere between the determinism alleged by the "CNN Effect" (see Cohen 1994) and the dismissiveness of the suggestion that media outlets are primarily mouthpieces for governments. The study is therefore based on the assumption that mass media have a definite, if imprecise and varying, impact on all aspects of political life, including international relations. In the view of the authors, repetitive, ongoing media coverage (agenda setting), and the way in which critical events are explained in that coverage (framing), go a long way toward revealing why not all humanitarian crises are treated equally (see Soderlund et al. 2008)

Certainly both the volume of media attention that international crises receive and the opinions of the adequacy of whatever coverage occurs differ considerably. With respect to the Darfur conflict which began in 2003, for example, there is disagreement about both the extent and effect of media treatment (see Thompson 2007; Grzyb 2009; Sidahmed, Soderlund, and Briggs 2010; Hamilton 2011a), but there is virtual unanimity that the civil wars between north and south Sudan were severely under-reported by Western media (Livingston and Eachus 1995; Minear, Scott, and Weiss 1996; Livingston 1997; Soderlund et al. 2008; Prunier 2009). Both these cases involved the actual, ongoing, large-scale destruction of human life. How was the mere possibility of such an occurrence to be treated by media, bearing in mind that the Responsibility to Prevent became a recognized norm only in 2005, too late to impact either Sudan's civil wars or Darfur? It is hoped that what follows will shed some light on that question.

In summary, the book sets out to accomplish a number of major objectives:

1. To explain the background and complexity of the violence-prone relationship between Sudan and South Sudan (Chapter 1).

2. To trace the development of the norms of international intervention in areas of domestic conflict down to the imperatives enunciated by the *Responsibility to Protect* (Chapter 2).
3. To review approaches aimed at identifying situations calling for preventive measures and to assess the relative effectiveness of major strategies of conflict prevention, both long-term (development aid, capacity building, and trust and confidence building) and short-term (diplomatic efforts and the rapid deployment of peacekeeping forces to stabilize a developing crisis), when applied to dysfunctional societies and failed states (Chapter 3).
4. To review *agenda setting* (the transfer of "issue salience" from mass media to mass publics) and especially *framing effects* (media influence on how events are interpreted by mass publics) with respect to their relevance to the process which culminated in South Sudan's independence (Chapter 4).
5. To study US and Canadian mainstream press coverage of three key events in South Sudan's path to independence: the April 2010 country-wide elections, the January 2011 referendum in the south, and the July 2011 final declaration of independence. Reportage will be examined with respect to the identification of potential violence-producing problems and the framing of these in ways that might mobilize public opinion to support prevention efforts or other more forceful international interventions (Chapters 5–7).
6. To evaluate South Sudan's independence process in terms of the interaction between press coverage and international (especially US) diplomatic efforts to avoid a humanitarian disaster (Chapter 8).
7. To reflect on what constitutes "success" and provide readers with an account of the problems that faced the new state and region in the four-year period following independence (Postscript).

This book had its origins in the authors' collaboration on *Humanitarian Crises and Intervention* (2008), which compared the impact of mass media coverage of international intervention in ten humanitarian crises of the 1990s, including a chapter on the Sudan's Second Civil War. The idea of the project was reinforced by a second collaborative effort, *The Responsibility to Protect in Darfur* (2010), with Abdel Salam Sidahmed (updated and printed as a paperback in 2012), which noted important connections between Darfur and the Second Sudanese Civil War, some of which have reappeared in the contested area of Abyei and in the Nuba Mountains region. As the crucial referendum approached, therefore, we felt compelled to turn our attention to it.

We began work on the project in the spring of 2010 by studying the April elections that returned President Omar al-Bashir to power, and followed that up with a study of the January 2011 referendum, before completing it with a study of the potentially deal-breaking violence leading up to and including the declaration of South Sudan's independence in July 2011. During that period three conference papers were presented: "The South Sudan Referendum, Round #1: North American Press Coverage of the 2010 Sudanese Election" (Canadian Political Science Association, May 2011); "Framing the *Responsibility to Prevent*: North American Press Coverage of the South Sudan Referendum" (Canadian Communications Association, June 2012); and "The Responsibility to Prevent: From Identification to Implementation" (Canadian Political Science Association, July 2013). Comments of discussants, fellow panelists, and audience members helped to identify arguments in need of clarification.

Books do not, of course, appear without significant help from many whose names do not appear on the cover. In this case our thanks go in particular to Abdel Salam Sidahmed, who initially was slated to be co-author of the book. He contributed his expertise to the design of the project, but in 2012 he was asked by the UN Office of the High Commissioner for Human Rights to establish a country office in the Republic of Yemen to promote and protect human rights during that country's transition to democracy. As this required his full attention, he was unable to contribute further, but we are heavily indebted to him for the enlightenment he has provided over the years with respect to Sudanese history and politics in particular.

We also wish to thank our graduate research assistant, Kiran Phull, who on a number of key occasions used her considerable Internet skills to move the project along. As always, the University of Windsor was very supportive of our work. Thanks go specifically to Vice-President for Research Ranjana Bird; Dean of the Faculty of Arts and Social Science Cecil Houston; and Head of the Department of Political Science Tom Najem, all of whom held these positions during the time the book was being researched and written. In the fall of 2011 Professor Soderlund taught a graduate seminar on crisis intervention in Africa, in which some material appearing in the book was discussed, leading to useful clarification of concepts and arguments. The United Nations Map Library receives our thanks for the use of their maps of Africa, Sudan, and South Sudan as does the Aid to Scholarly Publications Program for the grant to Wilfrid Laurier University Press that made possible the book's publication.

At the Wilfrid Laurier University Press we are indebted to Ryan Chynces for encouraging us to pursue this project, and to Lisa Quinn, Blaire Comacchio, Leslie Macredie, and Rob Kohlmeier for ultimately managing the never easy process of getting a book into print. Craig Hincks did a superlative job of copy-editing the manuscript. Sergey Lobachev compiled the index.

Also deserving of our thanks are two conscientious reviewers of the manuscript who offered a number of very useful suggestions for revision, virtually all of which we adopted. Needless to say, whatever errors or imperfections remain in the work are clearly our responsibility.

Walter C. Soderlund
E. Donald Briggs
Windsor, Ontario
26 May 2014

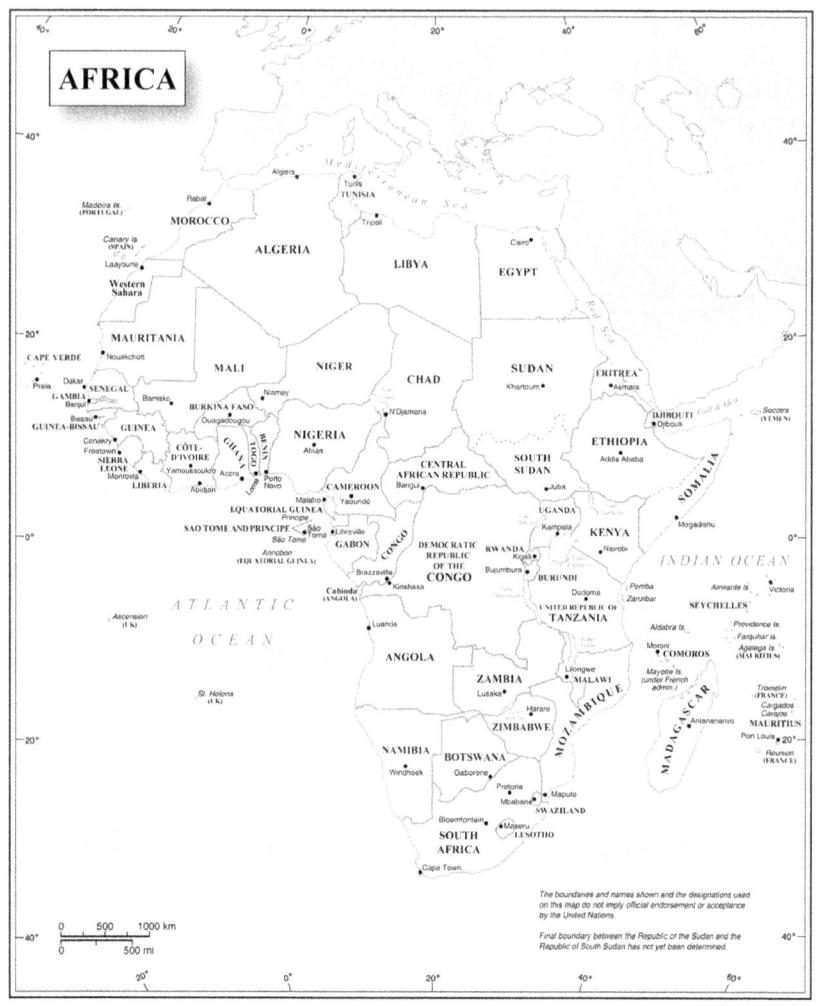

Map 1 Africa. The United Nations Map Library.

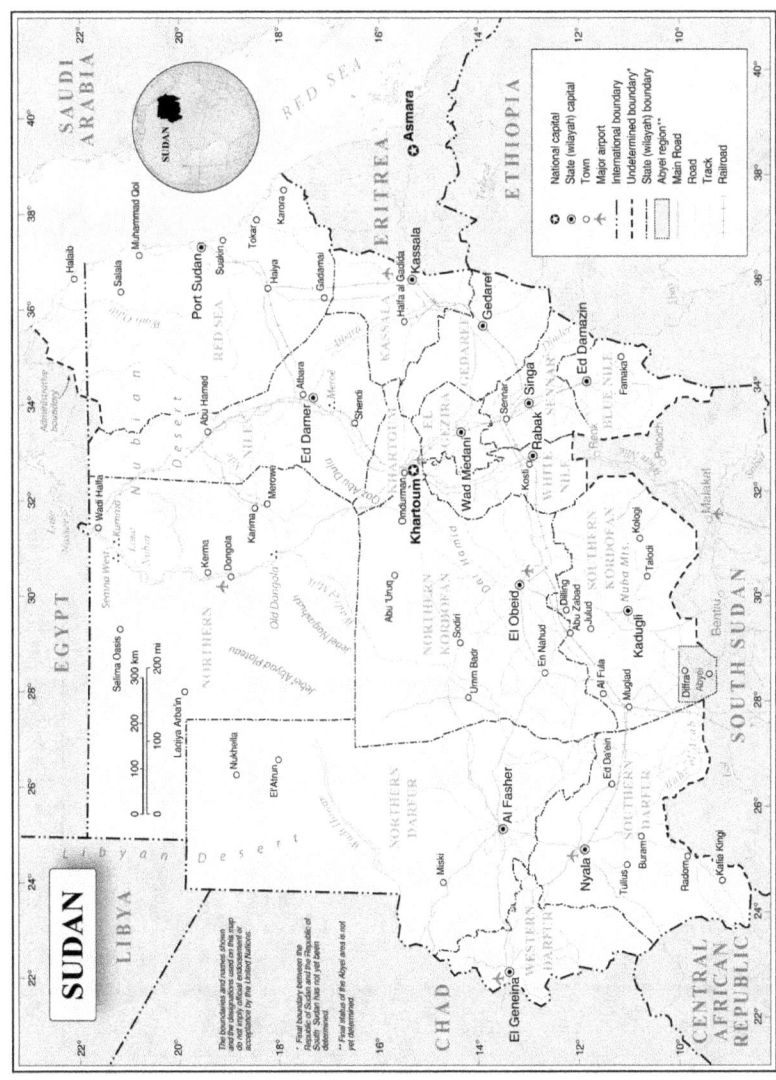

Map 2 Sudan. The United Nations Map Library.

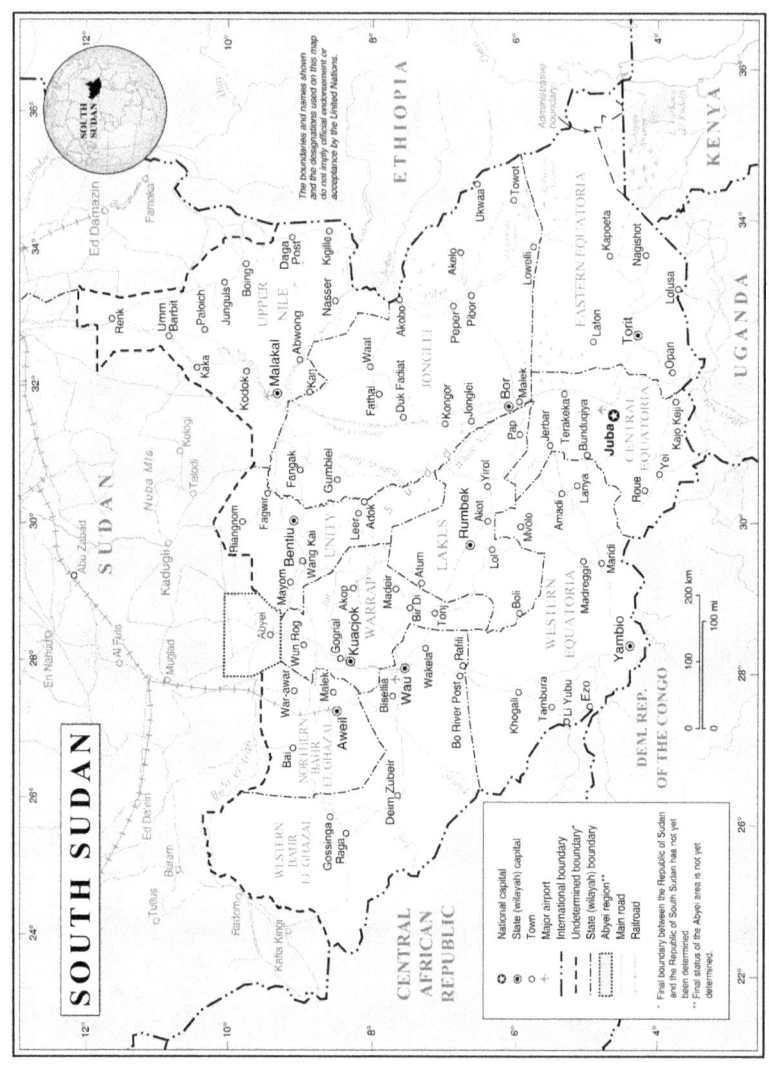

Map 3 South Sudan. The United Nations Map Library.

CHAPTER 1

SUDAN'S NORTH-SOUTH DIVIDE

It is the mission of social scientists with an international focus to unearth "the root causes" of undesirable or tragic events in the world in the hope that understanding these will improve the possibility of prescribing a cure for present ills, or at least a means of avoiding their future repetition. In carrying out this mission, however, they have a tendency to try to reduce complex situations to one or two intrinsically persuasive beginnings, both because parsimony is an academic virtue (especially when writing for publication) and because it is a natural human desire. Saying that something has multiple, interwoven, overlapping, mutually reinforcing root causes, after all, is neither very satisfying nor very helpful from a prescriptive point of view. It simply leaves the impression that one has failed to find the key to the problem, which, after all must be out there somewhere, unless one is to admit that the mission is in fact impossible.

In the case of Sudan, the tendency has been to fall back in one way or another on that reliable scapegoat British colonialism as the principal factor responsible for the fact that since independence in 1956 the state has been chronically unstable and mired in almost continuous civil war until 2005. Distinguished Sudanese scholar Francis M. Deng, for instance, began his 2002 essay "Sudan: An African Dilemma" with the observation that:

> The crisis of nationhood currently afflicting the Sudan represents two aspects of the dilemmas that confront African countries as they strive to build nations on the foundations emerging from the colonial state. One is the lack of cultural roots to the modern African state which was fashioned on the European model in virtual disregard for indigenous values and institutions.... The other aspect of the African dilemma is that colonialism separated ethnic groups and brought others together in the process of state

formation, creating diversities that were eventually rendered conflictual by gross inequalities in the sharing of power, natural resources, and development opportunities. (2002, 61)

That European colonialism in many cases had a less than benign influence on African states cannot be disputed, and Deng's two aspects in particular have acquired over time the status of conventional wisdom. No doubt instances may be found elsewhere in Africa where they have considerable validity, but it is questionable whether that can be said of Sudan. As another prominent Sudan expert has maintained, "the conflict between the northern and southern Sudan has usually been misunderstood, because the historic roots of the conflict have been misrepresented" (Johnson 2003, 1). Those historic roots indicate quite clearly that the blame for Sudan's modern troubles cannot be laid primarily at the door of its twentieth-century overlords; those roots go back much further in time. As argued by Matthew LeRiche and Matthew Arnold, "the social and political nature of the Republic of South Sudan draws heavily on the pre-modern experience" (2012, 8).

One must first recall that the Sudan that came into existence in 1956 was not an artificial creation of the British Empire so much as a reluctant acquiescence (on the part of the south at least) to the continuation of an unsatisfactory but long-standing relationship that it was hoped independence would improve. The beginning of the relationship is to be found in the fact that geography has dictated that Egypt and Sudan have been inextricably linked for centuries, while the same factor has "made it difficult for any government to tie [north and south] together through transportation or administrative infrastructure" (Natsios 2012, 9). Apart from anything else, the Nile River, the White branch of which rises in Uganda and flows the entire length of modern Sudan, is vital to Egypt's "agricultural, industrial, and human needs" (Natsios 2012, 5–6), and that has guaranteed continuing Egyptian interest in the lands and kingdoms south of its borders from earliest pharaonic times. Nubia, as the southern territories were then called, was of interest for other reasons as well; it was the source of ivory and, more important, slaves—so much so that "the terms 'Nubian' [Nubi], 'Nuba' [Nubawi], and 'Sudanese' [Sudani, i.e., black] entered the colloquial Arabic of the Nile valley as synonymous with 'slave'" (Johnson 2003, 2).

Penetration into the south by early Egyptian traders and slave raiders probably did not extend far into the territories of the present South Sudan, partly because the great Nile swamplands (the Sudd), extending as far as 240 kilometres, provided a natural and formidable barrier. But by the nineteenth century the south had become the prime slave hunting grounds for the now Arabized and Islamized state apparatus centred on Khartoum. Under Islam slavery was permissible as long as the enslaved were infidels, and the tribes of the south, who remained largely unconverted, were therefore a temptation not to be resisted.

Early in the nineteenth century, Egypt's ruler, Muhammad Ali (formally a viceroy of the Ottoman Empire, of which Egypt was then a part), embarked on a campaign to make Egypt an international power. To obtain the resources, especially the slave soldiers that would make this possible, he invaded Sudan in 1820. The ensuing Turco-Egyptian rule (the Turkiyya) lasted until 1881 and had profound effects on the development of the Sudanese territories. It was a draconian system, with the slave trade at its centre. According to Andrew Natsios, "the slave trade took an annual harvest of as many as 30,000 people captive among the [non-Muslim] African population in southern Sudan.... Some regions of the South were virtually depopulated by the slave trade during the nineteenth century" (2012, 18).[1] In essence the south was regarded as an uncivilized region fit only for the extraction of raw, uncultured resources, and certainly not a place a well-bred Arab would want to stay for very long, let alone settle in (see Deng 2002, 72). Indirectly that attitude was reinforced by the more formal and doctrinaire brand of Islam that was imposed by the Turkiyya (though not without difficulty) upon the indigenous and looser Sufi practices that had broad northern support especially in rural areas. Douglas Johnson notes the significant consequences of the Turkiyya: "the incorporation of the whole of the South as the state's exploitable hinterland, the intensification of racial stratification and the widespread identification of the people of the South with low status" (2003, 6).

Much has been made of the fact that when Sudan came under British rule (formally Anglo-Egyptian rule) in 1898 the south was administered differently from the north, a practice that in 1930 was formalized in the "Southern Policy." This policy "prohibited the settlement of northern traders, officials, and educators in the region to discourage the transmission of Arab culture. The south, however, was opened to Christian missionaries, thus strengthening its non-Muslim religious orientation" (Sidahmed and Soderlund 2008, 76). The policy also raised the possibility that the future of the south might better lie with the countries of British East Africa (Uganda and Kenya) than with those oriented to the Arab world.

If these factors are emphasized without placing them within the context of conditions that had already been established at the time, the implication is left that the Anglo-Egyptian Condominium (essentially British rule) was basically responsible for creating the north–south divide that has bedevilled independent Sudan. The fact is that there never was any degree of unity between the two territories. The "Southern Policy" statement merely "put into words what was already administrative practice" (Johnson 2003, 11), both in the sense of what had been done since 1898 and prior to that insofar as one could speak of there being such a thing as an "administrative practice" for the south during the

Turkiyya or before it. It is perhaps remotely possible that "imperial might" could have created a new fusion between north and south, but that does not seem very likely, and attempting it would in any case have flown in the face of both practical political needs and the principles of colonial administration (indirect rule) under which the British operated.

Britain became involved in Sudan in the first place as a means of preventing the area from "falling prey to another European power, with all the ramifications for the Nile waters and its control on Egypt—the safe route to the jewel of its colonies, India" (Sidahmed and Sidahmed 2005, 18). As the extremist Mahdist regime that had ousted the Turko-Egyptian administration in 1881 weakened during the following decade, and the French and Italians and Belgians sought to gain influence in the area, prudence seemed to dictate that the best policy for Britain was to use the Egyptians as proxies to reassert control over Sudan on the pretext that the latter were in fact its legitimate rulers. With the assistance of some Sudanese factions who were opposed to the Mahdiyya, a reconquest was completed in 1898. Thus began the period of the Anglo-Egyptian Condominium, "formalized in the Anglo-Egyptian Treaty of 1899, which recognized Sudan as an Egyptian possession administered by British officials on behalf of the King of Egypt" (Johnson 2003, 21).

The Condominium was faced with two immediate problems. The first, and in terms of security the most vital, was to guard against the possible resurgence of Mahdism, support for which remained strong in some northern areas. Urgent and long-term attention had to be given to such matters as replacing tribal leaders sympathetic to the Mahdiyya, or reinstating those who had been removed by it, and arranging to encourage and support "orthodoxy against fanaticism … by subsidizing the Mahdiyya's religious rivals" (Johnson 2003, 9).

The second problem was of course the south. It was clear even to the dimmest colonial administrator that that was an entirely different matter from political/religious manipulation in the north. The political and diplomatic needs in the north had no relevance in the south, and the south's situation was of little or no interest in the north. Indeed, centuries of slave raiding had left southerners with nothing but suspicion and distrust of northerners, and that was balanced by the latter's contempt for the former. It was undoubtedly hard for British or even Egyptian administrators to imagine how the two could be ruled other than separately, but in any case the divisions between them were not created by the Condominium. Indeed, the British view was that given the history of the region and the prevailing attitudes of the two populations, the south needed to be isolated from the north as much as possible, partly "to prevent Arab slave traders from harvesting their human quarry," but also, less altruistically, "to create a buffer zone containing the expansion of Islam in Africa, which [they] feared would destabilize their empire" (Natsios 2012, 31).

British policy toward south Sudan, therefore, might reasonably be described as benign, but it was also neglectful in that, apart from some efforts to improve education—mainly to provide low-level administrative personnel—it made practically no effort at development let alone reconciliation of the two historically conditioned solitudes. On this point Abdel Salam and Alsir Sidahmed have argued that the British felt no obligation to develop the Sudan at all, "since conquering [the territory] was done for external reasons and had nothing to do with the country itself" (2005, 23). Both administrative costs and developmental costs, if any, were the responsibility of the Egyptians, in whose name government was conducted, and the Egyptians had, if anything, even less interest in the south than the British.

Nor was this an instance in which colonial administrative convenience resulted in incompatible groups being forced together or cohesive ones being artificially separated. There are numerous references in the literature to Britain's proposed amalgamation of the southern Sudanese with the peoples of Uganda and/or Kenya, but it is unclear how seriously this was considered. At any rate, in the frenzy of nationalisms that arose during World War II and intensified thereafter, the principal issue as far as Sudan was concerned was whether it would become part of Egypt or an independent state.[2] An important subsidiary question, however, was what was to be done with the south. The British strongly favoured Sudanese independence over union with Egypt, but some officials held the view that the south should be held back, with self-government, and perhaps separate independence, coming at a later date (Johnson 2003, 25n6). That this was not insisted upon might in fact be regarded as the seminal mistake that set the table for the north–south violence that was to come.

Northerners were adamantly opposed to anything but a united Sudan and from the British point of view they were far more important than the southerners. Without northern cooperation, the colonial responsibility could not be ended and by the end of the war that was a prime objective of the British Colonial Office. A series of negotiations in which southern representation ranged from little to nil during the late 1940s ultimately led to Sudanese independence in 1956. The south's still apprehensive and ill-prepared leaders reluctantly acquiesced in this development, on the proviso that "full consideration" be given to the formation of a federal system, a condition they were promised would be fulfilled (Johnson 2003, 27, 29).

The problems that quickly developed were not the result of fashioning the Sudanese state "on the European model in virtual disregard for indigenous values and institutions" (see p. 1 above). The institutions of independent Sudan differed little from those that had preceded them, even before colonial times. It could be argued, in fact, that among the causes of later troubles was that the British had not insisted on a particular un-Sudanese structure (i.e., federalism) from the start. One of the south's major grievances early on in the independence period was that the promised consideration of a federal structure never materialized. In addition, at the time of independence, as Francis Deng observed, "the South found itself … the most marginalized and discriminated region of the country" (2006, 157). In the process of replacing British administrative functionaries with Sudanese nationals (the "Sudanization" policy), southerners received only four out of 800 posts available (Deng, as cited in Sidahmed and Soderlund 2008, 77). As well, "for form's sake … one or two Southerners were given ministries in successive governments, the Minister for Animal Resources becoming the token Southern seat in any cabinet" (Johnson 2003, 30). Perhaps most important, however, the issue of creating a federal state was shunted aside with little ceremony because some northerners feared that such an arrangement would be the first step toward southern secession, and others were too preoccupied with more important issues to give the matter much attention.

In retrospect it is not difficult to see why the whole southern issue could at the beginning have seemed little more than an annoyance to the politicians and religious leaders of Khartoum. They were from the outset embroiled in "persistent internal and partisan squabbles" (Sidahmed and Sidahmed 2005, 29) involving cross-cutting differences between supporters of the new independent state and those who still favoured union with Egypt, between those with left-wing tendencies and those of more conventional orientation, between military and civilian officials, and, perhaps most important of all, among a variety of Islamic movements. These were fundamental, nation-building issues, ones that would define what Sudan would be and who would rule it. Whether southerners were disgruntled and aggrieved or not could be dismissed as a trivial matter in comparison, or regarded as something that must be dealt with according to northern necessities rather than southern desires. That the northern schisms were deep and serious is attested to by the fact that since 1956 Sudan has had but three brief parliamentary regimes (totalling nine years in all), each of which was overthrown by a military coup. The three military regimes have so far totalled 45 years in office. The current one, while under stress from the "loss of the south" and more generally from the forces unleashed by the Arab Spring, is not likely to come to an immediate end despite an International Criminal Court (ICC) indictment against its leader, Omar al-Bashir, for his actions in Darfur.[3]

The south could not, of course, be entirely ignored. Apart from anything else, what is often considered to be the beginning of the First Civil War was under way before independence was even official. It lasted seventeen years, claiming an estimated 1.3 million lives and producing 5 million refugees (Poggo 2009, 192). For southerners, "the North's reneging on its promise to consider the federal option" (Sidahmed and Sidahmed 2005, 39), the niggardly allocation of positions during Sudanization, and the "rapid increase of Northerners in the South as administrators, senior officers in the army and police, teachers in government schools and as merchants" (Johnson 2003, 27), confirmed fears that they had exchanged a relatively benign form of colonialism for a worse one. On this issue Andrew Natsios quotes Joseph Lagu, who was to become the commander of the southern rebel army: "We felt this [Arab] occupation indicated a possible renewal of the slave trade after the British left. The southern Sudanese had always regarded the British as their deliverers and protectors, while they viewed northerners as slave traders and tormentors" (in Natsios 2012, 41).

One of the results of this deep distrust of northern intentions was that in 1955 the soldiers of the Equatorial Corp, having had their British officers replaced by northerners, and fearing that they might be disarmed and moved to the north (Johnson 2003, 27), or, as some suggest, had already been ordered to move north (Sidahmed and Soderlund 2008, 77), mutinied.[4] The mutiny, while it spread to a number of areas, and some 200–300 people (mostly northerners) were killed, was never a general uprising or an organized and coherent operation. It was more a matter of people lashing out in fear and frustration in a situation they did not fully understand. The mutiny was easily put down with the assistance of the British (who were still nominally responsible for the area). Reprisals followed, however, as the army undertook to track down those mutineers who had fled into the bush, and villages were burned, and all the previous fears were reinforced (Poggo 2009, 73–80).

These fears were bolstered again when the government headed by General Ibrahim Abboud, who had seized power in November 1958, undertook a campaign of Arabization and Islamization in the south. The activities of Christian missionaries (who had run almost all schools in the south) were first restricted and then proscribed. The language of school instruction was changed from English to Arabic and was henceforth to include Islamic instruction. The Sabbath was changed from Sunday to Friday. Quranic institutes were established to teach Islam to converts (see Natsios 2012, 43). As a result, in the early 1960s, senior political figures in the south began disappearing into the bush and into neighbouring countries, where they joined with the remaining mutineers from 1955 to form loose political and guerrilla organizations. These, Johnson maintains, were the true instigators of the First Civil War (2003, 31; see also Poggo 2009, chaps. 2 and 3).

First came the Anya Nya (poisonous snake) movement in 1963, which carried out sporadic ambushes and thefts of arms but did not manage to assert much sustained pressure. The situation nevertheless gradually escalated and the Southern Sudan Liberation Movement (SSLM) came into being in 1971 under the leadership of former army officer Joseph Lagu. Another military coup in 1969 had brought Colonel Jaafar Nimeiri to power in Khartoum, and he agreed to enter into negotiations with Lagu. These talks produced the Addis

Ababa Accord of March 1972, "which gave the South autonomy within a unified Sudan," incorporated Anya Nya soldiers into the national army (Sidahmed and Sidahmed 2005, 41), and created a Regional Assembly with very limited powers for the south. At the same time, it left a great many things undefined or open to misunderstanding. Officially, however, it brought the First Civil War to an end (to wide international acclaim) and ushered in an eleven-year period of peace that was uncertain, but that allowed some progress to be made in terms of economic development, infrastructural expansion, and education.

It is difficult to pinpoint exactly why that uncertain peace came to an end in 1983 and a conflict far more prolonged than the previous one, not to mention far more serious and deadly, began. The event that is frequently said to have precipitated it was yet another army mutiny, this time of Battalion 105 in July, but that was more a symptom of the general malaise that continued to exist than a cause of it. According to Douglas Johnson, a general uprising was already being planned for later in the year in any case, and the July mutiny was premature (2003, 62). The immediate reason for the mutiny was reported to have been "delayed salary payments, accusations of embezzlement from the funds allocated to the battalion and an order from the army's general command for the battalion to relocate north" (Sidahmed and Soderlund 2008, 79). However, it was also an expression of accumulated discontents concerning the implementation of the Addis Ababa Accord. The fact was that the Accord was never popular in the north, and Nimeiri's government, whatever it might have liked to do, had to minimize concessions to the south as much as possible in order to keep opposition elements at bay.

Not surprisingly, the Accord was not universally popular in the south either. Some Anya Nya guerrillas chose to continue their fight. Those who supported it, on the other hand, probably expected too much from the Accord, and were quick to interpret any difficulties that arose—for example, with respect to the integration of the guerrillas into the national army—as evidence of bad faith on the part of the central government. Certainly, however, Nimeiri's announcement of the "September Laws" in June 1983, modifying a number of the provisions of the Accord and imposing Shari'a law on all Sudanese, gave substance to southern suspicions.[5] It might also be mentioned that the 1978 confirmation of significant oil deposits, mainly in the south, substantially increased the incentives the south had to fight for greater independence, and for the north to prevent that development.

By July 1983, a force of 2,500 guerrillas had assembled in Ethiopia. The latter country was prepared to support them because Sudan had been supplying arms to Ethiopia's Eritrean rebels. By the end of the same month the guerrillas had brought into being the Sudan People's Liberation Movement/Army (SPLM/SPLA) under the command of John Garang.[6] The movement's manifesto proclaimed that it was "fighting to restructure Sudanese politics and society in a way that would tackle a wide range of historical inequalities, not just the 'southern problem'" (Sidahmed and Soderlund 2008, 80)—in other words, unlike the Anya Nya, it did not aim at secession, but at creating a better united nation. This may have been the genuine wish at least of the movement's leadership, but there were sound tactical reasons for it as well. In the first place, being almost totally dependent in the early days on Ethiopian funding, training, and arming (though Libya also contributed), the SPLM could hardly advocate state breakup when that was precisely what Ethiopia was fighting to avoid with Eritrea—and against which there was general international opposition in any case. Second, such a position held out greater hope for support from other sectors of Sudanese society that were also unhappy with the central government.

The Second Civil War was far more intense than the first, both because the SPLA was far more organized (despite high levels of factional infighting) as well as stronger than the previous guerrilla groups, and, importantly, because the central government became more and more insistent that the south must be Arabized and Islamized in order to create a united Sudan. In the words of Sadiq al-Mahdi, who became Prime Minister in 1986, "we wish to establish Islam as the source of law in Sudan because Sudan has a Muslim majority" (as quoted in Johnson 2003, 79). Compromise with the SPLA was therefore out of the question, and any tactic that would bring about its defeat was justified. Indeed, al-Mahdi's four-fold strategy for winning the war can only be described as chilling:

> First, ... the war must be kept at all cost in the South and away from Khartoum, limiting the damage and chaos of the war to the South. Second, the central government would organize, arm, and fund the Arab tribes along the North–South border to form militias as a supplementary force to the national army. Third, using these tribal militias, along with the northern military, the North would raid and burn villages, inciting massive population displacements, which would undermine southern culture and society, making people much more susceptible to ... forced Arabization and Islamization. Later, these displaced southerners would be driven into concentration camps run by the government, where they would hear the Quran read continuously from loud speakers all day, every day.... Fourth, ... the central government would use its resources—weapons, money, and jobs—to turn one southern tribe against another. (Natsios 2012, 72–73)

Allowing for differences of degree and emphasis, this could be said to describe the approach of successive governments in Khartoum throughout the ups and downs of the war. For northerners, the central need was to defend and extend the realm of Islam (see Deng 2002, 62, for a similar view)—perhaps not the only need, but certainly one that fuelled the turbulent politics in the capital much of the time. It had to be a central need because it was derived from Holy Writ, and there can be no compromise with the commands of whatever Allah/God/Zeus/Odin is thought to control one's destiny and eternal rewards. Moreover, Islam supported, and was supported by, the ideology of pan-Arabism, which was also important, in degrees varying with time, to northern leaders. To Hassan al-Turabi, who was one of the most influential figures in northern politics for thirty years, for instance, "the defeat of the SPLA was essential for the spread and consolidation of Islam in Sudan and the broader Salafist Islamization of Africa" (Natsios 2012, 112). For southerners, on the other hand, "the unity of the country could only be based on the exclusion of religion from politics" (Johnson 2003, 141). What southerners could not accept was what they considered to be a system of domination that required them to become something other than what they were. It was not a situation in which it was easy to see a solution—not even a military one since it quickly became clear that neither side was capable of defeating the other. As described by Robert Matthews, "with the extension of the war to the north, first to the Nuba Mountains, then to the southern Blue Nile, the eastern region, and finally to Darfur, Sudan ha[d] become a humanitarian disaster of epic proportions" (2005, 1049).

An early peace initiative, the Koka Dam Declaration, was signed in 1986 between the SPLA/M and various northern trade unions and political parties. "The declaration stated a consensus for a 'New Sudan that would be free from racism, tribalism, sectarianism, and all causes of discrimination and disparity.'" In short order, however, a proposed Constitutional Convention fell victim to northern political manoeuvring (LeRiche and Arnold 2012, 49–50). The Second Civil War might well have continued indefinitely had not external events forced re-evaluations, especially in Khartoum. The United States, in addition to its general reluctance to support revolutionary movements, had originally been suspicious of the SPLA because of its connections with Ethiopia and Libya and its communist-sounding rhetoric. It in fact had gone significantly in the opposite direction, supplying successive regimes in Khartoum with aid and arms which literally gave it the capability to pursue the war with the south. Sudan was the largest recipient of US aid in Africa during the 1970s and 1980s (LeRiche and Arnold 2012, 207). This began to change in the mid-1980s when Sudan concluded a mutual defence pact with Libya and began placing increased emphasis on seeking Arab unity. It changed dramatically in the 1990s as fear of terrorism increased, especially after the 1998 attacks on American embassies in Dar es Salaam and Nairobi, and the 2000 attack on the USS Cole. Since those who carried out these attacks were al-Qaeda operatives linked to Sudan (some of them carried Sudanese passports and Osama bin Laden had lived in Sudan until 1996), Washington launched diplomatic pressure on Khartoum in the form of sanctions and entered Sudan on the list of world "terrorist states" (see Natsios 2012, 113–16). When 11 September 2001 shocked the world and shook the United States to its foundations, greater attention was focused on the region from which terrorism was seen as originating, and that included increased efforts to find "areas of negotiation between the government of the Sudan and the SPLA" (Johnson 2003, 177). It took four years for that effort to bear fruit, but in 2005 the Comprehensive Peace Agreement (CPA) was finally signed. The CPA comprised six individual agreements that covered wealth-sharing protocols (the north and south were to share oil revenues on a 50–50 basis) and, as Abdel Salam Sidahmed explained, the following power protocols: "a protocol on security arrangements; a protocol on the resolution of the conflict in Southern Kordofan/Nuba Mountains and Southern Blue Nile; and a protocol on the resolution of the conflict in the Abyei Area." In addition, the CPA provided for a "six year transitional period during which the South [would] have full autonomy, its own government and constitution, and a separate army, flag and budget. At the end of the transition period in January 2011, the South [would] exercise self-determination through a referendum to decide whether or not to secede from the Sudan. The people of the Abyei area would do the same" (2010, 23).

The CPA was rightfully hailed as a remarkable achievement, but it inevitably set off a wave of speculation concerning whether it would actually bring an end to violent conflict in the region or merely set the stage for a third civil war. As might be expected, the views expressed varied from the pessimistic to the merely hopeful. Few if any were clearly optimistic. Francis Deng, for example, was uncertain how the future of the country might unfold, though he thought that there was a "likelihood, indeed the probability, of the north remaining committed to some version of the Arab-Islamic vision" (2006, 160). Writing four years later, Abdel Salam Sidahmed found both positive and negative signs: that there was for the first time in Sudan's post-colonial history a real attempt to provide people with democratic choices was positive; that there continued to be "human rights violations, lack of respect for the rule of law, a weak civil society, and media censorship" was less encouraging (2010, 25).

Long-time Sudan expert Douglas Johnson assessed the implications of problems related to the disputed Abyei region (a region that the CPA stipulated was to determine its own future status in a separate referendum in 2011), with one of the options being "incorpor[ation] into Southern Sudan" (2007, 8n2).[7] The Abyei region (co-inhabited by the Ngok Dinka and the Humr group of Misseriya Baggara Arabs in an increasingly conflictual relationship) was seen to be especially important both because it already had been a battleground between African and Arab groups during the civil wars, and because within its still-to-be-defined borders lie significant deposits of oil. Writing two years after the CPA was signed in 2005, Johnson reported that "there is a growing feeling, not only within the SPLM leadership and the [government in Southern Sudan] … that the Abyei area could be the flashpoint that brings the country back to war" (2007, 2).[8] It was noted that, early on, the Sudanese Government had reneged on commitments made in the CPA to accept the decision of the Abyei Boundaries Commission (composed of foreign experts, one of whom was Dr. Johnson) regarding "the definition of the area" (2007, 1).

Luke Patey, a researcher at the Danish Institute of International Studies, observed that the 2011 referendum was a "watershed fraught with political uncertainty and possible armed conflict" (2010, 634), primarily because 80 percent of the oil resources are located in the south or in disputed border regions, because oil accounts for roughly 90 percent of Sudanese exports, and because there was thus both reason for north and south to cooperate and incentive for them to avoid conflict (619–20). He concluded, however, that in fact there "is no need to make bleak forecasts on instability in Southern Sudan. Armed conflict is already rife in the region. The UN reported over 2,000 people had died and almost 400,000 were displaced in 2009 from violence between ethnic groups over water and other scarce resources" (628). Patey ended on the pessimistic note that even if rival elites managed to choose the route of compromise, this might not be enough to avert violence in the region. Citing misrule by the SPLM in the south, he claimed that "the lack of a peace dividend and environmental degradation from oil continue to spawn armed resistance at the local level," and he thus predicted that "low-intensity yet protracted conflict remains a likely condition for areas in and around Sudan's oil fields" (636).

Most observers, if pressed during the six years leading up to the referendum, would probably have given better than even odds that war between north and south would be resumed if the south actually opted for independence. Certainly no one could consider the referendum of less than seminal importance (see Deng, 2010). Given this outlook, how the unfolding of the CPA's provisions was treated by North American media outlets, and especially what, if anything, they urged their governments to do in light of the newly proclaimed international "Responsibility to Prevent" humanitarian disasters, seemed an obvious subject for examination. The pages that follow are accordingly devoted to that endeavour.

CHAPTER 2

INTERNATIONAL INTERVENTION

From *Peacekeeping* to *Humanitarian Intervention* to the *Responsibility to Protect*

Conceptions of how the international community can or should respond to incidents of destructive violence in the world, such as have occurred in Sudan and which were anticipated in the event of its likely division, have gone through several stages since the creation of the United Nations. In the first place, it is a truism to say that World War II ended with the victors attempting to restore the world to the "normalcy" of pre-conflict conditions, though it would perhaps be more accurate to say that what they hoped for was a safer and better protected normalcy. What was to be protected was the state system that had gradually evolved since the 1648 Treaty of Westphalia, and what it was to be protected from was the sort of ambitions that had fuelled Nazi Germany and made Dante's *Inferno* a reality in Europe for six long years. The means of that protection, as conceived mainly by a few Western minds, was the UN and a system of *collective security* that would serve as a bastion against military aggression everywhere, and ensure the maintenance of "international peace and security."

Political leaders of the time, in other words, thought more or less exclusively in *state-centric* terms, that is, in the preservation of state sovereignty. Such concerns as they had for the peoples who inhabited those political entities would, it was assumed, be addressed by their individual governments in the independence to which they were entitled. Whether the inhabitants of Argentina, Belgium, or South Africa were treated well or ill by their rulers was certainly not a matter in which international bodies like the UN should interfere, beyond the exceptional circumstance in which there appeared to be a danger to the wider world community.

It is also well known that the UN never functioned as its creators intended. When the victorious World War II alliance quickly splintered along ideological lines, any real hope of a Great Power Condominium to deter interstate conflict vanished and the new international organization became primarily a forum for verbal one-upmanship between East and West, and only incidentally relevant to more or less open interstate clashes like Korea. At the same time, however, the sanctity of the sovereignty principle was being buttressed by the clamour of Europe's extensive African and Asian colonies for independence and formal political equality with their former masters.

The Cold War and decolonization processes often overlapped and thus became confused, as they did in 1956, for example, when Egypt seized control of the Suez Canal and Britain and France reverted to colonial habits in an attempt to reverse that action. It was the Suez Crisis that gave the UN its first significant victory in its struggle to establish some sort of prestige in the eyes of the world, and that set it on a new and unthought-of path. Led by the US, but for once with the support of the USSR, the international organization embarked on "peacekeeping"—the deployment of a neutral, multilateral military force between former combatants until more permanent peace terms could be worked out.

Peacekeeping was in concept and design also essentially state-centric and limited in scope, though it proved vulnerable to what would later be referred to as "mission creep." In the Democratic Republic of the Congo between 1960 and 1964, what began as an apparent replay of the Suez operation was quickly and controversially transformed into something bearing a closer resemblance to peace*making* than peace*keeping*. Still, the principle objective in that instance was the preservation of the Congolese state in all its colonial-inherited essence, and concern for the Congolese population was at best incidental. There was, for example, much concern to prevent full-fledged civil war, but the fact that such an event would be vastly destructive of human life was less important than the possibility that it might trigger similar events elsewhere in Africa in particular, or, even more undesirable, lead to a direct confrontation between the two superpowers (see Soderlund et al. 2012, chap. 2).

Over the years, peacekeeping "served a substantial purpose in places like Cyprus and Lebanon" (Sidahmed, Soderlund, and Briggs 2010, 5), but its basic objective and format changed little. However, in the 1990s, two interrelated factors produced a surge of hope for international cooperation and organization. The first of these was the reduction in East–West animosity resulting from the collapse of the Soviet Union. This was seen by advocates of greater "Global Order" (including, but not limited to, enthusiasts for "World Government") as the opportunity for which they had long pined. The second was the unanticipated outbreak of intra-state violence that the end of the Cold War helped unleash.

With respect to the first of these, increased international attention to so-called domestic problems in fact has had an impressive history, a history that tends to be largely overlooked and is deserving of a brief review. During the 1970s and 1980s there had been a flurry of conferences and reports (most under UN sponsorship in one way or another) that focused on expanding international control over areas such as the environment, climate change, and economic development, and that brought into being a number of instruments for these purposes. For instance, in the 1970s, the UN Environmental Program spawned the Regional Seas Program (1973), the Conference on Trade and Development (1974), and the Global Framework for Environmental Education (1975). These were followed in the 1980s by the Independent Commission on Development (the "Brandt Commission," 1980), the UN Covenant of the Law of the Sea (1981), the World Conference on Environment and Development (1981 and 1987), and the World Conference on Environmental Management (1984) (see Lamb 2001, 17).

What all of these shared was the conviction that achieving "human security" involved far more than the deterrence of military hostilities. It involved addressing threats from environmental degradation, poverty, and economic inequality as well. All of these were seen not only as interconnected, but as the root causes of violence. As such they required global attention and management—that is, the advance of "Global Governance," with the UN as the foundational instrument for achieving this.

This trend continued and accelerated during the final decade of the twentieth century. It began with the World Summit of Children in 1990, followed quickly by the Conference on Environment and Development (UNCED—the "Rio Conference") in 1992, and the UN Conference on Human Rights in 1993. The Rio Conference was notable for producing the Convention on Biological Diversity, and the Framework Convention on Climate Change. The second of these proclaimed that "human beings are at the center of concerns for sustainable development," and, more significantly, that "*national sovereignty is subject to international law*" (Lamb 2001, 26; italics added). These events were followed in 1995 by the World Women's Congress, the World Summit on Social Development (which saw affluent states committing themselves to providing 0.7 percent of their GNP for development assistance), and, most important of all, the Commission on Global Governance. The last of these events notably observed in its report that (1) "all peoples, no less than all states, have a right to a secure existence, and all states have an obligation to protect those rights" (Commission on Global Governance 1995, 84); (2) "where people are subject to massive suffering and disasters ... there is a need to weigh a state's right to autonomy against its people's right to security" (71); and (3) "we believe a global consensus exists today for a UN response on humanitarian grounds in cases of gross abuse of the security of people" (89).

Among the sources of such abuses listed in the Commission on Global Governance Report was the "terrorizing of civilian populations by domestic factions" (1995, 79), but there was no suggestion that "sovereign governments" might also commit crimes of the same sort. That became an unavoidable fact, however, as a result of the second factor referred to above—the proliferation of intra-state violence that emerged at the end the Cold War. Of the 82 deadly conflicts that occurred across the world between 1991 and 1994, no less than 79 were of the internal, "civil" variety ("The 1994 UN Human Development Report" 1994, 18). These included the violent disintegration of Yugoslavia, the intensification of north–south hostilities in Sudan, the muddled disaster of Somalia, the political crisis in Haiti, and the appalling tragedy of government-orchestrated genocide in Rwanda (see MacKenzie 1993; Dallaire 2003; Soderlund et al. 2008, chaps. 3–6).

The UN endorsed some form of "peacekeeping" efforts in most of these situations, though with limited success and growing concern about the compatibility of these efforts with the principle of state sovereignty. Given that Article 2(7) of the UN Charter prohibits the organization from interfering within the "domestic jurisdiction" of states without explicit invitation, under what circumstances could international missions to rescue abused and endangered populations be justified? On the one hand, standing in mute observation as carnage raged and bodies piled up seemed to defy the essence of what it meant to be human. On the other hand, if international agencies could decide to meddle at will in any situation found objectionable, would not the very foundation of the international system be badly shaken if not destroyed? In particular, would it not open the door to new Great Power imperialistic ventures?

This dilemma was recognized by Secretary-General Boutros Boutros-Ghali early in the 1990s in his *An Agenda for Peace*. On the one hand he maintained that "respect for [the state's] fundamental sovereignty and integrity are crucial to any common international progress"; on the other he argued that "the time for absolute and exclusive sovereignty ... has passed" (1992, 203). Nonetheless, when humanitarian assistance to people was thought necessary, it "must be provided in accordance with the principles of humanity, neutrality, and impartiality ... and with the consent of the affected country" (207). But the most novel and far-reaching portion of *An Agenda for Peace* was the suggestion that consideration be given to the creation of "*peace enforcement units*" (210). The use of the word *enforcement* in this connection suggested, as Sidahmed and colleagues have maintained, "a quantum leap from the previous emphasis on peace*keeping*" (2010, 7).

The new term set off an intensive debate in academic circles during the 1990s concerning what *peace enforcement* could or should mean, and even what it should be called—"second generation peacekeeping," "assertive multilateralism," "robust peacekeeping," and "humanitarian intervention" were among the other labels suggested. There were of course critics. However, the idea of a more robust international effort to manage conflicts in the interests of their victims was generally embraced as logical and necessary, at least by the majority of Western commentators. No UN "peace enforcement units" ever materialized, or were seriously considered by any of the UN's political bodies, but the scope of possible responses to human tragedies was undeniably extended by the very suggestion of them, and the hunt, as it were, was consequently on for ways in which international interventions could be more certain and more effective (see Mackinlay and Chopra 1992; Greenwood 1993; James 1995; Jacobsen 1996).

In his report to the General Assembly in 2000, Secretary-General Kofi Annan accordingly challenged the world body to devise methods of responding "to a Rwanda, to a Srebrenica, to gross and systematic violations of human rights that affect every precept of our common humanity" (UN 2000, 5). The challenge was immediately taken up by Canadian Prime Minister Jean Chrétien, who announced at the UN Millennium Assembly in September 2000 that his government was creating an independent International Commission on Intervention and State Sovereignty (ICISS). This blue-ribbon panel, comprising academics and political nationals from eleven countries, produced a report entitled *The Responsibility to Protect* one year later, unfortunately at precisely the time the world was preoccupied with the ramifications of the 9/11 terrorist attacks on the United States. "R2P," as the report and the principle on which it was based came to be called, turned on its head the question of when international interventions within sovereign states might be justified. The traditional focus had been on *"when is it permissible for the international community to undertake interventions in crisis situations,"* whereas it should, in the Commission's view, be on *"when, and how, should the international community act to exercise its responsibility to protect suffering innocents"* (Sidahmed, Soderlund, and Briggs 2010, 12; italics in the original). In the words of the report: "Where a population is suffering serious harm, as a result of internal war, insurgency, repression or state failure, and the state in question is unwilling or unable to halt or avert it, *the principle of non-intervention yields to the international responsibility to protect*" (ICISS 2001, 11; italics added).

In elaboration, the report contended that the Responsibility to Protect contained three elements: a Responsibility to *Prevent*, a Responsibility to *React*, and a Responsibility to *Rebuild*.[1] In other words, the onus was on the global community to address the root causes of situations that might lead to populations being put at risk, to take action to mitigate damage when efforts at prevention failed, and to assist with "recovery, reconstruction, and reconciliation" following any such action (ICISS 2001, 39–40). Of the three responsibilities, the Commission identified the Responsibility to Prevent as the most important, arguing that "prevention options should always be exhausted before intervention is contemplated and resources must be devoted to it" (ICISS 2001, 11).

R2P was not immediately endorsed by any international body, partly because of the unfortunate timing of its release, but also because many governments needed convincing that it was not a step too far. Thus it was not until September 2005 that a somewhat generalized version was accepted by the High Plenary Meeting of the General Assembly, and not until seven months later that it was endorsed by the Security Council. Obviously, however, such endorsement did not imply universal approval of the new doctrine. There remained, and remain, critics on both right and left who consider it an instrument that enhances the domination of the powerful over the weak (Fenton 2005/2006; Podhur 2005). But even its critics would have to admit that R2P "introduced a new standard against which the protection of human rights will be measured and judged" (Sidahmed, Soderlund, and Briggs 2010, 14).[2]

It is from this position that it seems useful to consider the process by which South Sudan separated from the north and became an independent state. In our previous work on Darfur we examined in-depth the Responsibility to React (Sidahmed, Soderlund, and Briggs 2010) and continued that focus with a study of the UN's response to the Congo Wars (Soderlund et al. 2012). In that South Sudan offered a quintessential case for the Responsibility to Prevent—a great likelihood that violence would accompany any attempt by the south to secede—the following chapter will explore that concept at greater length. The goal of this examination is to gain an understanding of what conflict prevention means, how cases in need of prevention are identified, and, once they are identified, what strategies can be applied in difficult, multi-layered conflicts such as confronted the international community with the breakup of Sudan.

CHAPTER 3

THE RESPONSIBILITY TO PREVENT

Problems of Identification and Implementation

The Responsibility to Prevent

The Development Assistance Committee of the Organization for Economic Cooperation and Development (OECD) has usefully defined conflict prevention as "actions undertaken to reduce tensions and to prevent the outbreak or recurrence of violent conflict. Beyond short-term actions, it includes the notion of long-term engagement. It consists of *operational prevention*, i.e. immediate measures applicable in the face of crisis, and *structural prevention*, i.e. measures to ensure that crises do not arise in the first place, or, if they do, that they do not recur" (OECD 2008, Annex 1, 56; italics in the original).

As mentioned, the ICISS report gave top priority to conflict prevention, and as Sebastian von Einsiedel (2005) has pointed out, effective strategies for accomplishing that goal depend on two factors. The first of these is the *identification of cases* where humanitarian crises are likely to erupt, and, following that, the *selection and application of appropriate techniques of remediation*. While conceptually clear, as the discussion in this chapter reveals, neither of these tasks has proven easy to carry out.

Problems of Identification

The identification of impending crises through social science research was first singled out for attention in the mid-1960s in the form of "Project Camelot." Conceived of and sponsored by the US Army's Special Operations Research Office (SORO), Camelot's goals were to better understand violent social and political change associated with "wars of national liberation" and to suggest methods to deal with such situations (see Horowitz 1967). More specifically, the project's goals were to "devise procedures for assessing the potential for internal war within national societies ... [and to] identify with increased degrees of confidence those actions which a government might take to relieve conditions which are assessed as giving rise to the potential for internal war" (SORO, as quoted in Solovey 2001, 180–81). The project was based on the assumption of a "deeply rooted" partnership between military and academic communities. It came to grief, however, when the Vietnam War generated a sense of profound distrust among academics for all things associated with the military (Solovey 2001, 179). Project Camelot was cancelled within a year.[1]

A second US government agency took up the problem thirty years later. In 1994 the Central Intelligence Agency (CIA) commissioned a "State Failure Task Force" to address the "causal structure" underlying political instability by developing "methods of risk assessment and early warning systems in the hope that foreign aid could be directed to prevent states from failing" (King and Zeng 2001, 623). Unlike Camelot, field work was not a part of this project. Rather, an exhaustive data set of social, political, and economic indicators was to be compiled from non-classified sources in order to "assess and explain the vulnerability of states around the world to political instability and state failure" (PITF 2010).[2]

In that there were only a dozen or so contemporaneous cases of "complete collapse of state authority" (too few to permit statistical analysis), the Task Force initially decided to include within its data collection protocol "revolutionary and ethnic conflicts, regime crises, and massive human rights violations that are *typically associated with state breakdown*" (Esty et al. 1998; italics added). This resulted in a data set of 243 cases: 40 *revolutionary wars*, 75 *ethnic wars*, 46 *genocides and politicides*, and 82 *adverse or disruptive regime transitions*. These were subsequently reduced to 113 "consolidated cases" that were then compared against three times as many "control cases" where the problem conditions associated with violence and state failure were absent (Esty et al. 1998).

The Task Force collected data on 617 measures of demographic, social, political, and economic/environmental factors. In subsequent analysis these were reduced to 75 "high priority variables," of which 32 showed statistically significant differences between violence-challenged states and those in the more fortunate control group. Ultimately, three variables—"openness to international trade, infant mortality, and democracy"—predicted with 70 percent accuracy "which states would fail between 1955 and mid-1994" (Esty et al. 1998). These specific indicators were used as surrogate measures of broader concepts: *openness to international trade* tapped into a country's integration in the international system; *infant mortality* reflected the general quality of life in a country; while *democracy* indicated the conflict-dampening effects of open political institutions (Esty et al. 1998).[3]

The respected periodical *Foreign Policy* has also measured the extent of state weakness based on data collected for twelve *stress-causing* factors: demographic pressures, refugees and internally displaced persons, group grievances, human flight, uneven development, economic decline, delegitimization of the state, condition of public services, human rights, security apparatus, factionalized elites, and external intervention. Analysis of the resulting data set produced a "Failed States Index" (Foreign Policy 2010), which in the first decade of the twenty-first century showed that political instability was in fact remarkably enduring. Over the five-year period from 2007 to 2011 either seven or eight of the highest-ranking states on the index of state failure were located in sub-Saharan Africa, with Somalia, Sudan, Chad, the Democratic Republic of the Congo, Zimbabwe, and the Central African Republic making the top ten in every year, and with Somalia heading the list from 2008 through 2011. Côte d'Ivoire and Guinea made three of the five "top ten lists" as well (Foreign Policy 2011; Messner 2011).

What is also significant about this list is that while many of the states did in fact experience significant violence, not all of them did—Zimbabwe being a notable case in point. This brings to mind the observations of William Zartman in 1995, as well as the more recent ones of Gary King and Langche Zeng. Zartman argued that the defining characteristic of state failure or state collapse is a long-term decline of the ability to govern effectively (1995, 1–8; see also Rotberg 2002). King and Zeng, among others, rightly pointed out that while state failure and large-scale violence are often correlated, they are not necessarily the same, as the CIA Task Force's choice of its dependent variable would tend to suggest (2001, 654–55). First, violence can be either a *cause* of or a *consequence* of state collapse. Second, states can in fact continue to exist in a state of "failure" for significant periods of time without the eruption of devastating violence. Arguably more important, significant internal violence, as in civil war or the efforts of one group to eradicate another, does not necessarily imply state failure, as the case of the 1994 Rwandan genocide so brutally demonstrated. It took remarkable government-directed organization to orchestrate the killing of some 800,000 people in a matter of twelve weeks (von Einsiedel 2005, 24).

Compilations of data like those of the Task Force and *Foreign Policy* are undoubtedly helpful. They provide a better understanding of the problems underlying state failure (i.e., their "causal structure"), thus pointing to situations in need of long-term preventive measures, as well as flagging the need for short-term stabilization measures before deteriorating situations reach the point of disintegration. The latter is in fact quite valuable, for as von Einsiedel argues, "the more state institutions have eroded and the more a state is overwhelmed by chaos, the less the outside world can intervene effectively" (2005, 22).[4]

Useful as they might be, however, the approaches noted above are not, and perhaps never can be, conclusive: they cannot predict with certainty which unstable situation will result in either the collapse of state authority or the outbreak of violence within a state. Some have suggested that for such a purpose "triggers" and "accelerators," acting as "the straw that breaks the camel's back," must be identified; but again, as von Einsiedel has pointed out, in this dimension too, "knowledge is scant, and more research is clearly needed" (2005, 24). Indeed, we need to look no further than the unlikely and completely unpredictable trigger for the 2011 "Arab Spring" to demonstrate that even the most sophisticated models or compilations of indicators are unlikely to prove very productive in predicting when and for what reason violence will erupt.[5]

In truth, however, in determining the need for a preventative response, governments seldom, if ever, are dependent on academics (or for that matter, the press or other outside agencies) to alert them to impending problems, as these are generally well known. The crucial variable, as Rebecca Hamilton has argued, is *how governments react* to these problems (2011a, 193–205), and this reaction is in large part dependent on what *effective tools* are at their disposal (see Allison and Zelikow 1999, chap. 3). In the sections that follow we will assess the effectiveness of some of the major strategies available to the international community in operationalizing the responsibility to prevent.[6]

Problems of Implementation

Following the OECD definition above, conflict prevention measures are of two types: *long-term* "structural strategies" (those appropriate to deal with the "root causes" of conflict and state failure) and *short-term* "operational measures" (those designed to respond to signs of an imminent humanitarian crisis or state collapse). In the following pages we will assess the effectiveness of five of the most prominent of these measures: in the case of long-term structural strategies, *development aid*, *capacity building*, and *confidence and trust building*, and for short-term operational tactics, *diplomatic initiatives* and *rapid deployment of peacekeeping forces* to stabilize volatile situations. It was a combination of the two short-term tactics that the Obama administration used to prevent violence related to the independence of South Sudan, and in the book's conclusion their effectiveness will be evaluated.

Long-Term Structural Programs

Long-term approaches to conflict prevention are aimed at making fundamental changes to conflict-prone societies in such basic areas as culture, politics, and economics (see Goodhand and Hulme 1999). As Michael Brown and Chantal de Jonge Oudraat (2001) have pointed out, success of long-term measures depends on *cooperation* among all of the parties involved—the government at risk, contesting groups within society, and outside interveners—in order to implement what Séverine Autesserre (2010) has called "bottom up" strategies. To the extent this assessment is accurate, the *cooperation caveat* places clear limitations on the likely effectiveness of long-term strategies to deal with structural problems, especially as these exist in deeply dysfunctional societies.

Development Aid

Jonathan Glennie explains that "development aid seeks to make a difference in the short, medium and long term, fostering economic growth and reducing poverty." It focuses on improving conditions in areas like healthcare and education, as well as infrastructure through "large development projects such as hydroelectric dams and oil pipelines" (2008, 16). Indeed, since the end of World War II, "systematic aid ... government-to-government transfers ... or transfer[s] via institutions such as the World Bank" have ranked among the most popular strategies employed by the West to address the problem of poverty (Moyo 2009, 7). Partly on the assumption that there is a strong correlation between societal poverty and political violence and/or state failure, sub-Saharan Africa has been of particular concern in this respect since the percentage of the population there living on an income of $1.25 per day or less stands at 50.9, while that at $2.00 per day or less stands at 72.9 (World Bank 2011; see also UNDP 2011).

While overall the achievements of development aid have been significant, there are problems with the subset of states that are of specific concern to us. As Sebastian Mallaby observes:

> For decades, the aid intelligentsia was certain it had the solution to chaos.... But no magic key has yet been found. An obstinate group of dysfunctional countries has refused to respond to these approaches.... This is not to say that aid has failed. Since 1960, life expectancy in poor countries has risen from 45 to 64 years. The global illiteracy rate has fallen from 47 to 25 percent over the last three decades. And the number of poor people has fallen by about 200 million in the last two decades—a time when the world population has increased by 1.6 billion. Development institutions deserve more credit that they get.... *But donors must face up to their inability to shake the most dysfunctional countries out of poverty, especially in regions such as sub-Saharan Africa.* (2002, 3; italics added)

Nearly a decade earlier, Gerald Helman and Steven Ratner had come to the same conclusion: "Unfortunately ... [aid strategies] have met with scant success in failing states, and they will prove wholly inadequate in those that have collapsed. Western aid cannot reach its intended recipients because of violence, irreconcilable political divisions, or the absence of an economic infrastructure" (1993, 7).

Developments over the past decade present us with a paradox. Beginning with Millennium Development Goals in 2000, plus such efforts as the 2005 "Make Poverty History" campaign and Bob Geldof's "Live 8" concerts, the need for greater amounts of aid were popularized, especially for sub-Saharan Africa (see Live 8 2005; Glennie 2008, 115–20; Moyo 2009, 26–27). At the same time, some researchers were arguing that aid is not only ineffective in dealing with issues of poverty on the African continent, but may actually be contributing to problems.

Deborah Bräutigam and Stephen Knack examined the impact of aid on "poor governance" over the period 1982–1997 and their findings, based on *International Country Risk Guide* data, showed that "in Africa, higher aid levels are associated with larger declines in the quality of governance and in tax revenues as a share of GDP" (2004, 266). They identify "aid dependence" as a primary factor contributing to these problems and suggest that in parts of sub-Saharan Africa, "continued over long periods of time, large amounts of aid and the way it is delivered make it more difficult for good governance to develop" (255–56). They cite African Development Bank statistics showing that, in 1999, "27 sub-Saharan countries receiv[ed] at least 25% of net aid as a percentage of government expenditures…. Seventeen of these countries receiv[ed] net aid equivalent to more than half of all government expenditures" (257). They do not go as far as suggesting an end to aid programs, but argue that "aid needs to be delivered more selectively and in ways that reinforce a virtuous cycle of development rather than contributing to a vicious cycle of poor governance and economic decline" (256).

More recent studies support these findings. Jonathan Glennie, while acknowledging that "government-to-government aid will always have an important supporting role to play … [claims it] is becoming increasingly clear … that dependency on aid from foreign donors has undermined the development of the *basic institutions* needed to govern and the vital link of accountability between state and citizen" (2008, 3, 5–6; italics in the original). His conclusion is that "Africa needs less and better aid" (101). Dambisa Moyo's provocative and controversial book *Dead Aid: Why Aid Is Not Working and How There Is a Better Way for Africa* takes the case against aid a step further, asking the question "has more than US $1 trillion in development assistance over the last several decades made African people better off?" Her answer is an emphatic "No. In fact, across the globe the recipients of this aid are worse off; much worse off…. Aid has been, and continues to be, an unmitigated political, economic, and humanitarian disaster for most parts of the developing world" (2009, xix). She concludes that "at the end of it all, it is virtually impossible to draw on Africa's aid-led development experiment and argue that aid has worked. The broadest consequences of the aid model have been ruinous" (27).[7] She added that "what is perhaps most amazing is that there is no other sector, whether it be business or politics, where such proven failures are allowed to persist in the face of such stark and unassailable evidence.... The problem is that aid is not benign—it's malignant" (47). Moyo focuses on the consequences of aid dependency, among which she cites corruption and market distortions. Her views are extreme and not all agree with her position (see, e.g., Bunting 2009). First we must remember that causality (opposed to correlation) is hard to isolate in the real world. We must of course also consider the possibility that countries on the receiving end of aid would have been even worse off without international assistance. Most would probably agree that there have had to be at least some benefits resulting from what are massive amounts of dollars in aid. Whatever the case, the significance of these skeptical findings for the responsibility to prevent is that a strategy that experienced considerable success in other areas of the globe is seen increasingly as either ineffective or counterproductive in preventing tragic descents into violence and state failure in an area of the world where these outcomes are all too common.

Capacity Building

Merilee Grindle and Mary Hilderbrand define *capacity* as "the ability to perform appropriate tasks effectively, efficiently and sustainably. In turn, *capacity building* refers to improvements in the ability of public sector organizations, either singly or in cooperation with other organizations, to perform appropriate tasks" (1995, 445; italics added). Capacity-building strategies are therefore focused on the need to strengthen "the foundation" that underlies development, and as such can be seen as a non-monetary type of foreign assistance. According to the United Nations Development Programme (UNDP),

> capacity development helps to strengthen and sustain this foundation and is the "how" of making development work better. Put simply, it is about the "capable institution" that is able to better serve its mandate.... [It] is a process of transformation of leaders and managers, communities and organizations from the inside, based on nationally determined priorities and desired results. *It can be facilitated and supported, but cannot be driven from the outside.* (UNDP 2009, 2; italics added)

The UNDP suggests that capacity building programs follow a basic five-step process: (1) the engagement of stakeholders; (2) the assessment of assets and needs; (3) the formulation of "a capacity development response;" (4) the "implementation of a capacity development response;" and (5) the evaluation of the response in terms of an improvement in capacity (2009, 4).

In choosing strategies of prevention we are concerned primarily with countries that are recognized as being conflict-prone, and in this context "Security

Sector Reform" (SSR)—improvements in the capacity of institutions such as the armed forces, intelligence services, police, judiciary, and prisons—has emerged as a top priority program on the part of the international community (on SSR, see USAID 2009; and Hendrickson and Karkoszka 2002).

Rocklyn Williams has examined some of the problems entailed with the transfer of organizational behaviours from what are generally peaceful developed societies to ones that are neither, and agreed with the UNDP position regarding the limitations of outside input. With specific reference to Africa, he concluded that *"a rigorous and strategic indigenisation of the concept will be required on the … continent …* if any semblance of local ownership can be effected, and if any potential discrediting of the concept, from opportunistic and predictable political quarters, is to be avoided" (2000, 22; italics added). Williams's advice merits considerable reflection and attention.

David Beer, a Royal Canadian Mounted Police Officer involved in implementing a capacity-building project for Haiti's police force in the mid-1990s, has described some the difficulties encountered. The project in question was a UN-American-Canadian-French-Haitian initiative to reform Haiti's security sector, carried out under the auspices of the US International Criminal Investigative Training Assistance Program (ICITAP). Beer first pointed out that in 1994, following the removal of the de facto military government in power after President Jean-Bertrand Aristide's ouster in 1991, Haiti was an excellent candidate for SSR in that it "offered an environment generally free of violence in which to conduct development activities.… [Additionally, there was] no shortage of human or financial resources available for development, and the justice sector received particular attention" (2001, 2–3). In spite of these highly favourable circumstances, at the project's end Beer concluded that "the human rights situation, a principal factor in the international intervention throughout [the decade of the 1990s,] … had not improved significantly" (68).

Beer cited a host of problems both with the donors and on the part of the recipient state. Regarding the former, there was a lack of consensus on common goals and a failure to deal comprehensively with all components of the justice system (police, judiciary, and prisons). These shortcomings were complicated by the intrusion of national interests, especially the US focus on controlling drug trafficking, which distorted priorities. In Beer's judgment, "what should have been an 'international effort' soon developed into a series of poorly integrated independent programs" (2001, 35).

Beer noted not only differences between police practices in developed countries and Haiti, but between those in the United States and Canada (which followed a "community policing" model) and those in France where there was an emphasis on "maintaining order." As a consequence, at the point when administrative responsibility for the training program shifted from Canada to France, the basic principles underlying it shifted as well. An even more fundamental problem was that the type of policing practices characteristic of developed countries (heavily involved in the collection and analysis of forensic evidence) was a poor fit for Haitian needs. While the forensics training provided was deemed a "technical success," the evidence produced by those trained was not used since there was no corresponding training program for judicial agencies responsible for criminal prosecution. Further, as Graham Allison and Philip Zelikow noted in their explanation of "organizational processes" related to decision making in the Cuban Missile Crisis, complex organizations operate on the basis of "standard operating procedures" (1999, 143–53), and along with militaries, police forces are quintessential SOP-following organizations. As a consequence, "off the shelf" training modules that were used often had little relevance to the Haitian police recruits who were on the receiving end of the training.[8]

With respect to the behaviour of the recipient state, Beer pointed out that the "notion of partnership included a committed and responsive recipient state working with the international community in collective relationships with common goals of conflict prevention" (2001, 2). Unfortunately, there was a serious lack of commitment to the project on the part of the Haitian government. As a result there was little "sustainability" to the seemingly successful programs that had been initiated. For example, Beer noted that a training facility was built, furnished, and opened, but never used, because the Haitian government refused to pay the salaries of those who were to run it. Equally egregious was a refusal to pay for film to be used in the photographing of crime scenes and for motor oil needed to maintain vehicles donated to the police force. He concluded that "there was perhaps no factor more singularly important to limiting the success of development than the failure of the Haitian government to accept responsibility for, and contribute fully to its own development and its avoidance of a leadership role" (2001, 72–73).[9] There is little doubt that cooperation problems of this kind are multiplied many times in situations where lack of capacity is aggravated by ongoing violence.[10]

Trust and Confidence Building

A concise definition of trust is provided by James Notter, namely "to count on someone to do as they say they will do." He also notes that "just as trust lives at the heart of our personal, every-day relationships, *trust is at the heart of conflict transformation theory and practice*" (1995, 3, 17; italics added).

In the context of conflict resolution, international trust-building strategies can be applied to state actors as well as to those at the sub-national level in cases where ethnic, religious, cultural, or regional groups have come to expect the worst on the part of enemies, real or perceived. Trust-building strategies are premised on changing reciprocal expectations of bad behaviour, but according to Notter no one should expect any quick fixes: "In deep-rooted conflicts, where parties are not simply disputing over material interests but are suffering from deeply damaged social relationships, rebuilding trust is a key step towards resolution and transformation." This, however, is described as a "daunting" task (1995, 9–10).

Notter reviewed a trust-building program carried out in Cyprus by the US-based Institute for Multi-Track Diplomacy. The program had a time frame of "at least five years" and began with the organization having "to earn the trust and respect of the Greek and Turkish Cypriots [participating in the program]," a process that in itself "took several years." Even more difficult was the "attempt to foster the creation of a trust relationship between two different parties engaged in a deep-rooted social conflict." Notter outlined the process thus: "(1) making a long-term commitment; (2) showing up; (3) establishing familiarity; (4) listening; and (5) being perceived as neutral and fair" (1995, 11). The project operated on the clear understanding that "the Cyprus conflict is theirs to resolve, not ours, and that they know best, among them, what a fair and just solution would entail" (12). Notter acknowledged that training a total of thirty Greek and Turkish Cypriots in techniques of trust building was just the beginning of a long process, and he noted that despite the island being relatively free of "significant violence" for twenty years, "great psychological distrust" remained (15).

If there are that many problems in building confidence in a situation in which there are only two clearly defined parties who have not been in actual violent conflict for many years, it is difficult to imagine the problems involved for such a process in a multi-level quagmire such as that in the Democratic Republic of the Congo (DRC). Not only are there a varying number and type of contenders for the keys to the kingdom in the DRC, but as Séverine Autesserre has convincingly pointed out, there is also a plethora of localized village against village and ethnic group against ethnic group problems that are only occasionally and incidentally related to national issues. She is extremely critical of international peacekeeping operations in the country because she maintains that they have concentrated exclusively on the "Big Picture" (the "Top Down" approach in her terms), and ignored the many on-the-ground, community-based issues (the "Bottom Up" approach), which feed into and exacerbate the larger one (see 2010, chaps. 4 and 5 for more details of her argument).[11]

If Autessere is even partly correct (and in the view of the present authors she is more than partly so), attempting to utilize confidence-building techniques in complex and long-lasting conflicts like that in the DRC would not only be a mammoth task, but probably less effective than would the removal of tangible local grievances, though that would also be by no means easy.

While not wishing to draw too many parallels between South Sudan and the DRC, the situation confronting the international community in South Sudan is far closer to that in the DRC than it is to Cyprus (see LeRiche and Arnold 2012, chaps. 5–7). We find it difficult, therefore, to avoid the conclusion that as a method of conflict prevention or conflict remediation, trust and confidence building is at best a supportive instrument, and one that is likely to be useful mainly in the simpler kind of circumstances that are rarely seen by the international community in dealing with violent, multi-level intra-state conflicts.

Short-Term Operational Measures

Preventive Diplomacy

Diplomacy has traditionally been seen as a set of measures (both positive and negative) whereby one state attempts to alter the behaviour of another, the end goal being either the pursuit of or the retreat from a given policy. Diplomatic initiatives to deal with immediate conflict situations include the passing of UN Security Council resolutions, the dispatch of fact-finding or observer missions, and the offer of "rewards" for state behaviour that contributes to bringing violence under control or threats of punishment, such as sanctions, for failure to do so. In evaluating the effectiveness of coercive diplomacy in changing problematic state behaviour, we must bear in mind Jack Donnelly's sobering assessment that especially in hard cases, those where "comprehensive material sanctions seem appropriate ... they are unlikely to have much effect" (2013, 204). In fact it was rewards that the Obama administration used in attempting to influence Sudanese President Omar al-Bashir to agree to allow the pending independence to South Sudan (see Chapter 8).

One of the problems involved in evaluating the effectiveness of diplomacy as a tool of conflict prevention is that much of it is done "behind the scenes," more or less out of the eye of the press and the public (Soderlund et al. 2012, 145). There is of course good reason for this. Especially when one or two key players can be identified, "quiet" diplomatic pressure, which avoids public "loss of face," has a far greater chance of success than open accusations and demands. For example, Andrew Natsios revealed that, prior to the end of March 2004, President Bush had made eleven phone calls to Sudan's President Omar al-Bashir pressing him on CPA negotiations (2012, 157–58), though we cannot of course know how influential those calls might have been. The reality is that diplomatic successes are rarely easy to identify, not least because it is hard to know what crises have been averted, let alone why they were averted. Failures, obviously, are far more readily apparent, though the cause of failure also must usually be guessed at. Clearly, good, quiet diplomacy is useful, and may be successful, but there is no guarantee that it will be, and much will depend on the particular circumstances involved.

Counted among short-term diplomatic successes is Secretary-General Kofi Annan's mission to Kenya in early 2008, which was judged to be instrumental in constructing a power-sharing agreement that curbed the ethnic violence following a disputed election in December 2007 (Murithi 2009, 97). As well, UN and international actors pressured Zimbabwe's Robert Mugabe to agree to a transitional government in 2009 (Howard-Hassmann 2010; International Crisis Group 2010). Among prominent failures, on the other hand, were the negotiations to end the Kosovo Crisis in 1998–1999, and efforts in 2012 by the Arab League and the UN to curb fighting in Syria, which had to be abandoned due to the persistence of violence. Earlier, the 1993 effort to end the sporadic civil war in Rwanda was an ironic mixture of success *and* failure. The effort was successful in negotiating a power-sharing agreement that theoretically ended the conflict, but that success prompted extremist elements within the government to orchestrate the genocide that may have resulted in more deaths than the continuation of the civil war would have (Soderlund et al. 2008, chap. 5). The lesson here is that diplomacy should not be expected to force parties involved in a conflict to accept half a loaf if one of them remains convinced there is a possibility of obtaining the whole. Likewise problematic were the separate UN and US fact-finding missions to Darfur in 2003–2004; they came to different conclusions on whether genocide was occurring, thus complicating any consistent response (Sidahmed, Soderlund, and Briggs 2010: 103–5). What has to be recognized is that there was a vast difference between the situations in Kenya and Zimbabwe and those in Syria and Rwanda. Diplomatic pressure tends not to be successful when multiple parties are involved in conflict and nobody has decision-making authority, or when violence has already become entrenched.

Diplomatic persuasion, bargaining, and compromise rightfully are the first-order methods of dealing with violence-threatening differences in the international community. They are, moreover, constants that will always be deployed because in a world that grows smaller on a daily basis significant conflict anywhere is everyone's concern, and diplomacy is by far the cheapest means of responding to it. But no one should expect that such methods will always be sufficient, which means that other responses, like physical interventions of various kinds, must be held in reserve.

Rapid Deployment of Peacekeeping/Stabilization Missions

One such response is the rapid deployment of stabilization missions. The UN Charter (Chapter 7, Article 43) envisioned that member states would provide the Security Council with "armed forces, assistance and facilities ... necessary for the purpose of maintaining international peace and security" (UN 1945). Early on, the UN's Military Staff Committee addressed the issue of a standing force and, "at least in theory," achieved agreement regarding the desirability of creating one. There were, however, "significant disagreements among the Permanent Five about the size, composition, and basing arrangements of national contributions ... [and as a result] the whole enterprise was abandoned" (Roberts 2008, 100). In the years that immediately followed, despite numerous initiatives by the UN's first Secretary-General, Trygve Lie, little progress was made in resolving these differences. Within a brief time the idea was largely forgotten, though occasionally mooted as desirable (see, e.g., Frye 1957; Boutros-Ghali 1992). Thus, when they have been needed, UN peacekeeping missions have had to rely on voluntary contributions, sometimes led by a major power with assistance from others (the "lead nation model"), sometimes by a regional organization, and sometimes by the UN itself.

As UN peacekeeping expanded from dealing primarily with interstate conflict to include the far more complex cases involving the *human security* of persons at risk within sovereign states, the need for some sort of standing force, capable of being deployed to an emerging conflict site on short notice, became an even more urgent priority. There have been a few occasions when, if not a standing force, then at least a rapidly formed international deployment has been possible. For instance, Australia led a multilateral peacekeeping force, "INTERFET," into East Timor in 1999 (Soderlund et al. 2008, chap. 11) and France led "Operation Artemis" into the Congo's Ituri region in the spring of 2003 (Soderlund et al. 2012, 95–96). Both of these missions were possible, however, only because the lead states had particular interests in the situations and had the means at hand to undertake them. Many have long felt the need is for multilateral global (or at least regional) standby forces that can be rushed to trouble spots at more or less a moment's notice. Work in this direction has, in fact, progressed for some time. In the following pages we will briefly review four organizational structures that have been advanced to deal with the UN's need for a Rapid Deployment Capability (RDC): a Western-led rapid reaction force, an African standby force, a UN "Emergency Peace Service," and private military contractors.

A Western-Led Rapid Reaction Force: SHIRBRIG

In 1996, in response to a Danish initiative, the Standby High Readiness Brigade (SHIRBRIG) was formed by seven nations (Austria, Canada, Denmark, the Netherlands, Norway, Poland, and Sweden)—and by 2008, the year prior to the organization's termination, it counted 23 states in various categories of membership (Koops and Varwick 2008, 14–15, table 3). As described by Joachim Koops and Johannes Varwick, this multinational brigade of a maximum of

4,000 to 5,000 troops was "dedicated to rapid deployment (within 15–30 days of approval) for UN Peace Operations ... [and was to be] self-sustainable in theatre for up to 60 days.... [It was] to be deployed for not longer than six months, allowing regular long-term UN units to form and succeed the brigade" (2008, 6). SHIRBRIG was never intended to be "a formal organ of the UN System," but was developed in coordination with the UN's Department of Peacekeeping Operations (DPKO), which was its only client. In theory it should have provided the needed capacity to move quickly into an area of developing crisis and stabilize the situation. Indeed, in 2003, Peter Langille and Tania Keefe referred to SHIRBRIG as "the most advanced multinational mechanism for UN peace operations to date" (quoted in Koops and Varwick 2008, 7).

For a variety of reasons, however, SHIRBRIG failed to live up to expectations. Its principal success was its first deployment in the Chapter VI peace monitoring mission to Ethiopia and Eritrea (UNMEE) in 2000, when it responded with 1,200 to 1,500 personnel.[12] But this was the closest it ever came to "full-brigade deployment," largely because when it came to delivering troops earmarked for the undertaking, states rarely followed through by providing them (SHIRBRIG 2009, 15). At least partly because of this difficulty, SHIRBRIG's mission underwent significant changes almost immediately. And at least one of these changes, an emphasis on planning activities, placed it in direct competition with the UN's Department of Peacekeeping Operations (DPKO). As Koops and Varwick noted, "the DPKO want[ed] troop contributions, not planners" (2008, 24–25). In addition, problems in SHIRBRIG's decision-making structure regarding deployments led the UN to deal directly with member nations; SHIRBRIG "was not perceived as an organization, but a group of countries negotiating individually" (SHIRBRIG 2009, 51). The relationship between SHIRBRIG and DPKO became increasingly dysfunctional. By 2006, "it became increasingly clear ... that the organization's cumbersome decision-making process as well as the persistent absence of resources and political will ... [had undermined] SHIRBRIG's overall effectiveness" (SHIRBRIG 2009, 8). The organization was terminated in 2009.

SHIRBRIG nonetheless made a positive contribution by serving as a model for the development of an "African Standby Force" (ASF). SHIRBRIG's deployment to Côte d'Ivoire in 2003 (as a part of the UN Operation in Côte d'Ivoire—UNOCI) brought it into contact with the Economic Community of West African States (ECOWAS), and this subsequently led to SHIRBRIG serving as a model for the organization of two African standby forces—the Eastern Africa Standby Force (EASBRIG) and the West African Standby Force (ECOBRIG)—under the umbrella of the newly formed African Union (AU) (Koops and Varwick 2008, 29–34). The two new forces were described as "almost identical" to SHIRBRIG in organizational structure (2008, 22).

SHIRBRIG's significant efforts at capacity-building among these African forces also appear to have been both effective and appreciated. However, the SHIRBRIG report on "lessons learned" pointed out the obvious: "the decision to disband SHIRBRIG forced an end and limit to the support of the SHIRBRIG AFS partners" (2009, 25), and it lamented that the level of trust enjoyed by SHIRBRIG would not easily be transferred to other organizations (2009, 30–31).

Thus, while not without significant accomplishments, SHIRBRIG's stated goal of providing the UN with "a pre-pledged and ear-marked pool of troops on 'standby' and on a 'high level of readiness,' deployable at a short notice request by the Security Council," unfortunately was never realized to anywhere near the extent envisioned by its founders (Koops and Varwick 2008, 8). The SHIRBRIG lessons-learned report added emphasis to this conclusion: "it has become clear that its original aim of providing a rapid reaction capability at brigade level *was impossible to put into practice*" (2009, 97; italics added).

An African Standby Force (ASF)

Edmond Keller offered a bleak assessment of peacekeeping operations under the sponsorship of Africa's first pan-continent body, the Organization of African Unity (OAU):

> The OAU has from time to time been willing to try and engage in peacekeeping in domestic conflicts that have become regionalized, but it has not had the wherewithal to do so effectively. Such was the case in the first major peacekeeping effort in Chad in 1981–82. It was under financed and plagued by logistical problems. Most recently, the OAU has more or less stood helplessly on the sidelines as the conflict in the DRC has further conflagrated, drawing in neighbouring states such as Namibia, Zimbabwe and Angola in support of the Kabila government, and Rwanda and Uganda in support of rebel opposition groups. (2002, 10)

We will briefly review the record of African contributions to peacekeeping on the continent prior to the efforts of the African Union (successor organization to the OAU) beginning in 2003.

The OAU Mission in Chad (1980–1982). Given the OAU's twin commitment to "the right to national sovereignty and the concomitant principle of non-interference in the internal affairs of another sovereign state" (May and Massey 1998, 50), its intervention in the ongoing Chadian civil war in 1980 appears to have been on unsure ground from the very start. A lack of funds was apparent even as the operation began: "the OAU, without any single state, or group of states, to underwrite peacekeeping initiatives, was the most populous, yet poorest regional organization in the world" (May and Massey 1998, 58), and the mission to Chad quickly became dependent on foreign support, resulting in the organization becoming "just another actor in its own operation." As explained by Roy May and Simon Massey, "the extra-continental protagonists, notably France and the United States, treated the OAU as a necessary evil, rather than as the instigator of the mission. Likewise regional actors, including members of the IAF [Inter-African Force], worked to their own agenda. The layers of confusion and intrigue multiplied as the OAU acted as a conduit for self-interested international political realism played out on the Chadian stage" (1998, 55).

The organization also lacked the critical capability to move troops. Initially, three countries, Benin, Congo, and Guinea, were to furnish troops for the mission:

> The Congolese contingent, consisting of 550 soldiers, arrived in N'Djamena on January 18, 1980.… Congo lacked the transportation assets to move the battalion-sized element to Chad and relied upon assistance from Algeria. The Congolese reportedly arrived in N'Djamena aboard Algerian aircraft piloted by Angolans. The contingents from Benin and Guinea failed to arrive in Chad, with both countries claiming logistical and transportation problems as the cause. (Mays 2002, 48)

Finances, logistics, and issues of command continued to be major problems throughout the mission, with the first being the proximate cause for its abandonment in June 1982. As reported by Yvonne Kasumba and Charles Debrah, "the peacekeeping mission in Chad … ended abruptly with the withdrawal of United States and French support for the OAU, the latter of which was no longer able to sustain its deployment" (2010, 18).

Following that, the OAU demonstrated little interest in getting involved in peacekeeping operations. May and Massey concluded that this was probably for the best as "a reoccurrence of the Chad intervention could demolish the possibility of a valid *Pax Africana*" (1998, 62). Terry Mays, however, points out that with the OAU's retreat from peacekeeping, Nigeria turned to the Economic Community of West African States (ECOWAS) for its mission into Liberia in 1990, and South Africa to the Southern Africa Development Community (SADC)—"a smaller organization where it wielded considerable influence"—for stabilization missions in Botswana and Lesotho (Mays 2002, 157).

The ECOWAS Mission in Liberia (1990). When Liberia disintegrated into chaos in the summer of 1990, many thought that the United States, the world's only remaining superpower, would step in to restore order since there were historic connections between the two countries. For better or worse, this did not happen. Instead, the regional organization ECOWAS, led by Nigeria, undertook a military intervention. Herbert Howe notes that ECOWAS's intervention arm, the Economic Community of West Africa Cease-fire Monitoring Group (ECO-MOG), was the first sub-regional organization with which the UN cooperated on a formal basis (1996/97, 159).

While not the disaster experienced by the OAU in Chad, ECOMOG's intervention in Liberia (and later encompassing Sierra Leone as well) cannot be considered a success either. Problems related to the unity of the organization itself (ECOWAS was split along English–French lines), a misreading of the complex situation at hand (seen initially as classic peacekeeping rather than peace enforcement), questionable command decisions, plus what were seen to be inadequate numbers of troops, led most observers to question the overall wisdom of the intervention (in addition to Howe 1996/97, see Adeleke 1995; Alao, Mackinlay, and Olonisakin 1999). Lacking the strength to defeat its opponents, ECOMOG became in effect another long-term contender for power. For example, Michael Innes describes the period following the ECOMOG intervention as "a seven year campaign to seize control of the state" (2004, 11), while Yekutiel Gershoni concluded that "the prolongation of the war ... was partly due to the divisions within ECOWAS, and the inefficiency of ECOMOG" (1997, 57).

Peacekeeping under the AU. As Kasumba and Debrah have pointed out, "the OAU was not carved out to manage the complex security threats and the international concern for human rights and good governance that faced the continent after the Cold War." However, in the early years of twenty-first century, the African Union (AU) emerged as the pan-African organizational replacement for the OAU, and it had a different focus—namely, "the achievement of peace and security in Africa" (2010, 11). In this revised context, the AU began as early as 2003 to consider its peacekeeping options, especially the development of an African Standby Force (Cilliers 2008, 1). Such an initiative followed recommendations contained in the 2000 Brahimi report, which maintained that "a brigade (approximately 5,000 troops) is what is required to effectively deter or deal with spoilers of a peace process.... [Moreover] the military component of that peace operation ought to deploy as a brigade formation. It should not deploy as a collection of battalions that are unfamiliar with one another's doctrine, leadership and operational practices" (Kent and Malan 2003, 72).

A protocol for the establishment of an AU Peace and Security Council (PSC) "came into force in December 2003," and following this, planning began for "five standby level forces, one in each of Africa's five regions [East, West, Central, South and, North] ... supported by civilian police ... and other capacities.... The ASF [was] intended for rapid deployment for a multiplicity of peace support operations that may include, inter alia, *preventive deployment*, peacekeeping, peace building, post conflict disarmament, demobilization, re-integrations and humanitarian assistance" (Cilliers 2008, 1; italics added).

Six deployment scenarios were envisioned, with each having its own reaction time:

> **Scenario 1:** AU/regional military advice to a political mission ... deployment within 30 days.... **Scenario 2:** AU/regional observer mission co-deployed with a UN mission ... deployment within 30 days.... **Scenario 3:** Stand-alone AU/regional observer mission ... deployment with 30 days.... **Scenario 4:** AU/regional peacekeeping force for UN Chapter VI and preventive deployment missions and peace building ... deployment within 30 days.... **Scenario 5:** AU peacekeeping force for complex multidimensional peacekeeping missions, including low-level spoilers ... deployment within 90 days.... **Scenario 6:** AU intervention, for example in genocide situations where the international community does not act promptly ... deployment within 14 days. (Cilliers 2008, 3–4; emphasis in the original)[13]

While the term "African Standby Force" is frequently used in the literature, in reality there are five relatively distinct standby forces, and, importantly, these are at different stages of development and have different structures. Some regions are lagging "far behind" others: "There are resource disparities amongst the different regions, both in financial and human resource terms—all owing to inherent peculiarities in the political and economic backgrounds of the different regions. Different regions have also opted to adopt varying forms in terms of standby forces" (Kasumba and Debrah 2010, 14).

Development of the AFS was to occur in two phases: the first, originally scheduled to end in 2005 (but extended until 2008), primarily involved planning regarding areas such as "*Doctrine*; *Command, Control, Communications and Information Systems* (C^3IS); *Standard Operating Procedures*; *Logistics* and *Training* and *Evaluation*.... [By 2010] it was envisioned that ... the AU would have developed its capacity to manage complex peacekeeping operations" (Kasumba and Debrah 2010, 15; italics in the original).

While Tim Muritihi contends that the AFS "will effectively project the responsibility to react" (2009, 93), it is not clear where the overall ASF concept stands in terms of operational readiness. As of 2010, Kasumba and Debrah noted that "a lot of good progress" had been made, but they also pointed to a number of factors working against "the ASF achieving its initial operational capability by 2010" (2010, 16). Among these, serious by any standard of evaluation, was an "apparent lack of conceptual buy-in by the relevant stakeholders.... Without conceptual and political buy-in, the ability to achieve the ambitious vision of the ASF will be severely weakened.... National-level support is particularly important as, without it, the ASF—and indeed, the entire [African Peace and Security Architecture]—will likely not be able to succeed" (17). They also note as problematic "a high degree of dependence by the AU on external partners for logistics and general service support management capabilities.... [As a consequence] if the AU is reliant on unpredictable funding sources there is danger that, when required, essential capabilities may not be available" (18–19).[14]

At the beginning of the ASFs development process, Vanessa Kent and Mark Malan outlined a series of problems that they would face, and advised that "for its part the AU will need to undertake a realistic assessment of member capabilities, to clearly articulate its needs and to set realistic and achievable goals." Cited as particularly important was "the political will to fund and implement a long list of recommendations" (2003, 71). Given reports of a lack of "conceptual and political buy-in" by member states and the 2009 termination of SHIRBRIG (which operated with a similar structure and in circumstances far more favourable to success), it is probable that only some, or possibly none, of the regional brigades will become operational in the near future.

African Union Mission in Sudan (AMIS). Although not dispatched early enough to prevent the conflict and not deployed under the banner of an African Standby Force, the AU did contribute to attempts by the international community to bring the Darfur crisis in Sudan under control. Beginning in June 2004 (almost a year and a half into the crisis), the AU sent 29 peacekeepers as part of a ceasefire commission. Rebecca Hamilton reports that not much appears to have changed from the days of the Chad mission in that "AMIS relied entirely on contributions from donor countries to finance its operations." The UN was forced to beg and borrow funding "from other sources on an ad hoc basis. The result was that the small AMIS contingent that arrived in Darfur had neither the manpower nor equipment to cope with the massive violence" (2011a, 46). As time passed, while the number of AMIS authorized personnel increased significantly (to 2,314 in October 2004, then to 7,731 in April 2005),[15] the consensus among observers was that "the AU [was] not up to the task" (US Lt. Col. Ronald Capps, quoted in Hamilton 2011a, 74). An unnamed US State Department official was of the same mind: "Those of us working closest to the AU realized that you could expand ten times over and they still wouldn't have the capacity.... You can't run a peacekeeping operation on voluntary contributions and have your partners do all the logistics for you" (quoted in Hamilton 2011a, 75). Hamilton added that "by late 2005 it was clear that the merits of their early deployment notwithstanding, AMIS could not protect civilians. Indeed, they were increasingly unable to protect themselves" (2011a, 75). Similar evaluations of AMIS's capabilities filled news reporting on Darfur from 2005 to 2007 (see Sidahmed, Soderlund, and Briggs 2010, chap. 5). In January 2006, for example, *New York Times* reporter Marc Lacey reported that AMIS was running out of money, and that if none were forthcoming, the mission would be terminated by the end of March (Lacey 2006).

AMIS was eventually integrated into a hybrid African-UN peacekeeping force, the United Nations–African Union Mission in Darfur (UNAMID), in the spring of 2008. Although the level of violence in Darfur has decreased, as of this writing (over ten years from its outbreak) the conflict is still not resolved. Just as troubling, Hamilton notes that UNAMID's centre of operations in el-Fasher "was guarded by Sudanese police, who had been sent from Khartoum for the job and were being paid for by UNAMID" (2011a, 175). A UN official described UNAMID troops as "internally displaced people in uniform. They cannot protect themselves" (quoted in Hamilton 2011a, 175).

UN Emergency Peace Service (UNEPS)
One of the more interesting (if unrealistic) proposals for addressing the lack of an operational quick response capacity is the idea of a UN Emergency Peace Service (UNEPS), advanced in 2006 in a report edited by Professor Robert Johansen on behalf of Global Action to Prevent War, the Nuclear Age Peace Foundation, and the World Federalist Movement. UNEPS was to be organized by "civil society, working with allies in the UN and interested governments." The organization was envisioned to have between 12,000 and 15,000 personnel "individually recruited from among volunteers from many countries, ... carefully selected, expertly trained, and coherently organized and commanded." It would include "civilian, police, judicial, and military personnel prepared to conduct multiple functions in diverse UN operations" (Johansen 2006, 21). The organization would be "permanent, based in UN designated sites, and include mobile field headquarters," and as a "quick response force … [it would be capable of deploying] *to quell an emergency within 48 hours after United Nations authorization.…* [Furthermore it is] designed to complement—not replace—other essential national, regional, and United Nations efforts" (Johansen 2006, 21–22; italics added). The start-up costs of UNEPS were estimated at "$2 billion, with an annual recurring cost of $900 million or more, depending on field operations" (Johansen 2006, 30).

In spite of criticism that "the report overreaches by allotting a role for the General Assembly and the Secretariat in deploying force" (Levitt 2010), the proposition has gained some rhetorical support from humanitarian organizations. However, in terms of becoming operational, the idea of a UN Emergency Peace Service has moved forward slowly. For instance, in December 2010, the Ottawa-based Civilian Peace Service Canada (CPSC) was cited as having accredited the first "Peace Professionals." Global Action to Prevent War's Organizational Development Director Robert Zuber indicated that his organization "is excited about [the CPSC] program, in part that developing this cadre is a necessary supplement to UN-based efforts to implement … R2P" (quoted in Green Party of Canada 2010). Nevertheless, if a multi-government-supported organization such as SHIRBRIG failed, it is hard to envision the circumstances in which a far larger, more expensive, and more organizationally complex UNEPS can expect to see much success.

The fact is that, while the world is growing more interdependent, even those states that could afford to do so are reluctant to commit resources to an *in case of* structure, when it might be argued that there are urgent *right now* needs to address. Their publics would probably be even less supportive of purchasing charitable insurance policies of this type. If this is true of the advanced countries of the world, it is doubly true of those, like all the African countries, that lack sufficient resources to satisfy domestic demands, and whose organizational structures are deficient for carrying out complex operations in any case.

Private Military Contractors

Perhaps even more controversial than UNEPS, in light of the murky reputation that "mercenaries" have established over the years, is the idea of using what are now referred to (using more sanitized terminology) as "private military contractors" (PMCs) as conflict preventers. The case has been made that PMCs can serve as "first responders" in instances of civil conflict. Although in the final analysis PMCs are not likely to be employed as full conflict-preventing operatives, there is a history in Africa of states successfully employing mercenaries to deal directly with conflict waged against them by insurgent groups.[16] In addition, the supporting role contributions of PMCs to UN peacekeeping operations is already well established. As noted by Jakkie Cilliers,

> At present the UN has contracted out most of its logistic requirements to commercial companies. For example, Los Angeles based Pacific Architects and Engineers (now part of Lockheed Martin) that provided the logistics backbone for the AU Mission in the Sudan (AMIS) (and recently Dyncorp) provides 34 base camps in Darfur as well as vehicle maintenance and telecommunications equipment based on a series of contracts, the most recent of which was valued at $21 million. (2008, 6)

The idea of the private sector assuming military tasks previously falling under the purview of the armed forces of nation-states was given standing with the publication of P.W. Singer's book, *Corporate Warriors: The Rise of the Privatized Military Industry* (2003). Singer distinguished between three types of private military firms on the basis of how close their operations were to "the tip of the spear," that is, to "active combat operations." Those at the tip of the spear were referred to as "military provider firms." Further removed from the tip were "military consulting" and "military support firms," which provide advice and training and "non-lethal aid and assistance" respectively (2003a, 92–93).

The key question is whether the first category of PMCs, the *military provider firm*, offers "a twenty-first-century business solution to the world's twenty-first-century security problems" (Singer 2003b, 60). Could private military contractors in fact be used as "the tip of the spear" in the form of a rapid reaction force to be deployed as a preventive measure in early stages of intra-state conflict? Singer recognized that "the idea of military provider firms replacing blue helmet troops on the ground is one of the most controversial proposals to emerge from the [security] industry's growth" (2003b, 63), and in discussing their use he presented a range of arguments for and against.

The most persuasive argument for the use of PMCs revolves around their availability and effectiveness: "Whenever recalcitrant local parties break peace agreements or threaten the operation, military firms would be hired to offer the muscle that blue helmets are unable or unwilling to provide" (Singer 2003b, 64). Scott Fitzsimmons presented the case that in terms of three criteria of military effectiveness—"the ability to project force against belligerents, the ability to rapidly transport elements of an intervention force into and within conflict areas, and a commitment to the success of a military mission"—the record of PMCs stacks up well against that of UN peacekeepers. For example, he argued that the South African PMC "Executive Options" demonstrated these capabilities to a far greater extent in dealing with Foday Sankoh's Revolutionary Front (RUF) in Sierra Leone and Jonas Savimbi's National Union for the Total Independence of Angola (UNITA) in the early 1990s than did UMAMIR (deployed to Rwanda) and UNAVEEM III (in Angola) (Fitzsimmons 2005). Singer agrees that PMCs have demonstrated an ability to get the job done, and have done so at a financial cost that appears to be no greater than conventional peacekeeping operations (Singer 2003b, 65; see also Shannon 2000, 105–11).[17] On the negative side, there are questions regarding who hires PMCs and who pays them.

In the case of Sierra Leone, the government appears to have paid Executive Options through concessions for mineral exploitation (Shannon 2000, 107–8), a practice not likely to appeal to organizations with a humanitarian focus. Clearly, the wording of a contract, who signs it, who pays the bills, and how these are paid, are all critical decisions. There are also possible contractual difficulties related to changing circumstances on the ground that could make the mission far more dangerous than the one initially contracted for. To these problems are added questions of who ultimately controls what a private military force actually does on the ground, to what system of laws (if any) it is answerable, not to mention the uncomfortable truth that many privately paid soldiers are not recruited on the basis of their respect for human rights. As Singer noted, "the industry cannot be described as imbued with a culture of peacekeeping" (2003b, 66). Not least on the list of reasons why PMCs are not likely to be used is that "the U.N. Department of Peacekeeping … may have a vested bureaucratic interest in opposing the privatization of forces" (Singer 2003b, 67). In short, while PMCs appear unsuited to carrying out full peacekeeping missions, there do appear to be some reasonable arguments pointing to their being able to successfully defuse violent outbreaks relatively quickly. In the final analysis, however, we agree with the assessment of Christopher Spearin that, "while pragmatic and not without its benefits, [the use of PMCs] is a highly problematic solution for humanitarians" (2001, 20).

Conclusion

The International Commission on Intervention and State Sovereignty (ICISS) was emphatic that the most desirable approach to conflict is to prevent it. While it is obviously difficult to identify instances of successful prevention, many commentators appear to believe that there have been too few. David Carment argues that the overall record of success is "not good," citing failures in the Congo, Guinea, Liberia, and Sierra Leone (2003, 408), and Edmond Keller adds, somewhat more charitably, that efforts in this direction have achieved "mixed results." He nonetheless maintains that pre-empting the eruption of violence where the most severe ethnic and cultural divides exist (like Rwanda, Somalia, Liberia, or the Democratic Republic of the Congo) should be a priority (2002, 12). Regardless of how much or how little success in prevention has occurred so far, it is certainly easy to point to instances in which millions of people continue to suffer through the failure or refusal of their governments to protect them. At the very least, therefore, the conclusion must be that much remains to be done. As the OECD argues, "a clear need for *a better strategic policy framework for conflict prevention and peacebuilding* work has been demonstrated" (2008, 10; italics in the original).

Just what "frameworks" might be effective or appropriate is difficult to imagine, though some suggestions have been put forward. Gerald Helman and Steven Ratner, for instance, suggest that "a more systematic and intrusive approach" in the form of a resurrection of the UN trusteeship system might be considered. They envision a three-level "United Nations Conservatorship" in which the most intrusive, full UN trusteeship, would be utilized for "failed states" (1993, 12–18). Sebastian Mallaby somewhat similarly proposes the creation of a new "International Reconstruction Fund" (along the lines of the World Bank and International Monetary Fund) to deal with "the growing danger of failed states." Such an organization would "assemble nation-building muscle and expertise and could be deployed wherever its American-led board decided" (2002, 6–7). Nearly half way through the second decade of the twenty-first century, however, there is little evidence that these or any other new mechanisms are being given serious consideration. Nor does it appear that any soon will.

In this circumstance there appears to be little alternative to a continued reliance on trying to improve the mechanisms already accepted, however reluctantly, as norms of international politics. First of all, constant and careful monitoring of situations perceived as potential trouble spots must be carried out in order to allow diplomatic and, if necessary, more assertive forms of intervention to take place as early as possible.[18] Rebecca Hamilton is undoubtedly correct when she observes that *"the effectiveness of any action will often depend upon early engagement"* because delay often means that the situation on the ground becomes more complex (2011a, 202; italics added). The UN and the international community at large must therefore be urged to focus on potential, as well as ongoing, conflicts.

Second, it is crucial (as we are not the first to point out), that those acting as "conflict-preventers" have the operational capacity to carry out their missions effectively. What this might mean would of course vary with the circumstance, but ideally it would involve having adequate "stabilization forces" available for deployment early enough following the outbreak of violence to prevent it from becoming a way of life, as it arguably did in Somalia and in the eastern Congo (DRC), and perhaps in Darfur. Efforts have been made in this direction, of course. As was noted earlier, SHIRBRIG appeared to be a near ideal model; however, in practice it did not deliver. It is not encouraging that at least some of the African Standby Forces are built on the same model. Nor is it encouraging that the difficulties the AU's AMIS mission in Darfur has encountered echo those encountered by the OAU's intervention force in Chad more than twenty years earlier. On the other hand, in 2011 it was possible for a trained, organized, and ready Ethiopian Standby Force of 4,000 to 5,000 troops to successfully deploy to Abyei within weeks to defuse a situation that might have derailed South Sudan's independence and thrust the region into renewed warfare. That could not have happened even ten years earlier, so it may be argued that progress is being made. Progress, however, is certainly going to be slow and halting, and unfortunately never sufficient.

CHAPTER 4
INFLUENCING PUBLIC OPINION AND FOREIGN POLICY DECISION MAKING
The Role of Mass Media

Introduction

In the wake of the humiliating end to the Vietnam War, the role played by mass media in US foreign policy decision making came to occasion significant attention by scholars (see, e.g., Mueller 1973; Braestrup 1977; Wyatt 1993; Schmitz 2005). The issue again picked up momentum following the end of the Cold War, this time focused on *whether, to what extent*, and *how* the international community should respond to the formidable challenges of humanitarian crises in far-off lands.

In explaining the 1992 US intervention in Somalia, Bernard Cohen presented the case for what has been called the "CNN effect," arguing that a mass-media–aroused public opinion had the power to pressure governments to launch humanitarian interventions in situations that they otherwise most likely would have avoided. According to Cohen, "by focusing daily on the starving children of Somalia, a pictorial story tailor-made for television, TV mobilized the conscience of the nation's public institutions, *compelling the government into a policy of intervention for humanitarian reasons*" (1994, 9–10; italics added). Additional anecdotal evidence for the scenario of media pushing the elder President Bush into intervening in Somalia was provided by Lawrence Eagleburger (as cited in Minear et al. 1996, 54–55) and Jeffrey Clark (1993, 213). As well, Walter Soderlund and colleagues traced the possible impact of media on the president's policy, which had been opposed to US involvement as late as the summer of 1992 (see 2008, chap. 3).

In a report for the Montreal Institute for Genocide and Human Rights Studies, Frank Chalk, Roméo Dallaire, and colleagues likewise focused on the crucial role played by media in promoting what was termed the "will to intervene" on the part of the international community in what might be seen as remote humanitarian disasters:

> The "fourth estate"—the news media—exerts a powerful influence on government. The "CNN effect" is credited with persuading the U.S. and Canadian governments to intervene in Somalia in 1992, Bosnia in 1995, and Eastern Zaire in 1996. Policy experts argue that the process of "policy by media," or formulating policy in response to media coverage, is a contemporary phenomenon that arises from the government's sensitivity to media coverage. While news media reports influence policy, the inverse is also true: *an absence of reporting on mass atrocities in a particular country removes the pressure on the American and Canadian governments to act on their "responsibility to protect."* (2010, 48; italics added; see also Thompson 2007)

The idea of a CNN effect acting as a significant driver of foreign policy decision making has been challenged by a number of scholars, prominent among whom are Steven Livingston and Todd Eachus (1995), Jonathan Mermin (1997), Warren Strobel (1997), Steven Livingston (1997), and Piers Robinson (2002). The basic argument outlined by these critics is that media tend to follow, not lead, government policy, and that what may appear to be independent media influence is in reality media reacting to messages put forward by political elites to condition public opinion.

Our position regarding a possible CNN effect is that Cohen's view that a media-aroused citizenry can somehow seize control of and drive foreign policy should not be taken literally. Contrariwise, we believe that it would be equally ill-advised to maintain that mass media (held by most to be widely influential in virtually all other areas of political life) have no influence on foreign policy decision making. Specifically, more than thirty years of research have demonstrated consistent "agenda-setting effects" (the transfer of "issue salience" from mass media to mass publics), while a more recent stream of research has also confirmed significant "framing effects" (media influence on how events are interpreted by mass publics), with the latter seen as most likely occurring in cases where "advocacy framing" is used (see Aday 2006). Moreover, a long tradition of democratic theory, backed more recently by empirical research, tells us that governments (at least those aspiring to be democratic) do tend to pay attention to the wishes of those who elect them (see Page and Shapiro 1992; Page 1996; Jacobs and Shapiro 2000). The net result, as Karen Callaghan and Frauke Schnell have reminded us, is that mass media in fact do exercise indisputable influence in the mobilization of public opinion—this by deciding "which issues to cover" (agenda setting) and "which frame to use" to explain events (2001, 188).

In the following sections of the chapter we will review agenda setting and especially framing effects of mass media as they relate to South Sudan's independence and the role played in that process by the United States and Canada. On the latter question, it is important to note that Piers Robinson examined the impact of media on intervention decision making in the context of a "policy-media interaction model" and concluded that media influence is maximized in instances of "policy uncertainty" on the part of political elites (2000; 2002, chap. 5). As will become clear in the following chapters, US policy toward the upcoming referendum in the south of Sudan was characterized by uncertainty well into 2010, providing a possible opening for an effective campaign of media advocacy.

Agenda Setting

In terms of documented media effects no theory has greater standing than *agenda setting*. From the shrewd observations of Walter Lippmann regarding the link between mass media and "pictures in our heads" (1922), to Bernard Cohen's oft-quoted assessment that while the press "may not be successful much of the time in telling people what to think, ... it is stunningly successful in telling its readers what to think *about* (1963, 14; italics in the original), to Maxwell McCombs and Donald Shaw's study of voting in the 1968 US presidential election that provided the first empirically based evidence (1972), the idea that there is a *transfer of issue salience* from mass media to the mass public has generated a body of research that at this point is virtually unassailable (see Rogers and Dearing 1988; Salwen 1988; McCombs and Shaw 1993; Kosicki 1993; Rogers, Dearing, and Bergman 1993; Iyengar and Simon 1993; McCombs, Shaw, and Weaver 1997; McCombs 2005; and Weaver 2007). The majority of people get their information about the world beyond their personal knowledge from mass media, and a wide range of research shows that the issues that enjoy repeated media attention take pride of place among peoples' perceptions of what they consider to be the most important issues facing society.[1]

Other than when US or Canadian military personnel are involved in combat operations, issues of foreign policy do not occupy a high priority position in North American mass media (Emery 1989; Riffe et al. 1994; Utley 1997; Wu 1998; McChesney 1999; Halton 2001; Parks 2002; Sutcliffe et al. 2009).[2] This appears to be the case especially for Africa (see Livingston and Eachus 1995; Hachten 2004; Sutcliffe et al. 2009), where events are not only under-reported but often misunderstood (Hawk 1992; Keim 1999; Dunn 2003).[3] Thus for events in a country such as Sudan, in the absence of media attention most people would be largely unaware of what is taking place. For example, while the Sudanese-government-initiated attacks against insurgents in Darfur began in the spring and peaked in the summer of 2003, it was not until late in May 2004 that US television news ran its first story on the conflict (Secretary of State Colin Powell's use of the word "genocide" to describe what was happening)—and that is when Darfur began to emerge as an issue that demanded international attention (Sidahmed, Soderlund, and Briggs 2010, 61; Hamilton 2011a, 37–39, 44). This of course highlights the reality that governments use media to a far greater extent than media influence governments (see Robinson 2000; 2002).

Significant for this study of the independence of South Sudan is the proposition by Maxwell McCombs and Amy Reynolds that "establishing ... salience among the public so that an issue becomes the focus of public attention, thought, and even action is the initial stage in the formation of public opinion" (2002, 1). In the words of Robert Entman, "agenda-setting can thus be seen as another name for successfully performing the first function of framing: defining problems worthy of public and government action" (2007, 163). The implication of these assessments is that for an issue as remote to the general North American population as the future of South Sudan, one cannot even begin to think of an aroused public opinion pushing for international action to avert another catastrophic humanitarian crisis without a significant agenda-setting effort by mass media.[4]

Framing

Gadi Wolfsfeld reminds us that news stories have two components—factual material (the *what*, *who*, *when*, and *where*, comprising four of the five W's of journalistic practice) and framing (bringing into play the fifth W, *why*) (1997, 34). While agenda setting deals with the transfer of issue salience from media to the general public, framing addresses the *impact of media content on the direction of public opinion*—specifically, frames "supply citizens with a basic tool kit of ideas they use in thinking about and talking about politics. How events and issues are packaged and presented by journalists can in this way fundamentally affect how readers and viewers understand those events and issues" (Price, Tewksbury, and Powers 1997, 482). Similarly, Thomas Nelson and colleagues tell us that "in political communications research, framing typically has been depicted as the process by which a source (a newspaper or television news story) ... defines the essential problem underlying a particular social or political issue, and outlines a set of considerations purportedly relevant to that issue." Importantly, they explain that frames have the power to promote a particular course of action; for example, use of "the 'genocide' frame recommends immediate and decisive international intervention in the conflict, while the 'lingering dispute' frame counsels restraint, as nothing can be done about the situation anyway" (Nelson, Oxley, and Clawson 1997, 222).

Framing deals with the way information is presented by mass media and in this sense it is one of the "tools of power" wielded by political elites (Entman 2007, 163). In the process of story construction, certain sources of information are favoured by news organizations, with research showing authoritative government spokespersons placing high the list. For example, Jon Western notes that "the view[s] held by the president and ... core advisors will often enjoy a privileged position in mobilizing public and political support" (2005, 5). Moreover, as Nelson and colleagues caution, while "political elites may fail to influence public opinion among the most knowledgeable through direct propaganda campaigns, ... they may succeed in directing public debate in their favor through clever frames" (1997, 239). Vincent Price and colleagues further explain the framing process: "By activating some ideas, feelings, and values rather than others, the news can encourage particular trains of thought about phenomena and lead audience members to arrive at more or less predictable conclusions" (1997, 483). Callaghan and Schnell point out the consequences: "By promoting a particular frame, political elites, the media, and other players *can alter how an issue is understood and thus shift public opinion.* In other words, political elites can effectively use frames to promote their own political ends" (2001, 186; italics added). Western argues that "how the public perceives a crisis initially and in the near future depends on the information it receives about the nature and severity of the crisis or threat," a key function of framing (2005, 5). With respect to foreign policy decision making this framing process involves first *defining the situation* (does a particular crisis constitute a threat to vital national interests?), and second, *setting the limits of possible responses* (e.g., are military as opposed to diplomatic responses called for?).

The Literature

In terms of an overview of frame elements that are present in media coverage of crises—based on a systematic content analysis of 247 business crisis news stories appearing in 2006 newspaper coverage in *The New York Times*, *The Washington Post*, and *USA Today*—Seon-Kyoung An and Karla Gower identified five widely used generic frames. In order of frequency, these frames were "attribution of responsibility, economic[s], conflict, human interest, and morality," findings which the authors reported to be very similar to those found in a 2000 study by Holli Semetko and Peter Valkenburg (An and Gower 2009, 108). While we believe the study's "business crisis" focus might have influenced the prominence of the economic frame to some degree, there is no doubt that the issue of oil revenues led to significant economic framing of the South Sudan independence process.

In his research on 131 academic studies of framing, Jörg Matthes differentiated between "issue-specific" and "generic" frames, noting that 78 percent of studies focused on issue-specific frames and only 22 percent on the generic type. Among the latter, "the *conflict frame* was the most frequently reported" (2009, 356). Not surprisingly, perhaps, "textual elements were treated as the main constituents of frames rather than visuals,"[5] but significantly, "83% [of studies] … completely neglected visuals," including 72 percent of those that focused on television content (355–56).[6]

Among academic studies of framing effects, a significant portion of research has employed experimental designs, where test and control groups (usually consisting of university students) were exposed to different framing of information, then tested for differences in interpretation of the same factual content. The issues examined in this type of research have tended to be mainly domestic, with findings confirming that frames do make a difference in how information is understood (see, e.g., Aday 2006; Chong and Druckman 2007; Gross 2008). Studies focused on international events are not as numerous, but these studies likewise have demonstrated framing effects, although, as we will elaborate in the following pages, they tend to be more nuanced and complex than those seen with respect to agenda setting.

In their study of media effects in television news reporting of the Gulf War (1990–1991), Shanto Iyengar and Adam Simon (1993) focused on the concepts of *agenda setting*, *priming*, and *framing* and found significant effects for all three.[7] The authors treated framing in the context of "the connection between qualitative features of news about the Gulf (in particular, the media's preoccupation with military affairs and the invariably episodic or event-oriented character of news reports) and public opinion" (1993, 366). Framing could be either "episodic" (dealing with the events) or "thematic" (general information such as contained in "backgrounders"), while the qualitative features studied involved story lines, symbols, and stereotypes. These, in turn, were used to *assign responsibility* for the events reported on (e.g., what is the origin of the problem) as well as to discuss *appropriate treatment* of it—the latter focusing on "who or what has the power either to alleviate or to forestall alleviation of the issue" (369).

In terms of findings, Iyengar and Simon found that, "not surprisingly, television news coverage of the Gulf was heavily episodic or event-oriented" (1993, 377). As well, in a comparison of news coverage (which was weighted heavily toward military action), with National Election Study respondents' stated preferences for diplomatic vs. military solutions, the authors hypothesized "that exposure to television news would enhance viewers' preferences for a military as opposed to a diplomatic response to the Iraqi occupation of Kuwait" (379). The hypothesized relationship did indeed prove to be statistically significant (.03), indicating that "exposure to episodic news programming strengthened, albeit modestly, support for a military resolution of the crisis" (381).

Jill Edy and Patrick Meirick's study of framing was done in the context of US military action in Afghanistan in the wake of the 11 September 2001 al-Qaeda attacks. The research studied the effects of two media frames used to explain the nature of the attacks ("crime" vs. "war"), which the authors note "were not necessarily oppositional" (2007, 120). In correlating survey respondents' exposure to these two frames with support for the war in Afghanistan, the research posed the following question: "How does the frequency of different frames in the media correspond to the frequency of their adoption in the public?" (121).

The first major finding was that framing effects are far more complicated than the transfer-of-issues-salience principle underlying agenda-setting theory. The dominant "war" frame (appearing twice as often as the "crime" frame), did not correlate with greater support for the war. This, the authors pointed out, confirmed Dietram Scheufele's earlier conclusion that "framing influences how audiences think about issues, not by making aspects of the issue more salient, but by invoking interpretive schemas that influence the interpretation of incoming information" (quoted in Edy and Meirick 2007, 122).

Another significant finding was that when multiple frames were present in media accounts of an event (a research question we will pursue in our study of South Sudan's path towards independence) "robust framing effects ... are sharply attenuated" (Edy and Meirick 2007, 124). Overall, the authors presented a scenario suggesting that audiences do in fact tend to adopt the "mixed frames" that are often contained in media reporting. The role of media thus is seen "as making interpretive resources available to the public," which are then incorporated into a complex process of evaluation and decision making. In reaching conclusions audiences relied heavily on "their own moral compasses to evaluate and combine frame elements instead of deriving moral valences from the frames" (136). This of course makes any easy assessment regarding the likely strength and direction of framing effects an uncertain undertaking at best.

Three studies of framing, all employing experimental designs, relate directly to the research undertaken in this book—Adam Berinsky and Donald Kinder's study of *empathy* vs. *distance framing*, James Druckman's examination of *source credibility*, and Sean Aday's assessment of *advocacy framing*.

Berinsky and Kinder examined the process whereby "citizens organize and retain information" by linking media frames to "cognitive processes." In the context of the evolving crisis in Kosovo in 1998, they investigated how media framing of events led to "the creation of frames in cognition" among participants in the study. By altering the presentation of material—from "emphasizing the need to intervene" (empathy framing) to "highlighting the importance of staying out" (distance framing)—the researchers were "able to directly measure the effects of the particular media 'frame' on political understanding" (2006, 640–41). Their overall conclusion on the impact of even relatively subtle manipulation of framing deserves our close attention: "Compared to those who were assigned to the story that highlighted the risks of intervening, participants assigned to the story emphasizing the humanitarian aspects of the crisis were more likely to favor U.S. intervention, *not just in Kosovo but elsewhere around the world*" (653; italics added).

Druckman's study examined the key question of what constitutes successful framing, namely, "When do citizens 'accept' a frame?" He emphasized that the intent of the study was "*not* to suggest that framing effects are insignificant or irrelevant; indeed, it is because they are so important that understanding their limits can provide critical insight into public opinion formation" (2001, 1042; italics in the original). He suggested that framing effects work "through a psychological process in which individuals consciously and deliberately think about the relative importance of different considerations suggested by a frame (i.e., frames work by altering *belief importance*)" (1043; italics in the original).

In the process of establishing belief importance, the credibility of sources of information used in reporting is seen as a critical variable. Source credibility is derived from two criteria: "(1) the speaker's audience must believe that the speaker possesses knowledge dealing with considerations that are actually relevant to the decision at hand, and (2) the speaker's target audience must believe that the speaker can be trusted to reveal what he or she knows" (Druckman 2001, 1045). Findings based on a study using an experimental design confirmed the moderating effects of source credibility: "people seek guidance from sources they believe to be credible" (1061). Accordingly, in the studies of newspaper reporting of events in South Sudan that follow in chapters 5–7, sources of news were identified by their positions, views attributed to them were identified, and to the extent possible, the actual language used by them was quoted rather than paraphrased.[8]

Citing the literature on agenda setting and framing, Sean Aday argued "that not all issues, frames, or attributes have similar effects on audience attitudes … [and further] that the reach, and limits, of media influence are highly contextual" (2006, 769). Thus his research focused on why framing effects show up in some cases and not in others.

Aday looked at news stories specifically in terms of their use of "advocacy frames" vs. "objectivist frames." The former are characterized as "largely one-sided, often solution-oriented, and/or reflecting consensus."[9] He noted that such framing is often used "in coverage of foreign policy and, especially, war, where coverage has been shown to be uncritical and contributing to rally effects.… By contrast, objectivist frames are those that select two-sided narrative devices and/or a detached reportorial stance. These are most evident in conventional event-driven, or episodic, news stories, which typify modern news coverage" (2006, 769–70). Aday hypothesized that advocacy frames will have a greater impact on audiences than will objectivist frames: "We should expect that the narrative format that requires audiences to devote the least cognitive effort in judgment making—advocacy frames—to be more successful in creating attitude change than the format that demands more effort" (770). Aday's findings, based on an experimental design, "supported the hypothesis that stories utilizing an advocacy frame can have a framesetting effect on audiences," with the greatest effect seen in those "that include exemplars and vivid narrative language" (778–79). In that advocacy framing was relatively predominant in media coverage of Darfur (Sidahmed, Soderlund, and Briggs 2010), and nearly absent in coverage of the Congo Wars (Soderlund et al. 2012), the present study will pay particular attention to its use regarding how the press presented the role of the international community to North American audiences at the various steps marking South Sudan's progress toward independence, especially how news frames may have affected the international community's "will to intervene."[10]

Nancy Sherman has asked an intriguing question with respect to international responses to humanitarian crises in far-off lands: "How do we come to feel the ethical imperative to ally ourselves with those outside our borders?" (1998, 103). She argues that such an ethical imperative "depends upon understanding others' circumstances ... [and in this process] our private imaginations are fed by *public images and narratives*." This of course puts front and centre questions regarding "the influences of media on the shaping of foreign policy and, more generally, about the conception of morally responsible journalism" (110, 114).[11] Berinsky and Kinder tell us clearly that even in the absence of advocacy, "frames not only enhance understanding; they influence opinions" (2006, 654). How the press presented the roles of the US and Canada vis-à-vis their responsibility to prevent a humanitarian disaster in South Sudan to their respective audiences, is an issue we will address in the concluding chapter.

Research Methods

Historically there has been a low level of media interest in Sudan's civil wars (Livingston and Eachus 1995; Minear, Scott, and Weiss 1996; Prunier 2009). Additionally, Wolfsfeld has pointed out that media tend to focus on events, not processes (2004, 16–18). Thus, in an attempt to maximize instances of press engagement with Sudan, the following three chapters address the path toward South Sudan's independence by means of a content analysis of North American press reporting of three key events: (1) the nation-wide Sudanese elections held in April 2010; (2) the referendum on the south's independence held in the south in January 2011 (both of these called for in the 2005 CPA); with the results of latter culminating in (3) the declaration of independence by the Republic of South Sudan in early July 2011. In each case, a two-full-month period of press coverage surrounding the event is examined.[12]

As this project was initially conceived, both broadcast and print media in the United States and Canada were to be included in the research. Unfortunately television news had failed to cooperate, paying virtually no attention to the key events associated with South Sudan's path toward independence. Out of necessity therefore, we concentrated our attention on major agenda-setting newspapers in the United States and Canada. For the US, the newspapers studied were *The New York Times* and *The Washington Post*, while for Canada those studied were *The Globe and Mail* (Toronto) and the *Ottawa Citizen*. This sample includes the "newspapers of record" and the major capital-city newspapers in each country.[13] Over the three events studied, the data set collected consists of a total of 200 stories—127 (63.5%) appearing in the US papers and 73 (36.5%) in their Canadian counterparts. Stories from *The New York Times* were accessed through the newspaper's online archive and Factiva.org; stories for *The Washington Post* through Factiva.org and Nexus-Lexus; those for *The Globe and Mail* through Factiva.org and ProQuest; and those for the *Ottawa Citizen* through ProQuest.[14]

The research reported focuses both on *agenda-setting* and *framing* effects. The former were studied by means of quantitative measures (e.g., number of stories, date of publication, type of content, and affiliation of the reporter). For the latter we used a qualitative approach involving a narrative reconstruction of event coverage. This analysis centred on the identification of important issues, attribution of responsibility for problems, predictions regarding likely outcomes, and assignment of international responsibility to deal with these problems (i.e., "treatment frames" reflecting advocacy for action), as well as single vs. mixed frame presentations.

The combined data set of 200 items enables us to make reasonable comparisons between the likely understanding of issues surrounding South Sudan's independence among informed publics in the United States and Canada at three distinct time periods in the sixteen months prior to the actual declaration of independence in July 2011. The key research question addressed is: To what extent did North American press coverage, in terms of agenda setting and framing, match the expectations of Chalk and Dallaire in terms of influencing their respective governments to adopt "a will to intervene" posture in the event of a new humanitarian disaster in South Sudan? While readers will no doubt be able to reach their own conclusions, the definitive answer to the question will be provided in the concluding chapter.

CHAPTER 5

NORTH AMERICAN PRESS COVERAGE OF THE 2010 SUDANESE ELECTIONS

Methods

The first key event examined on South Sudan's path toward independence was the 2010 Sudanese elections held in mid-April 2010. As discussed in the preceding chapter the study focused on coverage in major agenda-setting newspapers in Canada, *The Globe and Mail* (Toronto) (N=6) and the *Ottawa Citizen* (N=9), and in the United States, *The New York Times* (N=15) and *The Washington Post* (N=10). In all, a total of 40 stories concerning the election appeared in the four newspapers during the two-month period of press coverage that began on 15 March and ended on 15 May 2010.

Findings

In view of the impact of increasingly stretched media resources,[1] and a low priority for foreign (especially African) news, the volume of coverage on the 2010 elections can be described as reasonable, especially in that three of the four newspapers studied had their own reporters on the ground in Sudan to cover the elections for at least some period of time.

The Globe and Mail

All election content in *The Globe and Mail* appeared as inside-page news stories. Reporting began on 7 April, five days prior to the beginning of the vote, with a report by *The Globe*'s African Bureau Chief, Geoffrey York. That story, datelined Khartoum, dealt chiefly with the conduct of the election campaign, noting that President Omar al-Bashir's hands were "in full control of the electoral levers ... [and that] the opposition has been squeezed off the political stage" (York 2010a).

The withdrawal and subsequent boycott of the elections by several opposition parties were reported. Implications of the elections for the upcoming referendum were also addressed. It was pointed out that their legitimacy was "rapidly dwindling … casting doubts on whether Sudan can navigate peacefully through the tense months leading to a January referendum on secession by South Sudan." The story cited a report by the International Crisis Group that reinforced the *likely violence* frame: "'The NCP [National Congress Party] has refused to create the conditions for free and fair elections.… It intends to continue to dominate Sudan, thus *leaving marginalized people to feel that they have no other option for challenging the status quo than continued armed resistance*'" (2010a; italics added). The report concluded with the observation that "a victory by Mr. al-Bashir in a fundamentally flawed election will make it even more likely that South Sudan will vote for independence in the referendum in January."

In a 10 April story filed from Juba, South Sudan's capital-in-waiting, York speculated that "southern Sudan is likely to win its independence within a year" and expanded on the *likely violence* frame: a "show of force by southern Sudan's former guerrilla army was a strong reminder that violence has not vanished in the semi-autonomous south.… There are fears that the three-day election that begins tomorrow could trigger more bloodshed in a region where at least 2,500 people died in fighting last year alone—more than the death toll in long-troubled Darfur" (York 2010b). The election was also portrayed as having created "a big boost" in momentum for the Sudan People's Liberation Movement's [SPLM] goal of independence for the south. South Sudan President and leader of the SPLM Salva Kiir noted that "We are running the final lap in our journey to the referendum" (quoted in York 2010b). York predicted that "within a few months of the referendum, if all goes smoothly, South Sudan could be the world's newest country."

There was, however, a note of caution that all might not go smoothly: "The birth of the world's youngest nation could be a troubled one.… *There are allegations that Khartoum is fueling the violence in the south by sending weapons to tribal groups and inciting the traditional cattle-raiding feuds in the region.…* Another potential flashpoint is Khartoum's reluctance to set up a commission to prepare for the January referendum." It was noted further that because of past experiences with secession referenda, Canada had offered "'technical assistance' on 'referendum and postreferendum questions'" (York 2010b; italics added).

A third York story, on 12 April, described the first day of voting and highlighted the absence of violence. However, high levels of poverty in the south and the idea that the election was likely a prelude to independence were highlighted: "Southern Sudan is among the poorest and hungriest regions of the world, yet its people showed that they were ready to endure any discomfort to express their will at the ballot box—a will that seems to be leading inevitably to secession from Sudan in the near future" (York 2010c).

A story two days later focused on the use of social media by political opponents and various techniques of intimidation employed by the regime. It was reported that while "Sudan's political freedoms have improved a little since 2005 when the government signed a deal with former rebels from southern Sudan," a crackdown was expected following the elections. A dissident group leader, Nagi Musa, claimed that "the security forces still have full authority to beat and kill with impunity" (quoted in York 2010d).

The final *Globe and Mail* story by York, on 27 April, was datelined Johannesburg and summarized the outcome of the elections and assessed their likely implications. President al-Bashir had won easily, capturing 68 percent of the vote; however, in that SPLM leader Salva Kiir had garnered 93 percent of the vote in the South, the overall outcome was seen as "pushing the country further along its path to a seemingly inevitable breakup." In York's analysis, "the elections show Sudan drifting into two solitudes, with Mr. al-Bashir dominant in the north and ... [Mr. Kiir] equally dominant in the south. Southern Sudan is now expected to vote for independence in a referendum in January, paving the way for the world's newest country to be created next year." Importantly, it was noted that Mr. al-Bashir had stated that the referendum "will take place on schedule" (quoted in York 2010e). Beyond Canada's offer of assistance in conducting the referendum vote, the issue of international action in the event of violence was not addressed in election reporting.

The Ottawa Citizen

Canada's capital newspaper, the *Ottawa Citizen*, was the only one of the four papers studied not to have covered the elections with its own reporters, relying instead on their then parent company, Canwest Global's corporate news wire service for five "news briefs," augmented by four inside-page stories from Agence France-Presse and Bloomberg News reporters, all of the latter datelined Sudan. Although nine election stories appeared during the study period, only four addressed the implications of the elections for the forthcoming referendum in any way, with only one hinting at *potential violence*, and none touching on the role of the international community should violence occur.

Election reporting began on 2 April with an inside-page story, datelined Khartoum, by Bloomberg News reporters Maram Mazen and Nicole Gaouette. The story drew attention to "concerns the election is rigged," and reported that the majority of opposition candidates had decided to withdraw. It was mentioned that the 2005 peace agreement had ended "a 20-year civil war between the Muslim north and the south" where it was noted that "Christianity and traditional religions predominate." Reported as well was that the SPLM, the government in "the semi-autonomous region of Southern Sudan, ... was withdrawing its presidential candidate from the vote and boycotting the polls in the western region of Darfur" (Mazen and Gaouette 2010). There was no mention of the 2011 referendum; hence there was no assessment of the implications of the elections on that event.

A day later another Khartoum-datelined story, this one by Agence France-Presse reporter Guillaume Lavallee, covered much the same ground, citing "allegations of fraud and a major opposition boycott." The story also noted that the SPLM's presidential candidate, Yasser Arman, had withdrawn from the race, but that he had indicated "the SPLM would still contest the regional and legislative elections 'across Sudan, except for Darfur'" (quoted in Lavallee 2010). A third election report, on 10 April, was written by Agence France-Presse reporter Jailan Zayan, and it updated developments in the campaign: the SPLM "was withdrawing not only from the presidential vote, but also from simultaneous parliamentary and state elections in all northern areas except disputed districts of Blue Nile and South Kordofan." It was further reported that "the SPLM is still campaigning to head the autonomous regional government that will rule the south up to the promised referendum next January" (Zayan 2010).

The only *Citizen* story that addressed the implications of the elections on the referendum in any way was a "news brief" that appeared on 12 April, which portrayed them as testing "the fragile unity of Africa's biggest country.... [The elections] *could also show whether Sudan can avoid more conflict and humanitarian crises as it heads toward a 2011 referendum on independence for the south*" (Canwest News Service 2010; italics added).

The New York Times

The New York Times featured the most extensive reporting on the elections and their implications; a total of 15 items appeared between 23 March and 14 May, including six inside-page stories, six "World News Briefs," plus one each op-ed article, editorial, and letter to the editor.

Reporting began on 23 March with a Reuters "World News Brief" highlighting President al-Bashir's response to suggestions by international election monitors that the elections be delayed. The Sudanese leader's reaction was less than diplomatic: "We wanted them to see the free and fair elections, but if they interfere in our affairs, we will cut their fingers off, put them under our shoes and throw them out" (quoted in Reuters 2010b).

On 2 April, *New York Times* East Africa Bureau Chief, Jeffrey Gettleman reported from Nairobi that a number of opposition parties, including the SPLM, had withdrawn from the presidential election due to charges of "rigging," but that the SPLM "would continue to participate in the parliamentary and local elections across the country, except for Darfur." Implications of the election for the future of the country, where a civil war between the north and south had "killed more than 2 million," were addressed as well: "the real risk to the country's stability—and the stability of the wider East Africa region—is a planned referendum scheduled for early next year in which southern Sudanese will vote on whether to secede. If that referendum is tampered with, many analysts say, it could be a recipe for another war between the north and the south" (Gettleman 2010a).[2]

Gettleman's next story, datelined Khartoum, appeared on 12 April, the day following the start of voting. Polarized views of President al-Bashir and his government were presented. In the north these were favourable—("'Without him ... this country would turn into Somalia. He's the only one who can hold it together'"), while in the south the judgment was unfavourable—("'Election? We don't consider this an election.... Around here ... people are still treated like slaves'"). In Gettleman's view all sides stood to lose as a result of the election—for the south, because its leadership had given up "trying to position themselves as the spearhead of national resistance, connecting with rebels in the west, north and east, ... [and had instead] focussed solely on getting their independence." As for the Sudanese president, "his victory will be tainted"; indeed, Gettleman pointed to the irony that with the economy doing so well, al-Bashir "may not have needed a heavy hand to win this election" (Gettleman 2010b). The International Crisis Group's E.J. Hogendoorn addressed implications for the referendum, explaining that "if the voting had been handled properly ... [the elections] could have helped ease the longstanding and dangerous tensions between Sudan's center and its periphery [that] ... 'everyone recognizes ... [as] the root cause of conflict in Sudan'" (quoted in Gettleman 2010b).

In a 15 April inside-page story, Gettleman reviewed Sudan's recent impressive economic progress, noting that "Sudan's gross domestic product tripled since Mr. Bashir took power." However, not all of Sudan benefited equally: "There are also large sections of the country, especially in southern Sudan and Darfur, that remain desperately poor and where well-worn images of stick-thin children are still true. Around 40 percent of Sudan's 40 million people live below the poverty line" (Gettleman 2010c).

Gettleman's election-summary article on 27 April, datelined Nairobi, framed the elections as "essentially Step 1 of what could be a messy divorce ... [as the expected secession of the south] could bring turbulence to the largest country in Africa." In terms of predicting a peaceful vs. a violent outcome, he noted that "the track record of Mr. Bashir ... raises troubling questions" (Gettleman 2010d). Also troubling was an assessment that a post-referendum government in the south would likely be no more democratic than the one that ruled the north, as it too was accused of being "seemingly allergic to dissent." Unfortunately, according to Project Enough's John Prendergast, "autocracy is the expected outcome on both sides of the border" (quoted in Gettleman 2010d). Oil was seen as both problematic and beneficial. On the problematic side, Sudan's president would be loath to give up the revenue stream driving Sudan's economic engine; on the beneficial side was the reality that the two halves of the country "are reliant … on each other … tied together by a 1,000 mile pipeline." Gettleman also mentioned the potential impact of a Sudanese split on Africa as a whole—namely that secession "could embolden separatist movements in other parts of Africa" (2010d).

Possible US responses to a predicted southern secession were addressed in four items of content: an op-ed column, an inside-page story, an editorial, and a letter to the editor. The op-ed article, datelined Juba, was written by *New York Times* columnist Nicholas Kristof and appeared on 22 April. The piece was critical of President Obama's lukewarm condemnation of Sudan's elections, which Kristof described as having been "deeply flawed.… Memo to Mr. Obama: When a man who has been charged with crimes against humanity tells the world that America is in his pocket, it's time to review your policy." The article also focused on the implications of the elections, not only on the outcome of the upcoming referendum, but also on the threat of renewed violence and an appropriate American policy to avert it. Kristof maintained that "the real game isn't, in fact, Darfur or the elections but the *maneuvering for a possible new civil war.*" In that the south is "expected to vote overwhelming to form a separate state … *the question becomes will the north allow South Sudan to separate?*" With most of Sudan's oil located in the south, Kristof claimed that "it's difficult to see President Bashir allowing oil fields to walk away." He cited the blunt assessment of Sudanese human rights advocate Mudawi Ibrahim Adam: "*If the result of the referendum is independence, there is going to be war*" (quoted in Kristof 2010; italics added). Kristof added that Adam believed that "America's willingness to turn a blind eye to election-rigging … increases the risk that Mr. Bashir will feel that he can get away with war." Kristof's own view was that "the north hasn't entirely decided what to do, and *that strong international pressure can reduce the risk of another savage war. If President Obama is ever going to find his voice on Sudan, it had better be soon*" (2010; italics added).

The only Washington-datelined *New York Times* story appeared on 28 April. It was written by Mark Landler, and focused on the views of retired General Scott Gration, the Obama administration's newly appointed Special Envoy to Sudan. Gration believed that the referendum vote would be in favour of independence, thus bringing into play two issues: (1) would the Sudanese government "let it go without a fight," and (2) "even if it does … how will the new nation survive, with virtually no government institutions, few paved roads and desperate poverty?" General Gration claimed that the US needed to step up and "pour in resources to help southern Sudan build its government and economy by July 2011, … [adding] 'We really haven't had a good history birthing nations. We sure don't want a failed state or a country at war.'" He noted as well that although the US could not "'avoid having a leadership role ... the problem is so big that it's not an American problem ... it's a global problem.'" Andrew Natsios, former Envoy to Sudan during the Bush administration, specifically addressed the issue of a response to violence: "We need to set outer limits on what's acceptable in terms of violence against civilians. ... *If the north attacks the south or attempts to take over the oil fields, we should have a response and it should not be rhetorical*" (both quoted in Landler 2010; italics added).

On 3 May, *The New York Times* weighed in with an editorial that skipped over the election, focusing instead on the upcoming referendum, which it described as leading to "*another potential crisis*." While leaders in both the north and south had pledged "to respect the results" of the referendum, "there is so much oil involved that they can't be depended on to keep their word—without strong encouragement from the United States and other major players.... [The international community] must make it clear—firmly and often—that renewed violence is not the answer." As for specific policy guidance, the editorial suggested "*what is most needed is sustained attention, and pressure, in this critical period*." Steps in the right direction were noted: "Washington is sending more diplomats to southern Sudan. They have a lot of work do—and not a lot of time—to help leaders improve their ability to govern and promote the rule of law. Otherwise, the desperately impoverished region runs the risk of becoming a failed state the day it is born" (*New York Times* 2010; italics added).

On 6 May, a letter to the editor from Refugees International's Dan Glickman also focused attention on the potential of "south–south violence." Citing reports of "voter intimidation and interference in opposition campaigns" on the part of the SPLM, Glickman suggested that "the United States and its international partners *must engage in a robust contingency planning process to prepare for politically grave humanitarian consequences if a large-scale resumption of violence takes place, whether between the north and south or within the south itself*" (Glickman 2010; italics added).

The Washington Post

The Washington Post covered the elections in ten items overall—five brief news "digest" reports, two inside-page news stories, two op-ed articles, and one editorial. As was the case with *The New York Times*, a full range of issues was examined.

Reporting began on 21 March with a "digest" report from Reuters indicating that a senior member of the SPLM had called upon President al-Bashir to "surrender to the International Criminal Court to face war crimes charges." It was noted that this request was likely to raise tensions prior to the election (Reuters 2010a).

Ten days later, columnist Michael Gerson filed an op-ed piece from southern Sudan. The elections were framed as setting the stage "for South Sudan's independence referendum … [the outcome of which] may determine if South Sudan becomes the world's newest nation—or a stillborn state, plunged back into one of history's bloodiest civil wars" (Gerson 2010a).

Interestingly, Gerson did not focus major attention on a possible renewal of the "north–south" civil war, but rather on problems internal to the south, claiming that "*it is politics that could destroy South Sudan even before its birth.*" Specifically, the SPLM was cited for a record of poor governance: "Most of South Sudan's budget goes to the creation of government ghost jobs, allowing the SPLM to pressure public employees for support like a big city political machine." As well, heavy-handed tactics employed by the SPLM during the election campaign were seen as having "encouraged internal division instead of ending it … [thus] allowing the skilled, brutal rulers of the north to play side against side, as they have done before." Gerson described the United States "as the main sponsor of the SPLM," and as such, it had an interest in promoting democratic legitimacy, which was seen to be "the surest way to avoid a failed state and renewed conflict." He ended the piece by pointing to the "terrible irony if South Sudan, a land that has survived by exceptional courage, should die by suicide" (Gerson 2010a; italics added).

Gerson's second op-ed piece a few days later, on 2 April, again focused on South Sudan's internal problems, indicating that "just months from South Sudan's likely vote for independence, its humanitarian challenges seem overwhelming." He called for greater direct international aid, arguing that "technical assistance to build specific capabilities might be the only way to avoid the destructive failure of a new nation." He also claimed not enough was being done to avoid catastrophe, citing the assessment of a unnamed US State Department official that "we are doing about 10 percent of what we need to do" (quoted in Gerson 2010b).

On 9 April, following these two op-ed articles, *Washington Post* coverage shifted to the elections themselves. US Ambassador to the UN Susan Rice described conditions as "quite disturbing" and suggested "a very brief delay" (quoted in Bases 2010). This idea was rejected by the Sudanese government.

The post-election assessment of the elections by the Obama White House was critical, but appeared to be carefully worded to avoid any across-the-board condemnation: "Political rights were circumscribed throughout the electoral process, there were reports of intimidation and threats of violence in South Sudan, ongoing conflict in Darfur did not permit an environment conducive to acceptable elections, and inadequacies in technical preparations for the vote resulted in serious irregularities" (quoted in Reuters 2010c). Another post-election news "digest" piece tied their outcome to the referendum and posed the questions "whether the referendum will actually be held or whether Sudan will once again descend into civil war." Pessimistically it was noted that "Bashir and his ruling party have a very poor record when it comes to allowing electoral competition, especially the kind that could reduce his grip on Sudan. And the south, home of most of the country's oil riches, plays no small role in Sudan's power structure" (Raghavan 2010).

International responses to possible violence in Sudan were discussed in an editorial and an inside-page story. In a 2 May editorial the newspaper minced no words, claiming that the "election was widely acknowledged to be a fraud." Moreover the Obama administration was criticized for timidity by holding the election "to a low standard." This was explained in terms of a deal: the US would "accept him as a legitimate president and set aside the war crimes indictment" in exchange for Mr. Bashir's commitment to follow through with peace in Darfur and hold the January referendum. However, the editorial was skeptical, citing the Sudanese President's past record of untrustworthiness, and questioning whether "Mr. Bashir will allow the oil-rich south to go without a fight or that he will give Darfuris the autonomy they seek." In the meantime, "*the United States should refrain from prematurely recognizing Mr. Bashir's claim to legitimacy. And it should be ready to respond when he breaks his word*" (*Washington Post* 2010; italics added).

On 8 May, two days prior to the end of our study period, an inside-page story by Mary Beth Sheridan reported on Special Envoy to Sudan Scott Gration's appearance before the Senate Foreign Relations Committee, during which he defended the administration against charges that preparations for the referendum were "behind schedule." The retired General explained that "'we have to redouble our efforts.... I think it's possible to get done everything we need to get done, but we can't waste a minute.'" Members of the Committee were not convinced and suggested that Secretary of State Hillary Clinton and Ambassador to the UN Susan Rice play a more direct role in moving things forward. The urgency of the situation was underlined by National Intelligence Director Admiral Dennis Blair's assessment "*that of all the countries at risk of experiencing a widespread massacre in the next five years, 'a new mass killing or genocide is most likely to occur in southern Sudan*'" (both quoted in Sheridan 2010; italics added).

Conclusion

Similarities in Canadian and American Reporting

- The elections themselves were portrayed as flawed to the extent that they denied President al-Bashir the legitimacy he both desired and needed.
- With the exception of the *Ottawa Citizen*, reporting in both countries featured the newspaper's own reporters on the ground in Sudan and linked the elections to the referendum. Moreover, both by their conduct

and outcome, the elections were seen to have further divided the south from the north, thus increasing the chances of a pro-independence vote in the 2011 referendum.

Differences in Canadian and American Reporting

- US reporting evidenced a greater use of opinion pieces: two editorials, three op-ed articles, and one letter to the editor.
- US reporting had greater focus on the referendum leading to renewed violence—with violence seen to be either potential or likely.
- US reporting also paid greater attention to how the US and the international community should respond to the situation—namely, the need for more "diplomatic action" and greater international aid, along with the assessment that not enough was being done. Nicholas Kristof was quite critical of perceived weakness on the part of the American president in dealing with Sudan's president; Dan Glickman called for "robust contingency planning"; and Andrew Natsios suggested the need for a non-rhetorical response. Beyond these criticisms, there was no discussion of what might come next—the *responsibility to react*, if the situation turned bloody.
- US reporting brought up the issue of internal divisions in the south as potentially leading to violence, as well as the pessimistic appraisal that the outcome of an independent south Sudan would be two autocratic governments in Sudan (north and south) instead of one.
- US reporting highlighted the south's poverty, lack of critical infrastructure, and experience in governance, pointing to the possibility of a "failed state" at birth.
- US reporting also included discussion of interesting "deals": Jeffrey Gettleman's suggestion that the SPLM did not run Salva Kiir as a candidate to oppose President al-Bashir nationally in return for an agreement to hold the referendum on schedule and *The Washington Post*'s editorial suggesting a deal between the Obama administration and the Sudanese president to soft-pedal criticism of the elections and to ignore the war crimes indictment in return for peace in Darfur and a guarantee that the referendum would be held on schedule.

The "Alerting" Function

While the question of what constitutes "adequate coverage" of any event is fundamentally subjective, a total of 40 stories (25 in the US and 15 in Canada) for elections in Africa, with three of four papers sending their own reporters to Sudan to cover the event, is probably as much as one could reasonably have hoped for. Moreover, three of the four papers did devote a significant portion of their election coverage to the implications for the upcoming referendum, with virtually all assessments pointing to a victory for the independence option.

The "Framing" Function

In coverage of the spring of 2010 elections, stories were by and large framed in terms of either a *potential for* or *likelihood of* a renewal of north–south violence following a referendum vote in January 2011, the results of which were universally predicted to lead to a declaration of independence on the part of the south in the following July. In this assessment, the reluctance of the north to part with oil revenues was seen as a critical factor.

Reporting in the United States discussed another troublesome problem—that of misrule in the south on the part of SPLM, perhaps leading to *internal fighting* or to a combination of a lack of good governance, poverty, and illiteracy that could result in a *failed state* at birth. On both these possibilities the international community's role was presented in terms of providing greater diplomatic support and aid. Moreover, there was a consensus that not enough was being done in terms of the *responsibility to prevent* violence that was seen as very likely to occur. However, in spite of the prevalence of pessimistic framing, a discussion of a possible scenarios involving the *responsibility to react*, should prevention measures fail, was ignored almost entirely.

CHAPTER 6

NORTH AMERICAN PRESS COVERAGE OF THE 2011 REFERENDUM

Methods

As was the case with the 2010 elections, coverage of the January 2011 referendum was studied in the same set of four newspapers—for Canada *The Globe and Mail* (N=17) and the *Ottawa Citizen* (N=21), and for the United States *The New York Times* (N=25) and *The Washington Post* (N=14). Voting in the referendum began on 9 January 2011 and continued for six days; our two-month study period began on 15 December 2010 and ended on 15 February 2011. Again our major interest was to determine whether and to what extent reporting went beyond describing what was happening day-to-day on the ground, focusing especially on the implications of the referendum for a major renewal of violence and what might be the responsibility of the international community to *prevent* that from happening. As the story totals indicate, the referendum attracted nearly twice as much press coverage as the election (77 vs. 40 items of content) pointing to a significant uptick in press interest regarding the fate of South Sudan, although, as with the election, there was again insufficient television news coverage to permit analysis.

Findings

The Globe and Mail

The Globe and Mail's reporting on the referendum consisted of two front-page stories, three op-ed articles, one letter to the editor, and eleven inside-page stories. Well over half of the material was contributed by the newspaper's African Bureau Chief, Geoffrey York, who covered the referendum from South Sudan.

Reporting began on 29 December, with an op-ed article by Senator Roméo Dallaire and Member of Parliament Glen Pearson. On the one hand, the authors, both active on issues of human security, praised Canada's past contributions to Sudan in the areas of aid, security, and diplomacy, and on the other, cautioned that not enough had been done in advance of the referendum. They mentioned a number of specific problems: that the UN peacekeeping force in the region (United Nations Missions in Sudan—UNMIS) and other UN agencies "lack sufficient staffing, [that] humanitarian access is an on-going issue, and [that] *a comprehensive plan to protect vulnerable minority populations has not been secured.*" Canada was called upon to "build needed relationships with the leaders of Southern Sudan," and to partner with the United States in a "joint Political Assistance Task Force." They offered the disquieting suggestion that the Khartoum government might well agree to the South's secession in order to have "a free hand … to crush Darfur" (Dallaire and Pearson 2010; italics added).

This op-ed piece was followed on 3 January by an inside-page news story by Jennifer Pagliaro that also focused on Canada's ongoing role in Sudan. The story assumed that independence would be the outcome of the referendum vote and, as with the Dallaire and Pearson article, it employed a *pending crisis* frame: "With South Sudan poised for independence in the coming weeks, *Canada is positioning itself for a possible humanitarian crisis in the world's newest nation.*" It was pointed out that along with Haiti and Afghanistan, Sudan ranked among "Canada's top three priorities for foreign aid," with $800 million having been provided to Sudan since 2006. As well, Canada had contributed "more than 400 soldiers and civilian peacekeepers to disarm rebel forces, train local police and help implement the post-civil war Comprehensive Peace Agreement" (Pagliaro 2011; italics added). However, MP Glen Pearson, who was in the region monitoring the vote, indicated that the real challenge for South Sudan was not the referendum itself, but what would come later: "After an event such as the referendum is over, 'the west has always had a tendency to move off and concentrate on other things. And when that happens, that's when the real need will begin to show.'" Among the problems facing the south was an expected influx of some 2.5 million people who had been displaced by earlier conflicts, and Pearson was skeptical that Canada had addressed the consequences: "'I think … [Canadian government agencies are] now realizing that there's a problem … [however] we've yet to see what the plan will be to address that problem'" (quoted in Pagliaro 2011).

On 6 January, in a Juba-datelined front-page story by Geoffrey York, the focus of reporting shifted to events unfolding in South Sudan. The story had a human interest focus, dealing with a man's return to the south from Khartoum after a nearly two-decade-long fruitless search for his father, last seen in the hands of Sudan's military intelligence service. York agreed that "the referendum is nearly certain to produce a landslide victory for the pro-secession forces, triggering a six-month negotiating process that could culminate in a declaration of independence in July." A note of optimism was struck in that Sudan's President, Omar al-Bashir, had "pledged to respect the referendum, regardless of the result.... His unexpectedly positive comments were a strong indication that Khartoum might allow secession without trying to sabotage it" (York 2011a). The optimism continued in another York story the following day. Michael Makuei Lueth, described as "a senior cabinet minister in the southern government and a key negotiator on issues with Khartoum," was quoted as expressing confidence that "the people of the south will take the right decision and vote for secession.... And there is no way that the north can sabotage it, unless they decide to declare war and invade the south." A veteran aid worker saw such a war as unlikely: "I think the north knows that it cannot go to war, because it would mean the end of the regime" (both quoted in York 2011b).[1]

In an op-ed article appearing a day later, York reflected on changes he had seen since his first visit to the region in 1993. He focused on what was described as the "unlikely outcome" of a long conflict, explaining that "it was difficult to imagine how these ill-equipped insurgents could win a small local skirmish, let alone a protracted war against Khartoum's powerful army and air force." While "the birth of a new nation" was now the assumed outcome of the referendum, the price that had been paid in getting there was described as "horrific." Moreover, "*independence is no cure for the misfortunes that lie ahead.*"[2] York went on to outline the major problems: "If the south gains its formal independence ... it will become one of the poorest and hungriest nations in the world," with an illiteracy rate standing at 85 percent, a maternal death rate among the highest in the world, with "almost half of the population ... dependent on food aid last year." Nor were South Sudan's problems with violence simply a matter of history. Citing tribal violence and cross-border raids by the Lord's Resistance Army that "killed about 2,500 people in 2009 and nearly 1,000 more in 2010," York pointed out "*the grim reality is that the bloodshed is not over, and the deaths have not ended*" (York 2011c; italics added).

York's inside news story on the same day surveyed the "myriad of potential flashpoints" involved in negotiating a "peaceful breakup" of Sudan: would the Khartoum government "co-operate" in negotiations that included setting the borders of the oil-producing region of Abyei, as well as the split in oil revenues, an issue on which the south was asking for 80 percent, a 30 percent increase over the 50–50 split established in the CPA. While not dismissing the potential for a renewal of war, German Institute for International and Security Affairs analyst Wolfram Lacher argued that "Khartoum seems to have 'gradually resigned itself' to the south's secession.... 'For the central government, the costs of preventing secession by force would be prohibitive, such as in the form of deepening international isolation and the emergence of a second front, in addition to Darfur'" (quoted in York 2011d). York also reported that the US had offered Khartoum the "tempting prize" of "a major package of concessions [including the lifting of sanctions] … if it allows the south to secede peacefully."

The first news story following the start of voting appeared on 10 January. York characterized the referendum as marking the liberation of the south "from a half-century of bloodshed and conflict under Khartoum's Islamic regime." In spite of long lineups, voting was reported as "proceeding smoothly in most places" and the participation rate was expected to far exceed the 60 percent needed to validate the vote (York 2011f).

An inside-page story by York on 10 January profiled actor George Clooney's most recent venture into celebrity diplomacy—the "Satellite Sentinel Project"—an "'early warning system' to scout for troop movements that could trigger war between Sudan's north and south." While Clooney's knowledge of Sudan's politics was praised, it was noted that his political activism had not been universally embraced; some believed the satellite image project could do as much harm as good. The actor showed signs of frustration and anger when asked about these criticisms: "I'm sick of it.… If your cynicism means you stand on the sidelines and throw stones, I'm fine. I can take it. I could give a damn what you think. We're trying to save some lives. If you're cynical enough not to understand that, then get off your ass and do something. If you're angry at me, go do it yourself. Find another cause—I don't care. We're working, and we're going forward" (quoted in York 2011e).

Stories by York on 11 and 14 January presented contrasting pictures of how the referendum vote might play out with respect to violence. The first reported clashes in Abyei between the nomadic Misseriya, an Arab tribe "who migrate into Abyei every year to seek pasture and water for their cattle … [and the Dinka] a permanently settled [African] people who grow crops." It was noted that the "Misseriya, armed with anti-tank weapons and artillery … are believed to be supported by the Khartoum government" (York 2011g).[3] By 14 January, the headline of York's story reflected a different tone ("Calm prevails as southern Sudanese vote"), with the report that followed indicating that northerners living in the south were being well treated: "There have been no reports of revenge attacks by the majority against the minority in most of southern Sudan. If the situation remains peaceful, it bodes well for a potentially smooth transition to southern independence by a July deadline" (York 2011h).

York's next report, a front-page story, appeared on 17 January and recounted a Christmas Day rampage in Juba by the newly Canadian-trained South Sudan police. The police cut off young men's dreadlocks with scissors and detained and slapped women wearing pants. Such actions were described as "police abuses" and the incident was framed as emblematic of the problems to be confronted by international efforts to help South Sudan: "Critics say the Canadian government was too quick to trust a training program that was deeply flawed and over-ambitious in a country with a shattered education system and high illiteracy. It may have been naive to think that a few months of training would produce a police force that understands the concepts of human rights." An unnamed security expert was quoted as saying, "it certainly seems like a disastrous international effort right from the beginning.... At the very least you can say that the amount of training was nowhere near enough" (quoted in York 2011i).

The only letter to the editor appearing in *The Globe*, written by Madeleine Cole (who had served as an aid worker in the south), was in response to Geoffrey York's 8 January news story. She commented on the problems faced by the new nation—"lack of civil society, ill health, illiteracy and more than 30 years of civil war"—and described these as "difficult to bounce back from." She expressed hope "that the international community helps with the post-referendum transition" (Cole 2011).

An op-ed article on 18 January by Rami Khouri, Director of the Issam Fares Institute for Public Policy and International Affairs at the American University of Beirut, dealt with the issue of change in the Arab world associated with the so-called Arab Spring, and focused on Lebanon, Tunisia, and Sudan. In contrast to the first two countries, Sudan's situation was described as "unique in being a rare case of citizens in an Arab country enjoying the opportunity to vote to determine their future status." Khouri went on to argue that

> two massive gaps in the modern history of the Arab world are corrected by this move which will probably see southern Sudan emerge as an independent country. Self-determination by citizens of an Arab state can define their borders, their national values and the governance system, and, a corrective mechanism that allows the countries and peoples of this region to reconfigure themselves into more natural sovereign states that correspond to their ethnic-national identities. (Khouri 2011)

Khouri did not discuss any possible negative outcomes of independence.

York's final two stories followed the referendum. The first, on 22 January, described the outcome: "a landslide of crushing proportions ... [presenting] an almost insurmountable obstacle for the Sudan government to overcome if it tries to resist the southern independence drive." Further, that the vote had been endorsed by both the European Union and the Carter Center meant northern legal challenges were "less likely." Key issues remaining to be resolved prior to the July declaration of independence were setting the borders of Abyei and the division of oil revenues. On the latter issue it was noted that "both sides have a strong financial interest in reaching agreement on the oil, allowing the money to keep flowing in" (York 2011j).

Three days later, the second post-referendum story explored the implications of the secession vote on the conflict in Darfur, where people "are wondering whether their own war-torn region ... could some day achieve the same result." York's assessment—not very likely: "The national government in Khartoum has shown no sign of easing its grip on Darfur." The irony that Muslim Darfuri refugees were being given protection in the non-Muslim south was noted in a statement by Barnaba Marial Benjamin, Information Minister in the South Sudan Government: "Ordinary Darfuris will not be harassed.... They have protection here" (quoted in York 2011k).

The Ottawa Citizen

With a total of 21 stories, the *Ottawa Citizen* exceeded by four the coverage of *The Globe and Mail*. However, of the total, nine items were of the short "news brief" variety, while the other twelve were inside-page news stories. Neither the *Citizen* nor its new parent company, Postmedia News, covered the referendum from Sudan with their own reporters. On balance, however, *Citizen* readers did get a wide range of perspectives on the referendum vote as well as its likely consequences from reporters working for a variety of media organizations: *The Times* (London), *The Daily Telegraph*, McClatchey-Tribune News (the successor to Knight-Ritter in the US), Agence France-Presse, and Reuters.

Reporting in the *Ottawa Citizen* began on 17 December 2010 with two reports, the first a story from Reuters that the Sudanese government had given up its attempts to keep the country together. Presidential Assistant Nafie Ali Nafie, described as "one of the most powerful men in Sudan," acknowledged that "efforts to keep the country united had failed.... 'we shall accept the reality and must not deceive ourselves and stick to dreams'" (quoted in Reuters 2010d). The second was a background piece, datelined Juba, by *Times* (London) reporter Jim Mclean. On the one hand, the story lead was that of fulfillment of a long-held dream—"a 55-year journey towards independence." On the other hand, possible pitfalls were reviewed: the north's penchant to exploit "tribal rivalries" in the south, citizenship issues, and the status of the oil-rich Abyei region. The result was a *potential conflict* frame: "The consequences could be bloody in a country riven by two north–south wars ... in which more than two million died" (Mclean 2010).

The first story in the new year was another backgrounder, this one datelined Khartoum, and written by McClatchey-Tribune News reporter Jeffrey Fleishman. The focus of the 6 January story was the outflow of southerners living in the north (total numbers there estimated at 1.5 million) back to the south. Fleishman indicated that due to racial discrimination, southerners had "never felt welcome in the north," but until recently remaining there was seen as a better option than returning to the insecurity they had fled. With independence in the wind, southerners were returning—an estimated 50,000 people to that point. Fears were also expressed that in the event of a vote for independence "the north would seek retribution against the south, which accounts for about 80 percent of [Sudan's oil output]" (Fleishman 2011). An Agence France-Presse story two days later placed the number of returnees to the south at 143,000, but also cited a UN assessment that "violent attacks were running at their lowest level since the 2005 peace agreement" and that preparations for the historic vote were "'on track'" (quoted in AFP 2011a).[4]

A Reuters story on 6 January assessed the negative consequences of the influx to the south of newcomers "who speak Arabic rather than southern languages, [and who] will lack farming knowledge and will want land allocated to them." According to International Relief and Development's Richard Owens, "there aren't enough resources and the institutional capacity of the government of South Sudan at the state, county and below level is not there and we think there needs to be a lot of emphasis put on assistance at the village level and tribal leadership level to help them" (quoted in Reuters 2011a). The following day, an inside news story by Postmedia reporter Steven Edwards, datelined the United Nations, shifted focus from South Sudan to what was termed the "escalating violence in Sudan's Darfur region." It was suggested by monitoring groups in Darfur that the preoccupation with the referendum had "caused the UN to take its eye off Darfur." According to the Global Centre for the Responsibility to Protect's Monica Serrano, "the international community must not repeat the mistakes of the past and allow conflict to flare up in Darfur when its attention is elsewhere" (quoted in Edwards 2011).

A pre-referendum story on 8 January by McClatchy-Tribune News reporter Alan Boswell dealt head-on with the implications of a possible secession. First, he pointed to south Sudan's grinding poverty: "The international community has focused heavily on aid to southern Sudan, and many wonder if a region so far behind the rest of the world and with its legacy of monumental violence can survive as a modern state." There were also fears that "the north's murderous history might reignite" (Boswell 2011a). Hafiz Mohammed, Director of Justice Africa-Sudan, cautioned that "the problem of Sudan will not be solved by southern secession.... Other problem areas remain, and nothing in the centre has changed." Second, Boswell pointed out that the north would also face problems, namely an economic crisis that could loosen President al-Bashir's grip on power. International Crisis Group's Zach Vertin agreed that "secession will certainly shock Sudan's political arena, particularly in Khartoum.... While it seems unlikely the NCP (National Congress Party) would be dislodged in the near term, the party does feel threatened, its political and economic future uncertain" (both quoted in Boswell 2011a). It was further noted that in the north "opposition parties are circling overhead, smelling blood."

The final pre-referendum story, also on 8 January, highlighted the activities of the international community, especially the United States, trying to ensure that the vote would take place as scheduled. Agence France-Presse reporter Steve Kirby reported visits to Sudan by Special Envoy Scott Gration and Senator John Kerry as signs that "Washington pulled out the stops to make certain no hitches block implementation of the peace deal in which it was so instrumental" (Kirby 2011).

While *Daily Telegraph* reporter Mike Pflanz acknowledged that voting had begun peacefully, he cited an unnamed Western diplomat's claims that "there are absurdly high expectations that—from the day after separation—schools, hospitals, jobs, roads, electricity, all of it will suddenly appear." Oxfam in East Africa spokesperson Alun McDonald agreed: "that is simply not going to happen. *The root causes of violence will not go away after the referendum*. The international community and the Northern and Southern governments have been working to resolve high-level issues, while the concerns of the local communities are in danger of being overlooked" (both quoted in Pflanz 2011; italics added).

At this point *Citizen* reporting shifted primarily to news briefs, updating readers to current happenings, culminating in a Reuters report on 22 January that "the website for the Southern Sudan Referendum Commission showed a 98.6 percent vote for secession" (Reuters 2011b).

A post-referendum story by Alan Boswell on 5 February gave an indication of future problems—clashes between southern militias within the northern Sudanese Army and the main body of that force, which was in the process of a mandated withdrawal from the south. During the civil war, the north had employed the southern militias against the SPLA, and a firefight in the city of Malakal was a sign that the integration of those militias into the SPLA-dominant armed force was not likely to go smoothly (Boswell 2011b).

The New York Times

Reporting in *The New York Times* featured more items of content on the referendum than any other newspaper (N=25) and consisted of one front page story, fourteen inside-page stories, three "World News Briefs," one editorial, five op-ed/news analysis articles, and one letter to the editor. For its coverage, the newspaper received reports from two journalists in Sudan covering the event—reporter Josh Kron and East Africa Bureau Chief Jeffrey Gettleman—while President Obama contributed an op-ed article outlining his views on the situation.

Josh Kron led off reporting on 19 December with a report that President al-Bashir had indicated that a southern secession would result in "a state governed by Islamic law" in the north. New American Foundation researcher Eliza Griswold was not surprised by what were described as his "incendiary comments." She claimed that "Bashir relishes the role of standing up to the West, and the South's secession gives him the chance to pander to his base in Sudan and beyond" (quoted in Kron 2010a).

Kron's second story appeared at the end of the month on 30 December and dealt with the failure to demobilize 180,000 soldiers and reintegrate them into society under a program set up as a part of the 2005 CPA. Each side had committed to demobilize 90,000 troops, but according to William Deng Deng, Chairman of the Southern Sudan Disarmament, Demobilization and Reintegration Commission, no more than 400 soldiers had been demobilized and reintegrated, leaving various armed groups "spread across the vast hinterland of Sudan" and likely to be a source of future problems. It was noted that international contributors to the program were looking to assign blame "and many ... are pointing toward the entity that is supposed to help the effort go smoothly: the United Nations" (Kron 2010b).

The early new year saw the first of Jeffrey Gettleman's reports from Sudan, a news analysis piece on 2 January datelined Khartoum. The question he asked was similar to the one that prompted our interest in studying South Sudan's march toward independence: "what ... are the chances that the independence referendum in southern Sudan, ... the culmination of a peace process that ended decades of civil war between north and south, will set off another one?" (Gettleman 2011a).

Despite US Secretary of State Hillary Clinton's description of the situation as "a ticking time bomb," Gettleman maintained that the chance of renewed war was "*slim and getting slimmer*" and he presented the situation to readers in the frame of *cautious optimism*. Simply put, both sides had too much to lose by renewing hostilities, and, in addition, "are more pragmatic than they are often given credit for." Northern leaders were seen as "especially eager to normalize relations with the West and know that interference with the referendum would torpedo any chance of that happening." Also, as Sudanese Professor of Political Science Mohammed Hamad pointed out, "Mr. Bashir will be reluctant to go to war because 'others will use it as an excuse, and Israel and the U.S. will try to depose the regime'" (quoted in Gettleman 2011a).[5] As for southern leaders, "they are on the verge of peacefully achieving what has taken decades of sacrifices ... [and] to keep their dreams of independence alive seem ready to make concessions. This includes sharing the oil." If there were to be an outbreak of violence it would likely be started by "uncontrolled elements"—tribal militias, referred to in another context by former US Vice-President Dick Cheney as "the unknown unknowns." Gettleman noted that in the disputed Abyei region "there are militias aligned to the north and to the south, but ... not necessarily controlled by either." And, if a "first shot" were to be fired, it would likely be by such militias, "possibly provoked by a land dispute" (Gettleman 2011a).

Gettleman's optimism was challenged by letter writer Jana Chapman Gates, whose negative experiences with the Sudanese president while serving in the preceding Bush administration prompted her to write. She agreed that the government of the north "was made up of rational actors," but that this didn't "preclude the possibility of violence." Specifically, "our focus should be on the protection of Sudanese civilians, and we can't afford to underestimate the dangers in the days ahead" (Chapman Gates 2011).

An Associated Press report on 5 January indicated that at least one "renegade general" in the south (Lt. Gen. George Athor) had made peace with the government prior to the referendum. The general had "defected from the southern government last year" after an unsuccessful run to become governor of Jonglei State. It was noted that his revolt had "represented a significant security threat as the country prepared for [the] weeklong referendum" (AP 2011a).[6]

In a pre-referendum editorial on 7 January, *The New York Times* maintained Gettleman's *cautious optimism* frame with respect to possible mischief on the part of the Sudanese president, who nevertheless was described as "the author of the murderous war in Darfur." It was argued that "months of mediation by the Obama administration and African leaders seem to have persuaded Mr. Bashir to forgo confrontation, for now." The standard range of problems facing the new nation—citizenship, borders, and oil revenues—were reviewed, and for them to be resolved "the United States, the United Nations and the African Union will have to remain deeply engaged, prodding both states to compromise." In terms of dealing with the north, the carrot was favoured over the stick: removal of Sudan from Washington's list of states supporting terrorism and a loosening of other sanctions. In addition, "if secession is peaceful, Washington should help the north by facilitating debt relief and foreign investment.… [However,] if Sudan resorts to force, sanctions must be tightened." In this respect, recent events in Darfur were described as "worrisome." As for the south, more aid would be necessary in order "to build a responsible and pluralistic government." Toward this goal, the referendum was seen as "an important start, but only a start" (*New York Times* 2011a).

Pre-referendum coverage continued with two op-ed articles, the first by the American president and the second by Kenyan journalist Murithi Mutiga, and both continued to express *cautious optimism* that events were on track to unfold peacefully.

On 8 January Mr. Obama argued that what was occurring in south Sudan had implications not only for Sudan, but beyond its borders: the "process will help determine whether people who have known so much suffering will move toward peace and prosperity, or slide backward into bloodshed. It will have consequences not only for Sudan, but also for sub-Saharan Africa and the world." He then made the US position clear: "the international community was united in its belief that this referendum had to take place and that *the will of the people of southern Sudan had to be respected, regardless of the outcome*" (Obama 2011; italics added).

Compromise on the part of leaders in both north and south was the order of the day. The south would require "partners in the long-term task of fulfilling the political and economic aspirations of its people," while for the north, *good behaviour* would result in Sudan's removal from the states-sponsoring-terrorism list and the lifting of economic sanctions. Importantly, good behaviour was extended to include Darfur: "there can be no lasting peace in Sudan without lasting peace in the western Sudan region of Darfur.... Here, too, the world is watching. The government of Sudan must live up to its international obligations. Attacks on civilians must stop." Leaders on both sides were reminded that "those who make the right choice will be remembered by history—they will also have a steady partner in the United States" (Obama 2011).

In his op-ed article on the same day, Murithi Mutiga stressed that the international community needed "to ensure the two sides resolve the outstanding issues amicably. Otherwise, a new, more brutal conflict is possible." He focused attention on the north, where the al-Bashir government was portrayed as being "at its weakest point since it assumed power in a coup in 1989." As a result, "if the north perceives it has little to gain from post-referendum agreements, it might return to fomenting troubles in the south.... *Fortunately, recent history shows that international pressure, and especially pressure from Washington, can lead to impressive results.*" Washington was encouraged to continue offering incentives to the north—incentives that were dependent on the continued good behaviour of the Sudanese president (Mutiga 2011; italics added).

Mutiga also tackled the thorny issue of the *moral correctness* of engaging "at all with Mr. Bashir, who is wanted by the International Criminal Court for the genocide in Darfur." He rejected such a position, however, and came down strongly on the side of engagement, pointing out that "the negotiations behind the 2005 accord took place as the massacres in Darfur were drawing world attention. ... [However,] the Bush White House recognized that, deplorable as the Bashir regime was, it was impossible to achieve peace in the south without engaging with Khartoum." Southern leaders as well had to recognize that, unpalatable as it might be, "they must now negotiate and even compromise with Mr. Bashir." It was assumed, however, that following the referendum, any southern negotiations with the north would be "on equal terms" (Mutiga 2011).

Reporting from Juba, Gettleman assessed the pre-referendum situation in an 8 January front-page news story: "A proud new African country is about to be born, but it will step onto the world stage with shaky legs. As it stands now, southern Sudan is one of the poorest places on earth.... Already aid agencies are ringing the alarm about a lack of food, water, health care and sanitation." The International Rescue Committee described the situation in the south as "an unfolding humanitarian crisis layered on top of an existing and forsaken one" (quoted in Gettleman 2011c). To make matters worse, in light of increases in "high-powered weaponry" in the region, Khartoum was suspected by many in the south of attempting to instigate violence, "just as it had in the past when [it] … fomented a civil war within a civil war." It was noted, however, that as of late incidents of violence were decreasing as various factions in the south were "trying to get along" (Gettleman 2011c).

In a *Week in Review* article appearing on the same day, Gettleman examined the likely impact of south Sudan's secession on wider Africa, which he described as a continent "wracked by separatists … [sharing] at least one thing: they direct their fire against weak states struggling to hold together disparate populations within boundaries drawn by 19th-century white colonialists." That history, he argued, "is a prime reason that Africa remains, to a striking degree, a continent of failed and failing states." It was noted that at its founding in 1963 the Organization of African Unity (OAU) committed itself to a strategy of recognizing "colonial-era borders," along with the assessment that "in hindsight, it is clear that the old boundaries often hurt prospects for state building" (Gettleman 2011b).

While this may well be the case, past Sudanese president Sadiq al-Mahdi offered a bleak assessment of the impact of the secession of the south for the rest of the continent: "to resort to self-determination to solve your problems will breakup Sudan, will breakup Ethiopia, will breakup Uganda, will breakup all of Africa, because all African countries are made up of heterogeneous elements. Pandora's box is now open" (quoted in Gettleman 2011b). In spite of such concerns, Gettleman maintained that "there was considerable international pressure on the African Union, the successor to the [OAU], to make southern Sudan an exception to the rule about preserving old borders." This pressure was attributed to "perceptions that southerners have long been Christian victims of Muslim persecutors" and suspicions that President al-Bashir was "reviving old contacts with the brutal Lord's Resistance Army in Uganda to destabilize southern Sudan." Northwestern University political scientist William Reno described recognition of South Sudan as "a very, very bitter pill," but that there was little doubt that the AU would have to swallow it, in spite of fears that such recognition would fuel other separatist conflicts (quoted in Gettleman 2011b).

Reporting on the largely uneventful voting process for the most part employed human interest frames and will not be reviewed in any detail. However, problems facing the new county continued to be embedded in this reporting. In particular, on 14 January Josh Kron cited a study by the United States Agency for International Development claiming "*there is no other post-conflict reconstruction challenge in modern times that is on par with Southern Sudan*" (Kron 2011a; italics added). In light of massive problems in Haiti, Somalia, Iraq, and Afghanistan, such a bold statement would lead one to believe that while the prospects for a renewal of civil war had to some degree faded, South Sudan would nevertheless face a truly massive set of problems in establishing itself as a viable nation-state.

Gettleman's story two days later, however, did reintroduce the possibility of renewed violence, and his focus was on Abyei, the "place in Sudan where Africa and the Arab world meet." He described Abyei as "the most contested, the most emotionally charged and recently, the most violent piece of land in this country of nearly one million square miles." While the issue of oil was mentioned in passing, the report focused on the long and antagonistic relationship between the Misseriya, a tribe of Arab nomads who used the region to water their animals in the dry season, and the Ngok Dinka who farmed in the region on a permanent basis. The area was described as heavily armed and "crawling with militias," with government official John Ajang claiming that "'there are no civilians here'" (quoted in Gettleman, 2011d). That in previous Sudanese civil wars "much of the violence was meted out by proxy forces and ethnic-based militias" made the situation in Abyei "worrisome."[7] Given the toxic mix of historic animosity between Misseriya and Dinka and a region awash with armaments and rival militias, Professor Mohammed Hamad's assessment went well beyond worrisome; in fact he predicted that "*the coming conflict will be set off from Abyei.*" He noted that the situation was complicated by the fact that "Sudan has always been a place where the center has no control over the periphery," thus casting doubts on whether the northern government had the ability to "reel in the Misseriya" (quoted in Gettleman 2011d; italics added). The end of the month brought news that with the arrival of ten transport helicopters, south Sudan was in the process of building an air force. While a southern spokesperson maintained that they would not be used "to antagonize the north," he acknowledged that the helicopters were capable of being used as gunships (Reuters 2011c).

February brought both good and bad news. The good news was President al-Bashir's promise "that his government would accept the choice of the long-embittered region of southern Sudan to separate from the north," and President Obama's indication that "'for those who meet all of their obligations, there is a path to greater prosperity and normal relations with the United States, including examining Sudan's designation as a state sponsor of terrorism'" (quoted in Kron, 2011b).

The bad news came in a report from Reuters indicating that clashes stemming from the called-for relocation of the Sudanese army to the north prior to the declaration of independence had "spread through the oil-producing Upper Nile State." This, according to Reuters, "illustrates concerns about how Sudan's northern and southern armies will separate their military hardware before July 9" (Reuters 2011d). Toward the end of the study period, on 12 February, Josh Kron also reported that the pre-referendum reconciliation between the renegade southern general George Athor and the SPLM government had ended: battles between forces loyal to the general and "the southern Sudanese military in recent days have left more than 100 people dead in southern Sudan, sending tremors through a heavily militarized region that only days ago celebrated the final results of a referendum to separate from the rest of the country." It was noted that "security is routinely singled out as the most important priority in southern Sudan right now" (Kron 2011c).

The Washington Post

The Washington Post ran fourteen items on the referendum, twelve inside-page stories, one op-ed article (a "news outlook" feature), and one short news "digest" item. Rebecca Hamilton—a "special correspondent working on a grant from the Pulitzer Center on Crisis Reporting" and author of *Fighting for Darfur: Public Action and the Struggle to Stop Genocide* (2011)—and Sudarsan Raghavan, the paper's African Bureau Chief, reported from Sudan.

Coverage began on 29 December with a news digest item describing the "Satellite Sentinel Project" promoted by George Clooney to detect large-scale troop movements in the region (Melendez Olivera 2010).[8] Also in late December, the first of Mary Beth Sheridan's two inside-page news stories focused on US policy toward Sudan and indicated that US officials increasingly believed the referendum would be held without major violence on the part of the north, despite its "stand[ing] to lose more than half its budget if the south, with its lucrative oil reserves, votes to split." A senior unnamed State Department official indicated, "I am far more optimistic about it than I was six weeks ago." The failure to deal with the Abyei region was again singled out for special concern, with US Institute of Peace researcher Jon Temin warning that "if the fighting starts locally around Abyei, the question becomes whether it escalates into a larger-scale conflict" (both quoted in Sheridan 2010b).

In a news "outlook" feature article on 2 January, Michael Abramowitz, Director of the US Holocaust Memorial Museum's Committee of Conscience, reviewed what he saw to be the less-than-adequate US responses to genocide in Rwanda and Darfur, pointing out that "now President Obama is trying to avoid having to issue his own mea culpa." A range of diplomatic efforts were reviewed and it was revealed that "the administration won't deal directly with President ... al-Bashir, who has been indicted for war crimes committed in Dafur." Samantha Power, author of the award-winning book on genocide *"A Problem from Hell": America and the Age of Genocide* (2002) and advisor to President Obama, offered that "this is the first time I have seen the U.S. government devote so many high-level resources to preventing violence before it happens rather than responding after the fact" (quoted in Abramowitz 2011). Abramowitz, however, was still not convinced that enough had been done to avert disaster. He argued that even though "the world's political and military leaders have had the luxury of giving serious planning and thought to how to avoid calamity ... there is virtually no limit to the possible scenarios that could lead to fighting in Sudan." For Abramowitz the future appeared grim: "Yes, the world is watching: In addition to Washington's diplomatic push, the African Union is trying to broker peace, European nations are sending economic assistance, and 10,000 U.N. peacekeepers are in southern Sudan monitoring the situation. *But the sad reality is that even an actively engaged international community may be unable to head off mass violence in the months or years ahead*" (Abramowitz 2011; italics added).

However, on 6 January, just prior to the referendum vote, Senator John Kerry offered another expression of official optimism: "Sudan is at a pivotal moment ... [and] the United States played an important role in ending the civil war ... making the vote this Sunday possible." And, he added that whatever the outcome, "our commitment to the Sudanese people will extend beyond the referendum" (quoted in Rogin 2011).

A second Sheridan story, on 7 January, reviewed the process of White House decision making on southern Sudan and focused on a key change of course made during the previous September. President Obama had grown concerned that Sudan "wasn't just another African country in turmoil ... [and] forcefully reminded his aides that 2 million people had died in Sudan's north–south war." Further, in light of the scheduled January referendum, time was seen as running out. According to Sheridan, "solving the Sudan crisis ha[d] been a tortured journey for a president committed to avoiding the kinds of genocide that erupted under his predecessors." She outlined the year-long debate within the administration over whether to strike a deal with the tainted al-Bashir government. In the end, Mr. Obama came full circle from his earlier hawkish position that had called for

> tougher action against Sudan and a no-fly zone over Darfur ... [and that] assailed as "reckless and cynical" a Bush offer to remove Sudan from the U.S. list of terrorism sponsors in exchange for allowing more peacekeeping troops.... Obama and his team [including genocide expert, Samantha Power] ... *wound up embracing elements of George W. Bush's approach that they had once criticized—specifically, offering incentives to a government accused of war crimes.* (Sheridan 2011; italics added)

Sheridan explained that in dealing with Sudan, reality had caught up with and overtaken morality: "the administration quickly ran into the constraints that had stymied the Bush administration. Military action would be difficult because of a lack of available U.S. troops and the risks of intervening in a Muslin country." Retired Air Force General and Envoy to Sudan Scott Gration outlined the rationale behind the new incentives offered to the north: "In order to fix these real problems that were threatening lives, human rights, physical property, there was no option but to engage and to build the relationship of trust" (quoted in Sheridan 2011). Sheridan maintained that the administration had in fact "adopted much of [Bush's] approach, offering to delist Sudan as a terrorism sponsor if the referendum is honored and the two sides resolve border, oil and other issues." Former Bush Envoy to Sudan Andrew Natsios noted that Obama's policy had "swung past the Bush administration in pursuing a conciliatory policy toward the north," and questioned whether in doing so, he had "'neglected the south,' a traditional U.S. ally." Samantha Power maintained that the "administration is 'sensitized to the importance of preventing violence before it occurs rather than responding after the fact.'… But with Sudan, 'there is a huge amount left to be done before anybody can say prevention worked'" (both quoted in Sheridan 2011).

In a front-page story just prior to the vote, Sudarson Raghavan emphasized the poverty of the region as well as the US commitment "to southern Sudan's future." Scott Gration noted that "President Obama has personally invested in Sudan.… He's briefed every day on what happens here.… That same commitment will continue after the referendum" (quoted in Raghaven 2011a). Senator John Kerry indicated that "he believes the likelihood of conflict, while still a concern, has diminished." However, Zach Vertin, International Crisis Group's Sudan analyst, was less optimistic: "If you don't resolve Abyei and you don't have some kind of solution for the border, you risk continuing a sort of low-intensity conflict along the border, which could spiral out of control" (quoted in Raghaven 2011a).

Reports on the vote itself were filed by Raghavan and Hamilton and these adopted a *human interest* frame, tending to focus on past hardships experienced in individual life stories. Animosity toward the north was commonplace: "Many villagers questioned the public pledge by the north's president … to recognize the south if it becomes a new nation. 'We don't trust the Arabs.… There will be no co-existence.… They mistreated the southerners. We cannot deal with them again'" (quoted in Raghaven 2011b).

On 24 January, Rebecca Hamilton provided a post-referendum update on Abyei, where the mood was described as "somber," as there was fear that the region might "'be left behind when the south gets its independence.'" Paramount Chief of the Ngok Dinka, Kuol Deng Kuol, stated his tribe's position: "We want to be clear that Abyei is part of the south and we want to belong to the south." According to Jon Temin of the US Institute of Peace, "if Abyei remains unresolved and the south secedes, the people of Abyei will be left in a very ambiguous and vulnerable position" (both quoted Hamilton 2011b). Although the 2005 CPA granted the Arab nomad Misseirya tribe continued grazing rights regardless of "whether the land ended up in the north of the south," Misseirya leaders were skeptical whether those rights would continue if Abyei were to be absorbed into the south. Hamilton reported as well that Ngok Dinka leaders were in turn "preparing their people for the possibility of a Khartoum-backed attempt by the Misseriya to take Abyei" (2011b).

On 6 February, McClatchy-Tribune reporter Alan Boswell, in a story similar to the one that appeared in the *Ottawa Citizen,* focused on the problems related to the mandated withdrawal of the Sudanese army from the south: southerners who had fought for the north against the south were resisting the move. A further complication was noted in that "the mutineers also are fighting to keep some of the heavy weaponry in the south—and in their hands" (Boswell 2011c). Reviewed as well was the continuation of the rebellion by former SPLA general and unsuccessful gubernatorial candidate, George Athor, described as "one of the south's largest security threats." An Associated Press report of the deaths of 105 people, including 39 civilians, "underscor[ed] the tenuous security situation in the region despite its successful independence referendum" (AP 2011b).

Hamilton's final story appeared on 12 February, and dealt with the problems that oil extraction was causing for the environment. While "southern Sudanese are pinning their hopes for prosperity on oil," there were serious problems of water contamination. State Minister for the Environment William Garjang Gieng hoped that independence would "give his fledgling ministry greater leverage over the industry.... 'Oil can stop at any time ... but the soil, the water—this needs to last forever'" (quoted in Hamilton 2011c).

Conclusion

Similarities in Canadian and American Reporting

- While renewed violence was by no means ruled out, compared to election coverage there was considerable optimism expressed in reporting in both countries—that somehow Sudan might avoid renewed conflict following a referendum vote that from the outset was seen to favour independence by a large margin.
- A wide range of contentious issues was covered. On the domestic side these included failures to demobilize troops, the impact of the return of southern refugees from the north, insurgencies in the south, and the impact of a southern secession on Darfur. Issues relating to the status of

Abyei and the impact of widespread poverty, hunger, and illiteracy on future development of the south were front and centre in both countries' reporting. On the international side the foreign policies pursued by both Canada and the United States were reviewed.
- Compared to election coverage, greater balance was evident in coverage in the two countries with respect both to the overall number of stories and to the placement of news in front-page stories, news briefs, and op-ed articles.
- Editorial commentary was scarce, limited to the one appearing in *The New York Times*. Letters to the editor were limited as well, one each published in *The Globe and Mail* and *The New York Times*.
- Beyond the call for more coercive diplomacy, there was virtually no discussion regarding what should be done by the international community if the optimistic scenarios for a peaceful independence failed to materialize and the region returned to a state of war.

Differences in Canadian and American Reporting

- Canadian reporting emphasized the problems stemming from the return to the south of those who had moved to the north to avoid the violence of the civil war.
- US reporting evidenced more optimism that widespread violence could be avoided. This was based largely on favourable assessments of the Obama administration's attempts to strike a deal with the Sudanese president to allow the secession to occur peacefully.
- US reporting assessed the implications of independence on violence in the region and on secessionist movements in other African countries.

The "Alerting" Function

A total of 77 stories dealing with the referendum, more or less equally distributed between the two countries, appear to have been adequate to alert both Canadian and American attentive publics to a potential crisis brewing in southern Sudan. This is particularly the case in view of the number of articles datelined Sudan and the wide range of serious problems discussed. However, as mentioned, television news, widely seen as critical in any alerting campaign, was significantly absent, thus calling into question any effective mass alert of the citizenry in either country.

The "Framing" Function

Referendum reporting can best be characterized by the use of "mixed frames." This was the case especially with US reporting. On the one hand, in terms of their potential for violence, problems facing a peaceful transition for south Sudan were seen as immense, with Abyei the most likely "flashpoint" (as identified by Douglas Johnson in 2007) for renewed violence. On the other hand, considerable hopefulness was expressed that a realistic appraisal of self-interest on the part of leaders in both the north and south, plus diplomatic pressure (especially the incentives offered by the United States), would be sufficient to get the participants to muddle through the independence process without a reignition of violence. The result, in our opinion, was mixed framing that gave readers no clear message of what likely lay ahead. This said, US readers, to a greater extent than their Canadian counterparts, were led to expect the best—in circumstances where, given all the possible obstacles, that outcome was still very much in doubt.

CHAPTER 7

NORTH AMERICAN PRESS COVERAGE OF THE DECLARATION OF INDEPENDENCE BY THE REPUBLIC OF SOUTH SUDAN

Methods

The final event in our assessment of how major newspapers in Canada and the United States reported on the probability of violence associated with the breakup of Sudan was the actual declaration of independence by the Republic of South Sudan on 9 July 2011. In this case the two-month period of study began on 15 May, allowing us to include reporting on the invasion and occupation of Abyei by the northern Sudanese army as well as fighting in Southern Kordofan and Blue Nile. The study period ended on 15 July, a week following what turned out to be the peaceful achievement of independence. Overall, the four newspapers offered 83 items of content, the most for any of the three events, by a small margin. Interestingly, both Canadian papers featured less coverage than they had given the referendum; reporting in *The Globe and Mail* fell from 17 to 3 items,[1] while for the *Ottawa Citizen* the decline was far less precipitous—from 21 to 17. This trend obviously was reversed for the American papers, with *The New York Times* increasing its coverage from 25 to 37 items, while *The Washington Post* also upped its coverage, by 12 stories, from 14 to 26 items. For both US newspapers, pre-independence hostilities in Abyei and the Nuba Mountains accounted for the increased attention.

Findings

The Globe and Mail

Reporting on the independence process in the paper edition of *The Globe and Mail* consisted of three items—an op-ed piece, an inside-page news story, and an editorial. Reporting did not begin until 6 July and did so with the publication of an op-ed article by Rift Valley Institute Senior Researcher Aly Verjee. The article presented background information on Sudan (both north and south) pointing out that the former (described as "a repressive and intolerant regime") was still involved in conflict in Darfur, while the latter was to become the first new African nation to emerge since Eritrean independence in 1993. The south's poverty and fragility were highlighted: "South Sudan will be one of the world's poorest countries in one of the world's poorest regions. On the United Nations Human Development Index, Sudan currently ranks 154 out of 169, so South Sudan will start even closer to the bottom. Independence brings to the fore the problems of weak state capacity, chronic insecurity and the difficulties of a postconflict transition from decades of war" (Verjee 2011). The centrality of oil to the economies of both north and south was discussed, with the assessment that there was "little transparency in the oil sector." Canada was noted as playing "a supporting role in both North and South Sudan, spending more than $100 million annually in development and humanitarian assistance." Other than a brief mention of "recent conflicts in Southern Kordofan," the potential for violence reoccurring following independence was not discussed (Verjee 2011).

Independence itself was marked by an inside-page wire service story that again focused on what were described as the "grim realities" facing the new nation: underdevelopment, illiteracy, poverty, lack of education and health care, plus a "legacy of mutual mistrust" between north and south, giving rise to "fears of renewed conflict" (Wire Services 2011h). UN Secretary-General Ban Ki-moon offered congratulations: "'the people of south Sudan have achieved their dream … [adding that] the UN and the international community will continue to stand by south Sudan'" (quoted in Wire Services 2011h). Initially this support would take the form of "a new peacekeeping force for South Sudan … [consisting of] up to 7,000 military personnel and 900 international police, plus an unspecified number of UN civilian staff including human rights experts." However, this was offset by information that "cattle raids and rebel battles have killed nearly 2,400 in the south this year." The story ended with a claim from an unnamed observer that "the problems South Sudan face are 'bigger and harder than what any other country in Africa faced' when most nations on the continent gained independence from the colonial powers in the 1960s" (quoted in Wire Services 2011h). An ongoing role for Canada was not addressed.

The Globe and Mail's "independence editorial" on 14 July echoed the frame of *caution* characteristic of earlier coverage: while there was "much to celebrate, once the independence party is over, Africa's newest country faces an almost unbelievable number of political, security and infrastructure challenges," among which was the unresolved Abyei border dispute with the north. The main focus, however, was on domestic problems in the south—namely internal conflict: "the government, dominated by the Dinka tribe, must work to resolve ethnic disputes. Without peace, aid and investment will dry up. The new government must show it can tolerate dissent, and that it is prepared to govern for all. A people beleaguered by years of conflict and loss deserve no less" (*Globe and Mail* 2011).

The Ottawa Citizen

The *Ottawa Citizen*'s seventeen items consisted of nine short "news briefs" (supplied by various wire services), five inside-page stories from Reuters and Agence France-Presse correspondents, plus one each editorial, op-ed article, and stand-alone photo. Coverage began on 23 May with a report that the northern Sudanese army had taken control of the disputed border area of Abyei. Coverage of fighting in Abyei, as well as in the border province of Southern Kordofan, continued until the end of the month. With a total of ten stories, overall coverage of pre-independence fighting surpassed that accorded South Sudan's actual declaration of independence. The latter was covered in seven items, beginning with an inside-page story on 8 July and ending with a 15 July news brief indicating that South Sudan had been accepted as a member of the United Nations (Wire Services 2011i).

The Abyei region, long felt to be the possible flashpoint for violence between the north and south, lived up to predictions. Following "weeks of growing tension and accusations of skirmishes by both sides," on 21 May the Sudanese army sent tanks into the region "forcing thousands to flee and bringing the country's north and south to the brink of full conflict" (Wire Services 2011a). Two days later, Sudanese President al-Bashir proclaimed that "'*Abyei is northern Sudanese land*' ... [and gave] the green light to respond to any possible 'provocation' by the army of south Sudan" (quoted in Wire Services 2011b; italics added). A day later another news brief reported a proposal for a UN peacekeeping force of 7,000 (United Nations Mission for South Sudan—UNMISS) for South Sudan to serve for a three-month period following independence. The existing 10,000-strong UNMIS was "expected to remain in place in the north," but its numbers were expected to be reduced over time (Wire Services 2011c).

Mid-June saw the first reports of fighting in the oil-rich northern border province of Southern Kordofan, in this case "between forces from the north and fighters aligned to the former southern rebel group the Sudan People's Liberation Army (SPLA)." Fighting had begun some ten days earlier when northern air strikes targeted Nuba peoples who had "fought on the side of the SPLA during the devastating 1983–2005 civil war" (Wire Services 2011e).

Both of these conflicts had obvious implications for the upcoming independence of the south, and the international community responded, especially former South African president Thabo Mbeki, who presided over talks to resolve them. Southern Kordofan was first on Mbeki's agenda. Reuters correspondent Aaron Maasho reported that Mbeki announced that "both sides have agreed that there should be a cessation of hostilities, and that negotiations should begin immediately" (quoted in Maasho 2011a). Fighting continued, however, and Mbeki gave no indication of when hostilities might cease.

On 21 June progress on Abyei was noted as Mbeki reported that following a week of negotiations in Addis Ababa "north and south Sudan have signed an agreement to demilitarize the disputed … region and allow in Ethiopian peacekeeping forces." He added that "a police service would be established for the region, with the size and composition determined by a joint committee co-chaired by northern and southern officials" (Maasho 2011b). Toward the end of June the UN Security Council followed up on this initiative by authorizing "a 4,200-strong Ethiopian peacekeeping force" to be sent to the disputed Abyei region. It was pointed out that "with fighting also flaring in the neighbouring state of South Kordofan, [north–south] rivalry is again an international concern ahead of southern Sudan's declaration of independence on July 9" (Wire Services 2011f). A day later, a further development on Southern Kordofan was reported: "The Sudanese government and the northern branch of the … (SPLM) … signed a deal to resolve their differences in the embattled border state" (Wire Services 2011g). Thus, just over a week before the scheduled declaration of independence by the south, major violence in the region appeared to be under control, at least temporarily.

Reporting on the actual independence process itself began on 8 July with an Agence France-Presse inside-page story that explored whether the newly ratified constitution in fact had placed too much power in the hands of the president. This was not the case, claimed Information Minister Barnaba Marial Benjamin. The Carter Center, however, disagreed: "The current draft of the transitional constitution contains a number of provisions that appear likely to concentrate power in the central government … [although] there is significant support for a decentralized system of government" (quoted in AFP 2011b).

On Independence Day, regular *Citizen* columnist David Warren's op-ed article recounted the impact of European colonization on Africa. Avoiding formulaic interpretations, Warren stressed the relative unimportance of Africa to European imperialist ventures, focusing instead on the flawed process of decolonization. Warren argued that "so much of today's sprawling political and economic catastrophe through sub-Saharan Africa can be traced not to imperialism, per se, but to the imperial authorities' eagerness to leave around the signal year of 1960. It was an appalling cat's cradle of quick fixes they left behind" (Warren 2011). And, with respect to Sudan, the "quick fix" in question was the abandonment of British plans to link up southern Sudan with its other East African colonies: "The British in fact saw the problem coming of putting millions of tropical rainforest-dwelling black Africans under the rule of desert-dwelling Arabized Muslims, at least a century ago. Their intention to make the region an extension of Uganda instead of Sudan was defeated by 'events'" (Warren 2011). While Warren's view of South Sudan's long-term future was somewhat hopeful, the immediate state of affairs was portrayed as bleak: "Contemporary journalism has given us a passing flavour of just how likely South Sudan is to become a failed state. It contains half a dozen extended ethnic groups or tribal formations which, with independence, will now recall that they do not like each other. The struggle for power within the new state will be, guaranteed, unedifying. Our guilt-strewn offerings of foreign aid will congeal layers of corruption" (Warren 2011).

Also on Independence Day, the *Citizen*'s editorial assessment of the situation was at best cautious: Just as resources were no guarantee for economic success, "political independence ... [was] sadly, no guarantee of peace or democratic self-determination for the people of South Sudan." Poverty and the legacy of "a long and bloody war with the north" were cited as strong impediments to progress. At the same time, independence was viewed as "a fresh start, a chance for decent governance—without which there can be no sustainable development—to take root." On the international side, it was noted that "Sudan is already a 'country of focus' for the Canadian International Development Agency. South Sudan will need our help, and Canada's work there should focus on effective projects to improve governance, guard against corruption and capitalize on the potential for a thriving agricultural sector" (*Ottawa Citizen* 2011).

On 10 July, Reuters reporters Ulf Laessing and Jeremy Clarke assessed the impact of southern independence on the north: "while the south rejoiced at finally getting its freedom from the dominant north, for people in Khartoum the secession brought not only the loss of a third of the territory and much of the country's oil resources, but also a profound feeling of sadness" (Laessing and Clarke 2001). While most of those interviewed in Khartoum expressed a feeling of loss, Al-Tayyib Mustafa, leader of the "Just Peace Forum" (a northern group in favour of secession), celebrated "the 'real independence' of the north. 'Sudan's unity was a mistake as history has proven. Now we can go our own way and don't need to listen to the needs of the south'" (quoted in Laessing and Clarke 2001). For the south there was dancing and celebrating as "for the moment ... [people forgot] the factional infighting, grinding poverty and lack of basic facilities that threaten the brave new dawn" (Laessing and Clarke 2011).

The New York Times

New York Times coverage of South Sudan's independence totaled thirty-seven items consisting of three front-page stories, twenty-four inside-page stories, five news briefs, two editorials, and three op-ed/news analysis pieces. The vast majority of this coverage (78 percent) focused on pre-independence fighting, first in Abyei and then in Southern Kordofan and Blue Nile, with about an equal amount of reportage addressing the two areas of conflict.

Coverage of the Abyei crisis began on 22 May with a Juba-datelined, Associated Press report that, following bombing attacks, northern Sudanese troops had occupied the town of Abyei (AP 2011c).[2] The next day Jeffrey Gettleman and Josh Kron, reporting from Nairobi and Kampala respectively, followed up with details: "After an air campaign … the north's ground forces staged a full-scale invasion of Abyei … with artillery, dozens of tanks and thousands of soldiers sweeping in from several directions."[3] South Sudan initially viewed the invasion as "'a declaration of war,'" with Information Minister Benjamin indicating that "'we will respond in self-defense.'" Project Enough's John Prendergast assessed the consequences: "'If not de-escalated, this could be the shot heard round Sudan.… On July 9, the Republic of South Sudan could be born in a state of war'" (both quoted in Gettleman and Kron 2011a). The reporters suggested that "southern forces in Abyei may have provoked the northern assault … [by ambushing] northern troops in Abyei, killing dozens." They described Abyei as "a clear potential spoiler in the separation of north and south Sudan" and noted that the United States response to the crisis was to seek a middle ground. On the one hand the US deplored "the southern aggression," and, on the other, termed "the northern invasion 'disproportionate and irresponsible'" (quoted in Gettleman and Kron 2011a).

Over the next few weeks, reports filed chiefly by Gettleman and Kron filled in the finer points. Abyei's importance lay not as much in its oil (at this point described as marginal), but rather in its "symbolic power"—both sides claimed it and both "have strong allies living there." For the north these allies were the nomadic Misseriya Arabs, used in the past by the government as "proxy militias," while for the south "Abyei is home to some of their top leaders" (Gettleman 2011e). International Crisis Group analyst Zach Vertin pointed to "tension in the south" between those who believed that war would undermine independence and those who felt that further capitulation to the north was intolerable. United States Special Envoy to Sudan Princeton Lyman called for negotiations: "'If we don't have Abyei negotiated, rather than occupied, it will be hard to move forward'" (quoted in Gettleman 2011e). For the north, the "move forward" referred to was the Obama administration's offer to normalize relations.

Vertin's opinion was that neither side really wanted war—the south was militarily disadvantaged while the north might "lose access to oil." His interpretation was that the northern invasion and occupation of Abyei was intended as a bargaining chip in continuing pre-breakup negotiations over "how exactly to split the oil; where to draw the border; [and] how to share Sudan's $38 billion debt" (Gettleman 2011e).

A more sinister interpretation of the move was that it represented a Darfur-like campaign of "ethnic cleansing" on the part of the north. UN officials reported "a relatively large influx of nomadic people into to the area ... in a bid to change its demographics permanently" (Gettleman and Kron 2011b). An unnamed UN official claimed that "'if the Sudanese government is intent on settling thousands of Misseriya in Abyei ... then last weekend's attack ... was planned as ethnic cleansing strategy.'" Eliza Griswold, a senior fellow at the New America Foundation, concurred: "'The north has begun to employ the same kind of scorched-earth tactics we saw Khartoum use in Darfur' ... [where] it sent notorious janjaweed militias ... to capture land belonging to dispossessed ethnic groups that the government was fighting." Griswold argued that "'all of these battles are brutal struggles for power and resources of land, oil, even water—waged by any means necessary'" (both as quoted in Gettleman and Kron 2011b). For their part, Sudanese officials and Misseriya leaders "denied any wrongdoing." Whatever their intent, a week following the invasion and occupation of Abyei, Salva Kiir, the soon-to-be President of South Sudan, indicated that war was not on the south's agenda—"*We will not go back to war. It will not happen*" (quoted in Gettleman, 2011f; italics added).

Toward the end of May the first *New York Times* editorial appeared since the beginning of the pre-independence escalation of violence. It cautioned that the "dispute over the Abyei region must not spin out of control ... [and urged] the United States, the United Nations and the African Union ... to press hard to get the two sides to back down." The editorial board was "'encouraged by reports that the two sides will meet with mediators from the African Union ... [adding that] another war serves no one's interest'" (*New York Times* 2011b).

In an end-of-the-month op-ed piece, long-time Sudan analyst Douglas Johnson offered contrary advice, arguing that "the international community—particularly the United Nations and the United States—have been spectacularly ineffective in getting the Sudanese government to honor its own agreements." He called instead for "*no more compromises over agreements already reached. All Sudanese armed groups should leave Abyei and the surrounding territory, and be replaced by international troops with a more robust commitment to protect civilians*" (Johnson 2011; italics added).

Johnson maintained that the US had "unwittingly encouraged the Bashir regime to take a hard line by supporting successive compromise proposals rather than insisting that Khartoum adhere to the [2005] peace agreement and abide by the court ruling [on Abyei's borders]." As a result, he felt there was "a real risk that the north will now simply occupy all contested border areas—and possibly the oil fields inside South Sudan—and refuse to leave unless pushed out.... To prevent the Abyei crisis from igniting other conflicts, *the international community must stop pretending that both sides are equally at fault*" (Johnson 2011;

italics added). Johnson contended that at this point the US had limited influence over al-Bashir. However, in that "the occupation of Abyei is threatening Chinese oil operations along the border and inside South Sudan," he saw China as the key player in moving the north toward compromise (Johnson 2011). In spite of Johnson's assessment, the US administration sent counterterrorism specialist John Brennan to Sudan, "where he 'underscored President Obama's deep concern over the continued presence of Sudanese forces in Abyei and urged a rapid and peaceful resolution to the crisis'" (White House spokesperson, quoted in Gettleman and Kron 2011f).

Whatever dynamic was in play, it appeared that the Abyei crisis was being contained in that it was reported that both north and south had agreed to "bringing in Ethiopian peacekeepers as a buffer between opposing forces." An unnamed Western diplomat appraised the solution: "We need something quick for Abyei, and the Ethiopians are it" (quoted in Gettleman and Kron 2011d). Some three weeks later, a ten-page deal was signed between north and south agreeing to allow about 4,000 Ethiopian peacekeepers to patrol Abyei. The agreement called for a peaceful negotiation of Abyei's "final status" as well as for the return of all people who had been displaced by the invasion (Gettleman 2011j).

However, just as the Abyei crisis was de-escalating in late May, Gettleman and Kron reported in a Juba-datelined story that "the northern Sudanese army is threatening two more areas along the combustible north–south border [Blue Nile and Southern Kordofan] weeks before southern Sudan is due to split off as a new country." While these two states had been recognized as part of the north since Sudanese independence in 1956, during the course of the civil wars they were bitterly contested territories. They remained home to a large number of troops who had fought for the south and were described as "still bristling with arms" (Gettleman and Kron 2011c).

The immediate problem was a decree by the north that "thousands of fighters allied to the south in these two areas" would be disarmed. Blue Nile's Governor Malik Agar "did not think the southern-allied fighters would surrender. 'It's like putting a cat in a corner.… They will fight'" (quoted in Gettleman and Kron 2011c).[4]

As with Abyei, the situations in Blue Nile and Southern Kordofan had been addressed in the 2005 Comprehensive Peace Agreement. But like the called-for (but aborted) referendum in Abyei, there was no follow-through on what was described as a "vaguely defined 'popular consultation' process" regarding their future status. And, in this instance, while southern leaders early on ruled out a military response, it was pointed out that they did not speak for the "possibly tens of thousands" of fighters in the two regions (Gettleman and Kron 2011c). Smith College professor and long-time Darfur activist Eric Reeves saw the move by the north into the Nuba Mountains in particular as likely to be explosive, given that the area was "one of the strongholds of the southern rebels during ... the 1980s and 1990s." Reeves claimed that "'the amount of weaponry and men under arms is tremendous'" (quoted in Gettleman and Kron 2011c).

Gettleman and Kron predicted that the situation in the border regions was likely to get worse: "Northern leaders have not been shy about their intentions to unilaterally annex large areas of contested territory. They amassed an enormous force of troops, tanks, and artillery pieces in the borderlands area and have publicly vowed to take control of all the disputed territory north of the 1956 border, regardless that the status of some of those areas was supposed to be decided by the people themselves" (2011c). Their motives were attributed, at least in part, to popular criticism over "losing the south, especially its oil.... By grabbing what little disputed territory remains, Mr. Bashir can make himself look strong even though he is still boxed in."

On 1 June, in the same story that explained that the north and south had agreed to establish "a demilitarized 12.4-mile-wide zone along the roughly 1,240-mile border," Gettleman and Kron also reported that the north "demanded that all southern-allied soldiers in ... [Blue Nile and Southern Kordofan]—and there are thousands—disarm [immediately]." At the beginning of June it was unclear whether force would be used in the disarmament of rebel fighters "or whether [the north] ... will heed the advice of Western and African officials to pause and give negotiations a chance to defuse tensions" (Gettleman and Kron 2011e).

Toward the end of the first week of June, Kron and Gettleman reported from Juba that fighting had indeed broken out in the Southern Kordofan capital of Kadugli. Unnamed analysts explained the north's motivation: "Sudan's government is concerned that rebel movements in other parts of the country, like Darfur, could be encouraged to fight harder for autonomy if the popular consultations in Blue Nile and Southern Kordofan are allowed to proceed" (Kron and Gettleman 2011a).

In a "news analysis" article published on the same day, Gettleman appraised the situation, describing Mr. Bashir's tactics as part of "a carefully devised strategy meant to ensure just one thing: that when southern Sudan declares independence next month, his government controls as much oil as possible, or at least is richly compensated." In addition, the Sudanese president's political position was judged to be tenuous: "If he hopes to keep his job—which may be the only way of staying out of jail—Mr. Bashir needs to keep the northern economy afloat, which he cannot do without southern oil." The soon-to-be-independent south was equally dependent on oil revenues, with analysts indicating that "the southern government, already racked by ethnic tensions and military problems, would implode if soldiers stopped getting their paychecks" (Gettleman 2011g).

According to an unnamed Western diplomat, "'it all adds up to one marvelous strategy.... I don't think a war's going to break out. These are calculated risks, though sometimes calculations don't work'" (quoted in Gettleman 2011g).

Within days, there were reports of air bombardments of villages in Southern Kordofan and UN spokesperson Hua Jiang described the situation as "very serious." US Ambassador to the UN Susan Rice indicated that the north was straying from the path leading to normalization of relations with the US: "They have put into grave jeopardy the implementation of the roadmap.... [b]ecause they have not only not fulfilled their obligations, they are doing the opposite" (both quoted in Kron and Gettleman 2011b).

The situation continued to worsen into the middle of June when it became clear that the Nuban people, who had supported the south in the civil wars, were being targeted. "They are killing black people.... The northern army is slaughtering people who supported the S.P.L.M." (unnamed Sudanese aid worker, quoted in Gettleman 2011h). International observers also expressed their concerns. Eric Reeves claimed "the ingredients for an explosion are all present.... The violence in South Kordofan threatens peace in Sudan like no other crisis, and there are many." Anglican Archbishop of Canterbury Rowan Williams likened the situation to Darfur: "The risk of another Darfur situation, with civilian populations at the mercy of government-supported terror, is a real one" (both quoted in Gettleman 2011h).[5]

Predictions of a new humanitarian disaster seemingly were coming to pass. In a front-page story on 21 June UN officials claimed that "the Sudanese army and its allied militias have gone on a rampage to crush rebel fighters in the Nuba Mountains in central Sudan, burning thatch-roofed villages, executing elders, burning churches and pitching another region of the country into crisis" (Gettleman 2011i). An unnamed American official predicted that things would get worse: "This is going to spread like wildfire … you're going to have massive destruction and death in central Sudan, and no one seems able to do anything about it." Other international observers agreed. Former State Department official Roger Winter reported that "today, again the Nuba people are positioned for liquidation by Khartoum forces," while Darfur expert Julie Flint claimed that "a new war in Nuba threatens to be a replay of Darfur" (all quoted in Gettleman 2011i).

By the end of June, however, a framework for an agreement had been worked out calling for the integration of "southern-allied fighters" into the Sudanese army "without resorting to force" (Gettleman 2011k). The agreement also called for "political partnerships and governance arrangements" that appeared to include the "popular consultations" called for in the 2005 CPA. However, "it stopped short of declaring a cease-fire in the Nuba Mountains." Blue Nile's governor, Malik Agar, who had signed the document, was less than enthusiastic: "Are we satisfied? Well, let's just say we can live with it'" (quoted in Gettleman 2011k).

Jeffrey Gettleman was also among the doubtful. On 1 July, in the second front-page story dealing with the crisis in the Nuba Mountains, he argued that "despite an agreement signed only days ago to bring peace to this part of central Sudan, it seems to be sliding inexorably toward war." A Nuban working for a World Bank project called the agreement "'meaningless.... We're never going to forgive them now.... Do you know how many people I've seen die right in front of me?'" (Caddy Ali, quoted in Gettleman 2011m). Gettleman described the fighting in the Nuba Mountains as "underscor[ing] how fractured Sudan will remain even after the south secedes. The same demands being espoused by opposition fighters here have been the kindling for major conflict—and major suffering—in several other corners of northern Sudan, where the government is determined to keep a firm grip across a country of diverse groups clamoring for their rights" (2011m).

Just days before South Sudan's declaration of independence, fighting in the Nuba Mountains remained unresolved. Gettleman reported that the Sudanese government "is scrambling to crush any rebellious chunks of territory that will remain its own. Its forces have been relentlessly pounding the Nuba Mountains from Russian-made Antonov bombers for weeks, demanding that tens of thousands of rebel fighters dug in here disarm and drop their insistence on more autonomy for the distinctive Nuba people" (Gettleman 2011n). He interpreted the north's policy as "a signal that even after the south breaks off, the result of decades of struggle for liberation, it will not tolerate other secession movements" (Gettleman 2011n).

The violence in the Nuba Mountains continued following South Sudan's independence. It was reported in mid-July that peace talks had broken off and a UN report suggested "that in its effort to stamp out any lingering rebellion in South Kordofan ... the northern government ... *has carried out widespread human rights violations that could amount to war crimes*" (MacFarquhar 2011; italics added). Ambassador Susan Rice told the Security Council that "the violence, the human rights abuses and the deliberate obstruction of access for humanitarian agencies must end" (quoted in MacFarquhar 2011). In spite of obvious parallels to Darfur, there was no discussion of possible consequences for northern non-compliance.

New York Times coverage of the south's actual declaration of independence paled in comparison to that accorded the conflicts in the border regions. It began on 7 July with an inside-page story by Josh Kron assessing its impact on Uganda as an important regional power: "In the last two decades, Uganda has helped bring three surrounding governments to power—here, in Rwanda and in Congo. In Somalia, it has dispatched thousands of troops to preserve another. And for southern Sudan, Uganda has been nothing short of a life-support system." It was explained further that even with independence, "South Sudan will be a nation in dependence," with Uganda (as a major exporter of goods) standing to benefit (Kron 2011d).

A front-page story on 8 July by Jeffrey Gettleman offered a pessimistic preview of the upcoming independence. He stressed that "from the moment it declares independence ... the Republic of South Sudan ... will take its place at the bottom of the developing world.... Beyond that, the nation faces several serious insurrections within its own sprawling territory and hostilities with northern Sudan, its former nemesis." On the former issue Gettleman added that "more than 2,300 people have been killed in ethnic and rebel violence this year, with at least a half-dozen rebel groups, some with thousands of fighters, prowling the bush, attacking government soldiers, terrorizing civilians, and stealing cattle and even children." In the context of rebel activity, he highlighted ethnicity, especially the historic conflict between the dominant Dinka and the Nuer peoples (Gettleman 2011o).

The New York Times independence day editorial continued to place South Sudan's future in a *pessimistic* frame, noting that "celebrations ... cannot obscure the sobering truth: building a functional new country will take decades of work" and that, in addition to efforts by South Sudan, the US and the international community had a continuing responsibility to make it work. The immediate problem was seen to be South Kordofan, where "Mr. Bashir's decision to order the United Nations to withdraw peacekeepers ... [was termed] deeply worrisome." The Obama administration was seen to have made the correct move in "not taking Sudan off its terrorism list and normalizing relations until Khartoum fulfills the peace deal and ends the conflict in Darfur" (*New York Times* 2011c).

In his Independence Day analysis article, Gettleman addressed the "interesting question why, of all the world's war zones and all the blood baths Africa has witnessed—Liberia, Somalia, the Democratic Republic of Congo, to name a few—this place has grabbed so much attention." In light of our research focus on creating the "Will to Intervene," his answer is thought-provoking: "American celebrities and religious groups teamed up with policy makers and helped a forlorn underdog region finally achieve what very few separatist movements achieve: independence." He pointed out that Christian missionary groups had long been present in southern Sudan; however, in 2001, with the election of George W. Bush, they "found a friend in the White House ... [and the Bush administration] pushed southern rebels ... and Sudan's central government to sign a comprehensive peace agreement in 2005, which guaranteed the southerners the right to secede." George Clooney was singled out for his role in urging "the Obama administration to stay focused on Sudan" (Gettleman 2011p). R. Barrie Walkley, the American Consul General in Juba, also stressed the importance of celebrity diplomacy in achieving the independence outcome: "Would this have taken place without celebrities? ... I think celebrities have a lot to do with it.... [They] focus attention on a problem. They do it in a bumper sticker fashion, perhaps ... [but] if you get millions of people sending blogs to the president, that will have an impact" (quoted in Gettleman 2011p).

In spite of the obvious achievement, Gettleman's post-independence assessment remained on the whole discouraging:

> South Sudan—Texas-size and with about eight million people—is already plagued by ethnic tensions and rebellions.... And relations with the north are still dicey. Negotiations have yet to agree on a formula to split the revenue from the south's oil fields, which have kept the economies of both southern and northern Sudan afloat. And Mr. Bashir's army has been pounding southern-allied rebels who have been refusing to disarm just north of the border in the Nuba Mountains, which some analysts worry could drag the whole region back into a full-scale war. (Gettleman 2011q)

New York Times reporting ended with a story on 14 July by freelancer Isma'il Kushkush dealing with the impact of the secession on the north, which was referred to as the "second republic." Kushkush's considered opinion was that beyond a greater emphasis on Islam and Shari'a, not much would really change: "'These are tactics; they want people to believe that they are going to change.... They are afraid of what happened in places like Egypt and Tunisia'" (Sudanese Political Science Professor Adlan el-Hardello, quoted in Kushkush 2011). Izdihar Juma'a, a member of the northern wing of the SPLM, was not optimistic that the north had learned much about how to rule an ethnically diverse country: "Northern politicians need to properly diagnose the problems of the outer provinces or the result will be similar to South Sudan.... It is not about who rules Sudan, but about how Sudan is ruled" (quoted in Kushkush 2011).

The Washington Post

The twenty-six items of *Washington Post* coverage consisted of eleven inside-page stories, eight news "digest" pieces, one editorial, and six op-ed articles, including one co-written by George Clooney and John Prendergast, one by Smith College Professor Eric Reeves, and one by Secretary of State Hillary Clinton. As was the case with the other events we examined, material in the US capital paper had a strong focus on the US contribution to the events unfolding in Sudan. And, while these efforts were judged to be impressive, they were not seen as likely to be enough to save the day. Thus *The Washington Post*'s framing of South Sudan's future was even more pessimistic than that offered by *The New York Times*.

Reporting began on 22 May with a short Associated Press news "digest" item indicating that northern Sudanese forces had attacked and occupied the disputed town of Abyei. It was noted that the attack had coincided with a visit by the UN Security Council to Sudan and that the international body "expressed concern about the recent violence in Southern Sudan and along the contested border" (AP 2011d). This initial report of fighting was followed two days later by an inside-page story from Reuters correspondent Ulf Laessing stating that the south had accused the north "of trying to provoke war and prevent the oil-rich south from becoming an independent country." It was noted as well that "the U.N. mission in Sudan 'strongly condemns the burning and looting currently being perpetrated by armed elements in Abyei town'" (quoted in Laessing 2011). Additionally, US Special Envoy to Sudan Princeton Lyman warned Khartoum that its actions put at risk normalization of relations with the US, but the north appeared uncompromising (Laessing 2011).

The one *Washington Post* editorial during the independence study period appeared on 25 May and adopted a worrisome tone. It acknowledged that south Sudan had been "a diplomatic success story for the Obama administration and the United Nations." This, however, was imperiled by the northern attack on Abyei: "The question now is whether the Obama administration, which has led international diplomacy on South Sudan, can bring enough pressure to bear on Mr. Bashir to end the conflict before it worsens." The US was seen as on the right track by demanding "'the immediate withdrawal of all military elements from Abyei'" (quoted in *Washington Post* 2011). More, however, was expected: "The administration must also move to restrain the southern Sudanese government from responding militarily, and urge Arab states and China … to use leverage on Mr. Bashir." The editorial ended with the observation that "no one, with the possible exception of Sudan's strongman, has an interest in the disruption of South Sudan's move toward independence, much less another war in Africa" (*Washington Post* 2011).

Reporting from South Sudan on 28 May, special correspondent Rebecca Hamilton explored the reasons behind the northern attack on Abyei. John Prendergast, she noted, saw it as an effort "'to intimidate the government of southern Sudan and the international community into deeper compromises at the negotiating table,'" while Fouad Hikmat of the International Crisis Group explained it as an attempt "to shore up support as it faces domestic pressure against its rule. 'Bashir can see Tunisia and Egypt and see the new winds of change blowing'" (both as quoted in Hamilton 2011d).

An op-ed piece by George Clooney and John Prendergast on the same day was critical of what was termed the "balanced international response—pressing both sides for compromise." They recalled "dishonored agreements and massive human rights crimes in Sudan … [which were described as] shocking in scope," and claimed that "the international community threatened real consequences during and after these incidents … but the consequences never came." In a rare use of *responsibility to protect* language in media coverage, they went on argue that "the world has recently shown some willingness to act in Africa" (specifically in Libya and Ivory Coast), and moreover, that "the objective of saving lives through robust military action, after other, non-military measures failed was successful." Clooney and Prendergast clarified that they were "*not advocating military intervention.*" However, they did claim that "*the evidence shows that incentives alone are insufficient to change Khartoum's calculations.* International support should be sought immediately for denying debt relief, expanding the ICC indictments, diplomatically isolating the regime, suspending all non-humanitarian aid, obstructing state-controlled bank transactions and freezing accounts holding oil wealth diverted by senior regime officials" (Clooney and Prendergast 2011; italics added). And, they argued, "we must proceed before Abyei ignites the next Darfur."

At the very end of May, Hamilton examined the impact of the northern military action on the largely Ngok Dinka population of Abyei—some 40,000 had fled from the town and another 40,000 from the surrounding areas. The plight of the refugees was complicated by what southern Sudanese officials called a "Khartoum imposed embargo of goods entering the south," a charge denied by the north. Fuel was in especially short supply: while "the south holds more than 80 percent of Sudan's oil, ... it is sent to refineries in the north before being transported back to the south for use. The trade blockade has left oil-rich southern Sudan with almost no fuel supply" (Hamilton 2011e). Furthermore, Nyandeng Malek, Governor of Warrap State (where most of the Abyei refugees had sought shelter), explained that "ninety-nine percent of the goods in our markets come from the north, so now we have nothing left in terms of food. How can you host when you yourself have nothing?" (quoted in Hamilton 2011e).

Some progress toward resolving border issues was reported at the beginning of June in the form of an AU-brokered agreement providing for "a jointly patrolled demilitarized border zone" between the two countries following the south's independence. Alex de Waal, who was serving as an AU advisor, took an optimistic view, seeing the agreement as "a necessary step between the two parties that will allow the Sudanese government to take the necessary action to demilitarize Abyei" (Fick 2011a). However, any optimism was checked by a UN human rights report warning "that Khartoum's seizure of Abyei 'could lead to *ethnic cleansing* if conditions for the return of the displaced Ngok Dinka residents are not created'" (quoted in Wire Services 2011d; italics added). It was further reported that "the Ngok Dinka and many of southern Sudan's senior leaders are pressing the region's president ... for *a robust response*" (Wire Services 2011d; italics added). In spite of this, Sudan made it clear that its forces were not about to leave Abyei (Hamilton 2011f).

Although the Abyei crisis appeared far from resolved, on 15 June coverage in *The Washington Post* shifted to what a State Department spokesperson described as "the worsening situation in the state of Kordofan." The Associated Press reported that "tens of thousands of people need assistance … Sudan was blocking flights from landing … [and] both northern and southern forces are obstructing humanitarian access by land" (AP 2011e). Two days later, President Obama "voiced 'deep concern' over the widening violence in Sudan." UN officials knowledgeable about the situation presented what was described as "a grim closed-door briefing to the … Security Council on events unfolding in South Kordofan, where more than 60,000 people have fled their homes.… [Fears were raised] of a resumption of all-out civil war" (Lynch 2011).[6]

On 18 June, Smith College Professor Eric Reeves offered a strongly worded op-ed piece on South Kordofan in which the trigger word *genocide* was added to the *ethnic cleansing* previously alleged to be taking place in Abyei:

> We are once again on the verge of a genocidal counterinsurgency in Sudan. *History must not be allowed to repeat itself.… Absent a vigorous international response*, there will almost certainly be a reprise of ethnically targeted human destruction in the middle of the country, specifically within the Nuba Mountains region of South Kordofan which has a rich mixture of African inhabitants.… Disturbing accounts have emerged of the African people of the Nuba being rounded up in house searches and road checkpoints, and subjected to indiscriminate aerial bombardment. *All signs point to a new genocide.* (Reeves 2011; italics added)

Reeves argued that "empty demands and threats" had a history of failure in dealing with Sudan's misdeeds and that "either the international community gets serious about preventing further violence in Abyei and the adjacent region of South Kordofan, or we will again see 'tens of thousands of civilians … die in the weeks and months ahead in what will be *continuing genocidal destruction*'" (UN Report, quoted in Reeves 2011; italics added).

Coverage of the actual independence of South Sudan began on 23 June with an assessment of China's likely role in the delicate process. The motivation behind the story was a trip to China by President al-Bashir, and the occasion was used to examine possible changes to China's foreign policy, which previously had been highly supportive of his government. This support was seen as "being undermined by a new reality. Roughly 75 percent of Sudan's oil lies in the south of the country" soon to become independent. Yin Gang, a researcher at China's Institute of West Asian and African Studies, predicted that China would have "to balance its previously wholehearted support for Bashir … with a 'close relationship with the south'" (quoted in Higgins 2011). It was also reported that China had already made diplomatic contact with the south and "as part of its outreach to a secessionist movement it long shunned, recently funded a hospital in the southern town of Bentiu."

Pre-independence reporting also focused on the long-expressed "passionate advocacy within the U.S. evangelical community" on behalf of Christians in Sudan. The reason behind the story was Sarah Palin's cancellation of plans to attend the independence ceremonies, reportedly due to scheduling difficulties. Trip leader, evangelist Billy Graham's son Franklin, explained the importance of celebrities in raising awareness of Sudan: "She would be a very good person to help draw attention to the plight of the Christians in South Sudan.... We've got George Clooney, we've got some Hollywood type people. I'm very grateful for what Mr. Clooney has done. But we need everybody we can find" (Franklin Graham, quoted in Gardner 2011).

Congressman Frank Wolf, who was described as "an advocate for more U.S. involvement in Sudan," also stressed the importance of popular engagement: "There is a genocide taking place.... The more people [who travel to Sudan] from the West, from the United States, the better.... We have a museum on the Mall, the Holocaust Museum. It says 'Never again.' What doesn't the West understand about this? If this were taking place in the south of France, do you think we'd let it go on?" (quoted in Gardner 2011).

A 4 July op-ed article by the newspaper's deputy editorial page editor Jackson Diehl reviewed the contributions of President Obama to the upcoming declaration of independence. His assessment was that "substantial credit should go to the Obama administration—which has demonstrated what can be achieved when U.S. power and influence are fully engaged under the president's direction." Key to the success of the process was the "road map" presented to Mr. Bashir's government: "If it would allow the south to go peacefully, it could earn a release from sanctions, debt relief and diplomatic recognition from the United States." And, when conflict erupted in Abyei and South Kordofan, "again the Obama administration ... responded aggressively" (Diehl 2011). As well, the US provided "some $300 million" to the south for building basic governmental infrastructure. Special Envoy Princeton Lyman praised the personal contributions of Mr. Obama and Hillary Clinton to the process: "The president has been very involved, as has the secretary of state.... Getting that kind of high-level involvement has been very important" (quoted in Diehl 2011).[7] Diehl commented as well that part of the reason for US involvement was that "the cause of southern Sudan (and Darfur) has galvanized liberal interest groups and Hollywood stars, not to mention prominent officials, such as Susan Rice, the U.S. ambassador to the United Nations" (2011).

Washington Post columnist Michael Gerson contributed two columns from South Sudan. The first, on 8 July, described President al-Bashir's attendance at the independence ceremony as an example of "the Sudanese paradox of deep hatreds and unavoidable ties." Gerson described the current state of affairs between Khartoum and Juba as "uncomfortable" as well as "fragile." To that point, southern president Salva Kiir was seen as having "skillfully de-escalated the situation. But it would be an easy slide from a border conflict to a general war—with a new flag carried into battle and new victims of a war that pauses but does not end" (Gerson 2011a).

Gerson's second piece followed independence and focused on internal southern politics. The tasks that lay ahead were seen as daunting: "[The South] … must construct a nation out of flawed materials—a weak economy, a strong military and fractious tribes." Gerson posed three questions: (1) "Can a guerrilla army transform itself into an effective governing class?" (2) Can the corruption associated with "patronage politics" be overcome? And (3) can the "centrifugal forces" of tribalism, "a long history of SPLM infighting and a tendency for North Sudan to fund and encourage internal conflict within the South" be contained? He pointed out that the style of leadership employed by President Kiir was a critical factor, and that the new president "models himself on the chiefs of his tribe, the Dinka." While this style (described as "aristocratic" and "oriented toward consensus") had to date "served Kiir well," Gerson argued that addressing South Sudan's problems "requires the making of enemies," particularly in dealing with systemic corruption. South Sudan's independence was described as "a large, unlikely achievement. But now it faces the hardest of historical tasks. The liberators of a nation must become the founders of a nation" (Gerson 2011b). Whether this would happen was left unanswered.

On the day before independence, Mary Beth Sheridan and Rebecca Hamilton co-authored an inside-page news story that reviewed US contributions toward south Sudan's path to statehood: "President George W. Bush put Sudan at the center of his foreign policy in Africa" (resulting in the 2005 CPA), and President Obama rescued the "accord as it risked unraveling." The impact of the violence in Abyei and Southern Kordofan was evaluated, with Susan Rice being quoted as commenting that the situation remained "extremely volatile." Reporters were told by the US Ambassador to the UN "that if Abyei and other issues weren't resolved soon it could 'swiftly destabilize the future relationship between these two states. So for our part, the United States will continue to be extremely active in supporting the implementation of the peace accord'" (Susan Rice, quoted in Sheridan and Hamilton 2011). Internal problems were reviewed as well and focused on pervasive poverty, described as the legacy of "decades of war." It was noted, for example, that "more than 80 percent of health-care services are provided by the foreign aid groups."

Secretary of State Hillary Clinton's op-ed piece the day after independence attempted to strike an optimistic tone in spite of the difficulties that lay ahead: "There is reason to hope for a better future—if the people and leaders of both Sudan and South Sudan commit themselves to the hard work ahead." First on the agenda was "a return to the negotiating table to complete the unfinished business of the Comprehensive Peace Agreement." Sudan was put on notice to fulfill "its obligations and demonstrate its commitment to peace within its borders [including Darfur and Southern Kordofan] ... and with its neighbors." As for South Sudan, it had to "address its internal challenges.... [And to succeed in this] South Sudan will have to begin building an effective, democratic and inclusive government that respects human rights and delivers services with transparency and accountability." Both governments were reminded "that they have the power to chart a better future for all Sudanese. As they do, they can be assured that the United States will be a steadfast partner" (Clinton 2011). It should be noted that in his speech at the independence ceremony, President al-Bashir indicated that he had done his part, and "prodded Obama 'to meet his promise and lift the sanctions imposed on Sudan'" (quoted in Fick 2011b).

The final *Washington Post* item in the study period was a news "digest" report on 15 July that the Satellite Sentinel Project had detected fresh evidence of mass graves in South Kordofan, "where Sudan's Arab military has been targeting a black ethnic minority loyal to the military of newly independent South Sudan." In addition to the photographic evidence, "a witness told the project that he saw 100 bodies or more put into one of the pits" (AP 2011f).

Conclusion

Similarities in Canadian and American Reporting

- A similar range of problems, generally associated with underdevelopment, was identified as confronting the south: poverty, internal conflict leading to chronic instability, weak state capacity, corruption, illiteracy, and tribal dominance by the Dinka.
- Likewise a similar set of problems was seen as facing the south in dealing with the north: questions related to oil revenues, control of Abyei, and the future of the Nuba peoples in southern Kordofan.
- Some attention in the reporting of both countries focused on the negative impact the southern secession would have on the north.

Differences in Canadian and American Reporting

- Canadian reporting brought up the question of the amount of power that the constitution placed in the hands of the southern president; the David Warren article also explored colonial history and assessed its impact on unfolding events.
- Canadian reporting focused to a greater extent on African diplomatic efforts, especially those by Thabo Mbeki and the AU to resolve the pre-independence crises in Abyei, South Kordofan, and Blue Nile.

- US reporting contained far more detail with respect to both motivations behind northern military actions and their likely consequences. US reporting also contained a greater amount of advocacy—as seen in language and argumentation—for a greater international (especially a US) role in sorting out Sudan's problems. In this context, US reporting used the important emotional trigger words *ethnic cleansing* and *genocide* in advocating greater international involvement.
- Although neither of the specific terms "CNN effect" or "celebrity diplomacy" were used, US reporting called attention to the critical role of established celebrities and non-governmental interest groups (especially evangelical Christians) in fashioning US foreign policy toward Sudan.
- While President Obama's role in getting Mr. Bashir to agree to a peaceful separation through incentives was generally praised, the alternative position, that "sticks" as well as "carrots" would be required to deal with the north, was presented by Clooney and Prendergast, Reeves, and Johnson.

The "Alerting" Function

That there was an absence on the part of *The Globe and Mail* in covering the final chapter of South Sudan's path to independence in its print edition, and that just over half of the *Ottawa Citizen*'s seventeen items were "news briefs," lead to questions regarding the likely awareness on the part of the Canadian attentive public of late-breaking critical events. Our assessment is that in terms of an "alert," Canadian coverage was less than adequate. As for the US papers, there appeared to be coverage sufficient both to draw elite readers' attention to what was happening in the area and to give them an adequate grasp of the serious issues that remained unresolved between north and south, as well as those internal to the south. Importantly, the new outbreak of conflict in the Nuba Mountains was framed as a genocide in the making.

The "Framing" Function

On the Canadian side, since coverage was marginal at best, it is difficult to address the likely impact of framing. However, both newspapers did run editorials marking South Sudan's independence and, in light of the multiple problems reviewed, both adopted what we term a *cautious* tone. In addition, the *Ottawa Citizen* called for continued Canadian governmental assistance to the new country, but neither paper addressed how the international community should respond to renewed violence, should it persist.

On the whole, independence framing in the two US papers appeared more *pessimistic* than *cautious*. First, the conflicts (both cross-border and internal) were explored in greater depth, thus giving readers a better appreciation for the multiple pitfalls lying in the new country's path to success. This was combined with an analysis of the ingredients involved in the achievement of independence: persistent and skilful diplomacy on the part of the Obama administration based on a series of rewards offered to Mr. Bashir for "good behaviour." However, both US newspapers featured op-ed columns that argued that such rewards were unlikely to be adequate in dealing with Mr. Bashir, thus offering important counter-framing of the situation. And, as his comments at the independence ceremony indicated, the Sudanese president was looking for payment on the basis of having carried out his part of the bargain.

However, as Hillary Clinton pointed out, while peaceful independence had come to the south, Mr. Bashir's rewards were dependent on his "good behaviour" not only with regard to the south's peaceful transition to independence, but also on the resolution of the Darfur conflict as well as disputes over Abyei and the recent outbreak of fighting in the Nuba Mountains. And on these conflicts, US reporting confirmed the north's determination to keep control of these regions, thus almost ensuring a continuing source of humanitarian suffering as well as motivation for renewed north–south fighting. In that *ethnic cleansing* on the part of the north was charged in Abyei and that *genocide* was alleged to be occurring against the Nuba peoples in Southern Kordofan, the international community was put on notice that these conflicts had implications for the doctrine of "responsibility to protect," and thus were likely to entail demands for some future international action that went beyond offers of rewards for good behaviour. There was, however, no elaboration on the nature and extent of such action.

CHAPTER 8
ASSESSING THE EFFECTIVENESS OF THE *RESPONSIBILITY TO PREVENT*
The Impact of Press Framing on Policy Choices

The Role of Preventive Diplomacy

President Obama ordered a review of policy toward Sudan shortly after taking office in 2009. This involved reconsideration not only of the north-south situation, but also the lingering issue of Darfur. Although the latter was no longer the subject of the massive public outrage evident a few years earlier, many still felt strongly that holding President al-Bashir accountable for genocide there should continue to be the primary thrust of American and world policy.

Not everyone, however, thought that increased toughness toward Khartoum was helpful in light of other pressing policy objectives. Retired General Scott Gration, the newly appointed Special Envoy to Sudan, for instance, thought that the immediate primary concern had to be bringing the CPA to a successful conclusion. Moreover, he was convinced "that al-Bashir, and al-Bashir alone, could ensure the referendum went forward. This meant that the United States had no option but to work with his regime" (Hamilton 2011a, 182).[1]

> When the Sudan policy review was released on October 19, 2009, it reflected the genuine disagreement between those aligned with Susan Rice, who believed that Khartoum's behavior was best influenced by sticks, and those aligned with Gration, who believed that carrots were the only way forward, and of a president who, in the face of these disputes, chose not to force the review to ... [an early] conclusion.... [In the end] the review stated that Darfur, the CPA, and counterterrorism cooperation were three co-equal priorities on Sudan and that a mix of pressures and incentives would be used to get progress on all three objectives. (Hamilton 2011a, 185)

However, as Hamilton concludes, "the United States had already reached close to the maximum of unilateral pressure it could apply, *short of military action*.… The consequence was that Gration's all-carrot approach became the policy enacted by default … [and] the U.S. government's Sudan policy under Obama in 2010 reverted to what the Bush administration's policy had been in 2003: Darfur was again sidelined in the service of the north–south problem" (2011a, 189; italics added). The question that remains is how did major media outlets, like the four newspapers included in this study, influence or contribute to the strategy of positive diplomacy that had been adopted?

In his discussion of the role of media in peace negotiations, Gadi Wolfsfeld has argued that "when violence breaks out … leaders come under great pressure to 'do something' and the press is an important agent for creating this sense of urgency" (2004, 13). It is reasonable to ask if the same might not be the case where violence is thought to be highly likely. In the sixteen months prior to South Sudan's independence in July 2011, did the press create or increase a sense of urgency, and did it advocate or oppose particular policies or actions?

The Role of Media

Table 8.1 reviews the agenda-setting performance of the four newspapers studied with respect to three key events related to the independence of South Sudan. There is significant evidence that international news (especially dealing with events occurring in Africa) receives relatively low attention in the North American press (see Chapter 4). In spite of this (with the exception of the dearth of material in the print edition of *The Globe and Mail* on the immediate pre-independence conflicts in Abyei and Nuba Mountains—see Chapter 7, note 1), the principal events leading up to the declaration of independence by South Sudan were given reasonably adequate, though by no means extraordinary, coverage.[2]

Table 8.1 South Sudan Coverage, by Newspaper

	Election	Referendum	Independence	Total
New York Times	N=15	N=25	N=37	N=77
Washington Post	N=10	N=14	N=26	N=50
Globe and Mail	N=6	N=17	N=3	N=26
Ottawa Citizen	N=9	N=21	N=17	N=47
Total	N=40	N=77	N=83	N=200

That 200 items of content appeared with respect to the high points in the independence process in just under a year and a half should have been sufficient to engage the notice of that portion of the public that is attentive to international affairs and enable it to lead public discussion on a subject with which the vast majority was unlikely to be knowledgeable or closely engaged (see Almond 1950; Katz and Lazarsfeld 1955; Auerbach and Bloch-Elkon 2005).

On the latter point it needs to be stressed that the absence of coverage on the part of major television networks suggests that the problems entailed in South Sudan's independence would not have penetrated very deeply into the consciousness of the Canadian or American mass publics. Although all traditional media have suffered losses of audience to the Internet, television remains by far the leading source of news and information for North American publics. For example, in 2009, 31.1 percent of Americans cited television as their primary source of news as opposed to 19.4 percent for both newspapers and radio. In contrast, 14.6 percent reported online sources (Marketing Charts 2009). Statistics Canada suggested that following an initial surge in popularity, use of the Internet stabilized, leaving it a secondary source of information (2003). A study by the Canadian Media Research Consortium confirmed this, reporting that 17.1 percent of respondents cited the Internet as a source of news, while 53.5 percent reported viewing national news programs and 18.9 percent reported reading the newspaper (2004). While the majority of people on both sides of the border get their news from television, those who favour more in-depth coverage, as is likely the case with those Hamilton has referred to as "elite advocacy circles" (2011a, 48), continue to rely on the printed media. It is precisely this group of people who are critical to the type of public mobilization such as occurred with respect to Darfur.[3]

Table 8.2 shows a breakdown of press coverage by type of content, and in this dimension we see conflicting evidence regarding the perceived importance of South Sudan. First, suggesting a lack of high priority, the problems confronting the soon-to-be new country only rarely found their way on to the front pages of newspapers, and, with the exception of *The New York Times*, did not engage the interests of editorial boards much beyond acknowledging the birth of a new country. The near total absence of letters to the editor on the matter seems to confirm that this was also true even for concerned internationalists and Africanists in the public at large. On the positive side, however, more than half (54 percent) of total coverage consisted of substantial, well-researched, inside-page stories written largely by reporters deployed in South Sudan, in contrast to only 25 percent consisting of one paragraph news briefs. This would appear to be an acknowledgement that developments in Sudan were of more than passing concern to editors. Op-ed treatment was relatively robust as well, especially in the two US papers (14 percent of content as compared with 7 percent in the

Table 8.2 South Sudan Coverage, by Type of Content

	New York Times	Washington Post	Globe and Mail	Ottawa Citizen	**Total**
Front Page	4	—	2	—	6
Inside Page	44	25	18	21	108
News Brief	14	14	—	23	51
Editorial	4	2	1	1	8
Op-Ed	9	9	4	1	23
Letter	2	—	1	—	3
Photo	—	—	—	1	1
Total	77	50	26	47	200

Canadian papers). These op-ed articles added depth to the analysis of problems that had been identified in reporting, but, until the eruption of violence in Abyei and the Nuba Mountains in mid-May 2011, offered few alternatives to dominant interpretive frames.

Optimistic vs. Pessimistic Framing of Outcomes

In his analysis of types of media influence on peace processes, Gadi Wolfsfeld has called attention to the importance of "defining the political atmosphere":

> Is the process moving forward or back? Does the overall level of hostility and violence appear to be rising or declining? Is the "other side" keeping its side of the agreements? Are those opposed to the peace process succeeding in their efforts to stop it? How much of the public supports what the government is trying to do? Is this process going to work? The answers to such questions—which are often provided by ongoing news coverage—help determine whether the political atmosphere is conducive to making peace. (2004, 11–12)

As our study of newspaper content reveals, the political atmosphere surrounding South Sudan's uncertain path toward independence was not quite one of pessimism, but at the same time it was a long way from optimism. It can perhaps best be described as *troubled* and *doubtful*. Press accounts of developments identified, and focused on, two major potential problems. First, would the north attempt to sabotage the attainment of southern independence, and, if so, what form would this take? The implication left by most commentators was that some form of deliberate sabotage, or accidental eruption of simmering animosities, was not at all unlikely, and that Abyei was the most probable location for such an event. As it turned out, the areas that proved to be among the most important generators of conflict in the weeks immediately prior to independence—the borderlands to South Sudan, South Kordofan and Blue Nile, where Khartoum launched campaigns of repression—were not identified as likely trouble spots.

The second principal cause for concern was the range of problems that a newly independent south was seen as having to face, quite apart from the matter of its relations with the north. Would these problems—identified as wide-spread poverty, ethnic divisions, corruption, and almost total lack of infrastructure—be severe enough to result in its becoming "a failed state at birth"? Simply asking such a question underlined, though from a different perspective than issues related to its relationship to the north, the uncertainty with which the whole independence scenario was perceived by reporters on the ground. The latter, as the preceding three chapters have pointed out, did not exactly lead their readers to expect violence to occur, but they certainly did not discourage such a conclusion. The framing of each event can thus best be described as "mixed," and this suggests that although the specific "mix" of frames differed to some extent by the event and country in which the events were reported, framing effects would be limited. However, to answer the question posed in Chapter 4, we can say with certainty that press framing was definitely not such as to arouse the international community's "will to intervene" militarily in the event of the outbreak of sustained violence. A small number of contributions came close to that line, but none crossed it. Press framing did, however, reveal a tacit agreement that, regardless of how things developed, the situation was such that international assistance in one form or another would be needed for many years to come.[4]

Dominant Policy Frames vs. Counter Frames

Coverage of the spring 2010 election in both countries highlighted the potential for violence and noted the absence of adequate international attention to readily identifiable problems—problems between the north and south as well as those related to the internal politics of the south.

In terms of policy framing, US National Security Director Admiral Dennis Blair's assessment that in the next five years southern Sudan was "most likely ... [to experience] a new mass killing or genocide" showed governmental awareness of the seriousness of the situation (quoted in Sheridan 2010a). At this point press coverage was generally critical of what was considered to be inadequate attention to easily identifiable flashpoints. President Obama's Special Envoy to Sudan, General Scott Gration, attempted to pre-empt possible criticism of US efforts (or lack thereof) by acknowledging that while not enough had been done, the US (along with the wider global community) understood the severity of the situation and would do what was necessary in time to avert disaster (Landler 2010). The press was skeptical. In two op-ed columns in *The Washington Post*, Michael Gerson focused particular attention on the possibility of violence erupting within the south, even if the north refrained from attempting to destabilize the new government. He suggested that the US had a responsibility to ensure that southern politicians understood the importance of democratic legitimacy (2010a). In a 6 May 2010 letter to *The New York Times* Dan Glickman called for "robust contingency planning" in the event of such adverse developments (2010). This appeared to hint that the US should be prepared to launch some sort of forceful intervention if that were necessary to prevent widespread bloodshed, but he was not specific on the matter.

Glickman was not, however, the first to point in the direction of greater involvement. On 22 April 2010 Nicholas Kristof had offered a *New York Times* op-ed article strongly critical of President Obama's Sudan policy. In the first place, he suggested that White House criticism of what he saw as a seriously flawed election had been far too weak. Second, he urged that the whole of US policy toward Sudan should be reconsidered, that cozying up to the Sudanese president was ill-advised, and that President Obama had better "find his voice" on Sudan, and do so quickly (2010).[5] As mentioned earlier, at this point American commentators generally tended to be more concerned with, and pessimistic about, likely developments in Sudan than was the case with their Canadian counterparts. The only reference to a possible Canadian involvement in the unfolding process in the two Canadian papers studied was Geoffrey York's report that Canada had offered technical assistance in conducting the upcoming referendum (2010b).

As the referendum approached, the pessimism of eight months before had been considerably tempered by what may have been a conscious campaign by the Obama administration to use the press to legitimize its approach to the Sudanese situation. Public reiterations of confidence that everything there was on the highroad to success were made by General Gration and by other government spokespersons such as Samantha Power and Susan Rice. High-ranking politicians like Senator John Kerry and celebrities like George Clooney visited South Sudan to deliver the same message. President Obama of course added his own views of what would be needed on the part of both north and south to achieve a positive outcome—"compromise" on the part of all Sudanese leaders (Obama 2011).

With the exception of Michael Abramowitz's pessimistic feature article (2011), this generally bright outlook was not one that was challenged in the press. While there were many concerns, little overt dissent appeared in print, and even less alternative policy advocacy. US reporting, especially that in *The Washington Post*, now saw Obama's so-called "road map" to a peaceful transfer of sovereignty to be working, and this became the dominant frame for policy evaluation (Gettleman 2011a; *New York Times* 2011a; Mutiga 2011; Kron 2011b).

This interpretation extended to some extent into Canadian reporting as well (York 2011d; Kirby 2011), though its tone was usually significantly more guarded. An op-ed article by Roméo Dallaire and Glen Pearson and a story by Jennifer Pagliaro focused chiefly on Canada's role in the region, and while Canada's generous aid program was acknowledged, both stories called for greater involvement. Dallaire and Pearson specifically called on Canada to establish a partnership with the United States to provide assistance to the south (2010), a suggestion to which there was no follow-up. Pagliaro focused on the problems returnees to the south from the north and elsewhere would pose for a new and fragile government. She cited Glen Pearson (who was serving as a referendum observer), to the effect that Canada had no plans in place to assist with this influx of people who needed land, housing, and jobs (2011). Geoffrey York weighed in with the suggestion that the Canadian assistance already provided had not been entirely satisfactory. Referring to unfortunate clashes between civilians and police in Juba on Christmas Day, he called Canadian training of police in the south inadequate at best, and the police program in general "deeply flawed and over-ambitious" (2011i).

All four newspapers emphasized that the dependence of both north and south on the oil industry gave them strong incentives to avoid violence that might interrupt oil flows and the all-important revenues derived there from. Problems internal to the south, noted above, also continued to be identified in both countries' reporting, but despite implicit and explicit warnings that much assistance would be needed to overcome these obstacles, there were few (if any) specific recommendations of how this might be accomplished.

Until the military operations launched by Khartoum in Abyei and the Nuba Mountains in May 2011, there was virtually no discussion in the press regarding the role the international community might (or should) play if the effort *to prevent* was superseded by the need *to react*. But as a consequence of those military attacks, language implying a need for the *responsibility to react* began to be used explicitly for the first time (Clooney and Prendergast 2011). It was charged that *ethnic cleansing* was being carried out in Abyei and that *war crimes* were being committed in the Nuba Mountains. These claims, along with the suggestion that the latter might easily escalate into a new *genocide*, gave the situation in Sudan a sense of immediacy and urgency it had lacked up to this point. Missing, however, was any call for a specific kind of response, least of all a military one.⁶ Thus, by implication, the appropriate response of the international community for keeping independence on track was an intensification of diplomatic pressures on the involved parties.

Pervasive as that attitude appears to have been, US reporting now exhibited a significant degree of elite counter-framing for the first time since Kristof's April 2010 article. George Clooney and John Prendergast maintained, for instance, that "incentives alone" were not enough to get the job done, and that these therefore needed to be supplemented by a range of coercive measures (2011). In a somewhat similar vein, Douglas Johnson argued that, rather than engaging in renegotiations with the north, President al-Bashir had to be held to agreements he had already signed (2011). Eric Reeves came very close to calling for a military response, though without actually doing so. Arguing that "history must not be allowed to repeat itself," and citing past failures of "empty demands and threats" to reign in the duplicitous Sudanese president, he called upon the international community to get serious in the form of a "vigorous international response" to avert "a new genocide," leaving unspecified exactly what a vigorous response might entail (2011).

Such arguments, and the mere use of language such as *ethnic cleansing*, *war crimes*, and most importantly *genocide*, seriously dampened optimism in American reporting, and suggested the process that was to complete the 2005 CPA was in grave jeopardy. But when, with the help of AU mediation, an agreement was reached to allow some 4,000 Ethiopian peacekeepers to be deployed to Abyei, confidence in the efficacy of positive diplomacy was restored once more. Faith in the road map to peace was further confirmed when, perhaps miraculously, independence was achieved in July without further violent episodes. At any rate there were no further calls for a change in policy, and following independence, Secretary of State Clinton offered a cautiously optimistic appraisal of what lay ahead (Clinton 2011).

In light of the absence of reporting by *The Globe and Mail*, especially on the outbreaks of violence in May 2011, it is frankly difficult to compare Canadian and American reporting on the final key event studied.⁷ *The Globe and Mail*'s editorial marking the independence of South Sudan did not mention any Canadian involvement, while the *Ottawa Citizen*'s editorial reiterated, somewhat lamely, that Canada would need to continue to play a supporting role in the country, especially in the area of agriculture. This might be said to have typified Canada's largely detached attitude to the matter. Canada was present at the creation of peacekeeping, and had long been front and centre in the promotion of human security as well as instrumental in creating the International Commission that brought forth the concept of Responsibility to Protect; however, there is nothing in the reporting of the Canadian papers to suggest that Canada (or the world) had any unusual responsibility with respect to the Sudanese situation, or should pursue any special preventive measures. It was much as if, from a Canadian perspective, what was developing, or might develop, in Sudan was a kind of "business as usual" about which it was unnecessary to get very excited—after all, the Americans seemed to be dealing with it.

Policy Advocacy

What was in the spring of 2010 clearly "policy uncertainty" on the part of the Obama administration provided an opportunity for what Piers Robinson has termed "policy-media interaction" (2000; 2002). Another such opportunity appeared when violence broke out in Abyei, Blue Nile, and South Kordofan in the months just prior to independence, with the latter two leading to a challenge to the US policy line. It is our conclusion, however, that while American, and to a slightly lesser extent Canadian, print media were attentive to, and apprehensive about, developments in Sudan, there is little indication that either attempted to spur their governments to greater action, or indeed to any form of involvement other than what was already being undertaken. Nor does it appear that the general public in either country became significantly engaged in the issue itself, or in the policies pursued by their governments in relation to it. This is demonstrated by the next-to-total absence of any advocacy-type letter writing by concerned citizens; and it is in startling contrast, for instance, to what occurred with respect to Darfur (Sidahmed, Soderlund, and Briggs 2010, 96–97).[8] It is perhaps surprising that hard-line justice advocates did not become more incensed over the perceived leniency shown to President al-Bashir. We suspect this may have been because by 2010–2011 most had become resigned to the fact that there was no easy way to compel him to answer for his crimes. In any case, as it turned out, the rewards promised the Sudanese president were apparently not delivered. According to Andrew Natsios, "because of the atrocities committed by Khartoum in Darfur and later in 2011 in the Nuba Mountains ... U.S. policy makers found it politically untenable to begin any improvement of relations with Khartoum or the rescinding of any sanctions" (2012, 169).

That the independence of South Sudan was achieved relatively peacefully despite fissures in southern leadership, the lack of agreement on the distribution of oil revenues, the unresolved status of Abyei, and late-breaking explosive conflicts along the border was undeniably a significant accomplishment.[9] The American president's controversial decision to negotiate with Mr. al-Bashir, offering him release from the "states sponsoring terrorism list" and other incentives such as the granting of debt relief, apparently persuaded him not only to recognize South Sudan's proclamation of independence on 9 July 2011, but actually to attend the ceremony marking the event. It could accordingly be argued that sustained diplomatic efforts, along with, importantly, the presence of large numbers of peacekeeping troops in the south as well as those deployed quickly to stabilize the situation in Abyei in May 2011, had prevented the almost certain large-scale violence many had expected a year earlier.

This could be seen as at least a temporary triumph for the prevention component of R2P. But above all else, it must be recognized that major efforts at prevention were made by many in the international community. In that sense the largely peaceful birth of South Sudan clearly demonstrates that the spirit of R2P's first principle was alive and well in national capitals and at the UN. It seems likely, moreover, that in this particular case little "push" from media or mass publics was needed. The urgency was already recognized by government bodies practically everywhere; the threat and need in South Sudan's case were so obvious as to be unavoidable. That is not likely to be true often, but that does not detract from the fact that the necessity to act to avoid the development of catastrophes appears to have been internalized in principle by governments. The circumstances surrounding the independence of South Sudan should therefore be encouraging for proponents of R2P, especially in light of the controversy over the application of its "military reaction" component in Libya and the failure to apply it in Syria.

POSTSCRIPT
DEVELOPMENTS SINCE INDEPENDENCE

How does one know when a conflict-that-might-have-been has been *prevented* as distinct from merely *postponed*? Any situation that threatens to develop into a serious conflict or humanitarian disaster is almost certain to be characterized by deep-seated animosities and/or a history of violent clashes that will not quickly be forgiven or forgotten. As a result, efforts to prevent such developments are, at best, more likely to suspend the violent pursuit of objectives in the short to medium term than to render them unthinkable. Even the temporary suspension or postponement of violent conflict is not to be derided of course, but the question remains: how long is it necessary for this period of suspension to last in order for prevention efforts to be termed "successful"?

It also needs to be recognized that trying to prevent conflict is rather like punching a pillow: producing an indentation on one side will result in a protrusion on the other. Similarly, pacifying one conflict situation has an unhappy tendency to cause, or to unleash, another in the immediate vicinity. If the latter happens, as occurred in eastern Congo following the end of the Rwandan genocide, has prevention occurred, or merely a kind of conversion? Or is the proper conclusion that prevention has failed entirely?

One has to ask how these considerations apply to the case of South Sudan. From the vantage point of 2014, it appears that international efforts to permit the more or less peaceful birth of the world's newest state have indeed been successful—if not miraculous. But clearly problems remain not only between the two Sudans but also within each of them, which make any predictions of long-term peace and security problematic at best. Already there have been a number of violent outbursts that have caused international concern and created doubts about the stability of the new state in particular.

The North–South Dimension

Needless to say, relations between the two Sudans continue to be strained and sometimes violent, though at this point it is difficult to say whether Khartoum or Juba is more to blame. Some of the difficulties centre, predictably, on issues relating to the sharing of oil revenues, but others relate to the ongoing operations of dissident groups on both sides of a border that is still unclear in a number of places. In the fall of 2011, for example, relations deteriorated over the alleged "stealing" of oil shipped from south to north. In response, South Sudan shut down its oil production of approximately 350,000 barrels per day in January 2012 (*The Guardian* 2012). Then, in mid-April, with oil production still shut down, southern military forces seized and occupied the Heglig oil field in the disputed border area northeast of Abyei. This resulted in a northern counter-attack. Whether southern forces withdrew voluntarily in the face of international criticism or were driven out is unclear, but in any case significant damage was done to oil infrastructure, for which the north demanded compensation (Laessing and Dziadosa 2012). The conflict escalated in a serious way toward the end of April when Sudanese warplanes bombed a market in Bentiu, capital of South Sudan's Unity State, some 80 kilometres from the border. US State Department spokesperson Victoria Nuland "called on Sudan to immediately halt the 'aerial bombardment in South Sudan' and on both sides to 'end all military support for rebel groups within the other country.'" UN Secretary-General Ban Ki-moon "condemned the bombings and called on the government in Khartoum 'to cease all hostilities immediately' … [and] resume dialogue" (both quoted in Bariyo 2012; see also Reuters 2012). The various oil issues appear to have been successfully resolved in a series of halting negotiations which began in August 2012 (see below, and also Boswell 2012; Quinn 2012).

In addition to squabbles over oil, the north–south relationship continues to be complicated by the fact that Sudan has been dealing with insurgencies within its own territory, insurgencies it is convinced can be sustained only by support from South Sudan. It is of course possible that there is some truth to this charge. Given the uneasy relationship between the two states, both are undoubtedly tempted to provide assistance to "rebel" groups within each other's territory, or, just as serious, accuse each other of doing so even when such groups are beyond the control of either government. A case in point is the continuing tension between the Misseriya and Ngok Dinka groups in Abyei. It is not at all clear that it is within the power of President al-Bashir to control the militias fielded by the Misseriya in particular, but President Kiir is unlikely to believe that he cannot, or be willing to admit it even if he does.

And of course the same is true in reverse with respect to South Sudan's alleged support for the SPLM-North in the Nuba Mountains. As was pointed out earlier, the Sudanese government launched a campaign of armed repression in the Nuba Mountains in mid-May 2011—in much the same way as it had long been doing in Darfur. Massive bombing raids "wreak[ed] havoc on the lives of the residents of the Nuba Mountains" and caused a reported 200,000 refugees to flee to camps in South Sudan (McConnell 2013). These events have not been widely reported in mainstream Western media, although they were observed and publicized by relief and humanitarian agencies to the extent allowed by the Sudanese government. The reality is that international access to all such trouble spots has been largely forbidden. But the Nuba Mountain situation engaged the attention of Darfur critics who in turn raised fears of a new genocide. In the fall of 2012, for instance, Gerald Caplan and Amanda Grzyb reported that "as in Darfur, the Sudanese government is targeting civilians in areas held by rebels from the ... [SPLM-North]." They also noted Doctors Without Borders had reported that the rate of mortality among children under five in refugee camps across the border in South Sudan was "more than twice the emergency threshold" (Caplan and Grzyb 2012). In late January 2013, Canadian activist Lorna Dueck inquired whether the Canadian government could not do something to help the Nubian people (2013) but there was little other comment. United Nations and African Union representatives have repeatedly attempted to negotiate a settlement to the crisis, or at a minimum to induce Khartoum to adopt less draconian methods of dealing with the rebels, but none of these has been successful. The extent to which Juba has actually encouraged or supported the SPLM-North is unclear, but it is reasonable to suppose that it would be difficult for the South's government to be entirely neutral on the issue, and impossible for Khartoum to believe that it is. The unfortunate reality is that both governments are likely to put the worst possible construction on the words and actions/inactions of the other for a long time to come.

Nonetheless, extensive open warfare between north and south has so far not developed, and is probably no more likely today than in, say, 2011 or 2012. It may be that the best one can hope for in the near future is the continuation of a festering hostility between the two countries, one that only occasionally erupts into explosions of violence. Clearly, however, the international community will have a significant and continuing role in trying to prevent anything more serious from developing.

Problems within the North

Khartoum is generally, and rightly, regarded as the cause of most of the problems that beset the northeast region of Africa, as well as the perpetrator of the most egregious violations of humanitarian standards of behaviour. But it should not be overlooked that it *does* have legitimate problems of its own, some of which are related to the loss of the South.

The Darfur conflict remains unresolved, and could ultimately result in further loss of Sudanese territory. The Nuba Mountain situation in South Kordofan and Blue Nile States presents the same, and perhaps a more imminent, threat of the same kind. It is not clear what the objectives of the SPLM-North are, but as an offshoot of the SPLM responsible for the independence of the South, it may be assumed at a minimum to seek greater autonomy from Khartoum and/or the replacement of the government in power there. It is not unreasonable to suggest that the SPLM-North is probably the principal security concern for the al-Bashir government at the moment. But it is not the only cause for alarm. There has also been unrest in the eastern states bordering the Red Sea, and in September 2013 there were riots in several cities, including Khartoum, as a result of cuts in food subsidies mandated by the International Monetary Fund due to the country's dire economic position. Inflation is said to be more than 50 percent annually, and more than 80 percent for commodities like meat. As a result professional people like doctors have been leaving the country in large numbers: 6,000 doctors left for Saudi Arabia alone between 2009 and 2013 (see Reeves 2013). The 2013 riots were put down with al-Bashir's customary brutality, with an admitted loss of 84 lives. Amnesty International, however, put the figure at more than 200 (*Sudan Tribune* 2013).

Clearly the al-Bashir government must fear the further disintegration of the country, as well as personal loss of power. In the view of Andrew Natsios, in fact, Khartoum "fears the breakup of the Sudanese state more than nearly anything else: more than ICC war crimes, more than UN resolutions condemning their atrocities, more than U.S. economic sanctions" (2012, 203). Equally clearly, the regime is prepared to go to extreme lengths to prevent such an eventuality, despite the fact that extreme tactics encourage, if not necessitate, precisely what they are intended to prevent.

There is also the question of the extent to which the issues driving the "Arab Spring" will affect Sudan. A number of reporters have mentioned that events in Egypt and elsewhere had the Sudanese president looking over his shoulder. Natsios, for instance, claims that, contrary to the common perception of al-Bashir as a "strongman" with an iron grip on power, his government is "now the weakest of any state since Sudan's independence in terms of its ability to exercise authority over the remaining regions of the country. Under the [National Congress Party], Sudan is becoming a failed state" (2012, 197). Perhaps that is overstatement, but it should nevertheless not be forgotten that weakness makes compromise difficult and encourages extremism, not to mention the search for convenient scapegoats. Consequently, Sudan's growing internal problems, and the current government's perception of these, create difficulties for the prevention of further hostilities in the region.

Problems within South Sudan

On the basis of evidence to date (May 2014) it might be concluded that the greatest danger of the renewal of large-scale or prolonged violent conflict lies within South Sudan itself. In addition to widespread poverty, illiteracy, lack of medical facilities, and a nearly total absence of physical infrastructure, there is an uneasy, often vengeful, relationship among many of the indigenous groups that inhabit the area. In 2012 LeRiche and Arnold in fact described South Sudan politics as "interwoven with low intensity warfare, inter-communal violence … and the ability to threaten violence" (2012, 158). According to a UN report, between December 2011 and February 2012 "at least 888 people lost their lives in violence involving the Nuer and Murle tribes" in Jonglei State. The report also noted that "South Sudan … failed to stop or investigate attacks, contributing to the fatal cycle" (Alpert 2012).

Without firm and effective control from the central government, including the creation of local mechanisms for conflict resolution, (neither of which seems likely to materialize soon), there is significant danger that violence will become a "normal" way of life among rival groups in South Sudan, as it has in the eastern provinces of the Democratic Republic of the Congo (DRC). That is a frightening thought because for well over a decade the international community, despite the input of significant military and other resources, has been unable to bring sporadic but persistent violence under control in the DRC (Soderlund et al. 2012, 147–154). The 2013–2014 period has given further cause for concern along these lines in South Sudan.

The central fact that must be recognized is that the fledgling government of South Sudan can only be described as fragile. Its leadership has been splintered from the beginning, but has become more so since July 2013 when President Kiir dismissed his entire cabinet, as well as Vice-President and long-time political rival Riek Machar. Machar had challenged Kiir's leadership with respect to the ongoing problem of Abyei in particular, and that may have been the motive for his dismissal. At least one source has suggested that his ouster was pleasing to Khartoum because it was thought to remove one obstacle to settling the Abyei issue (Al-monitor 2013), but Kiir's unexpected action did not please Washington or the international community in general. It was seen as a retreat from democratic principles, although Kiir had in fact acted within the wide powers granted him by the South Sudan constitution (see Chapter 7). Secretary of State John Kerry told President Kiir that "too much sacrifice has been made to see that effort [to achieve independence] … go backwards. The world is watching to see if South Sudan pursues the path of peace and prosperity, or the tragic path of violence and conflict that characterizes much of its past" (quoted in

Landler 2013). A new cabinet, smaller by one-third and minus Mr. Machar, was appointed within a week.

Unfortunately that was merely the beginning of a series of tragic events. On 15 December 2013, armed conflict broke out in the capital city between supporters of President Kiir and Mr. Machar within the ranks of the Presidential Guard. It quickly spread to other centres across eastern South Sudan. On 16 December, President Kiir accused Machar of plotting a coup, and ordered the arrest of eleven of his alleged co-conspirators. As Jehanne Henry reported for Human Rights Watch, "the violence took on dangerous ethnic overtones, with Dinka forces in the government openly targeting ethnic Nuer in neighbourhood round-ups and house-to-house searches, killing many in cold blood." She added that in the six weeks since it began, the conflict had "sowed distrust between Dinka and Nuer, polarized South Sudan's political elite … and wrought havoc on the communities of greater Upper Nile. Thousands of civilians have died, over 400,000 have fled their homes, and around 70,000 are now living in squalid conditions in UN compounds across the country" (Henry 2014). It was, in effect, open ethnic-group warfare, with the principal combatants the Dinka (Kiir's ethnic group) on one side and the Nuer (Machar's ethnic group) on the other.

Pressure from neighbouring east African states resulted in the signing of a ceasefire on 23 January 2014, but that had little effect as each side accused the other of failing to honour the agreement and demanded conditions for the resumption of the peace talks being urged upon them (*The Guardian* 2014). Both the UN and other humanitarian agencies have documented human rights abuses by both sides. According to Human Rights Watch, "each side, when in effective control of [a] town, attacked civilians, destroyed and looted civilian property—including food and humanitarian aid—and targeted people based on their ethnicity" (2014b). As of this writing there is little indication of improvement in the situation, despite threats by both the US and the European Union to impose sanctions on both sides (AFP 2014). Indeed, it appears that more and more civilians are arming themselves in a search for some kind of security—while others seize the opportunities presented by insecurity to settle old scores with neighbours or to steal livestock from them (Hatcher 2014). For observers of the DRC, this is an all-too-familiar picture.

The political-ethnic divide is arguably the major problem facing the novice government in Juba, but there are other difficulties as well. For instance, like most African (and many other) countries, one of these is corruption, which appears to afflict the government at high levels. In June 2012, President Kiir took the unusual step of announcing publically that "about $4 billion has been stolen by corrupt officials" since the 2005 CPA dictated a fifty-fifty split of oil revenues between the two Sudans. He did not name those who were guilty, but he asked them "to give the money back, please." This was likely to prove difficult since, as Geoffrey York reported, "most of the stolen cash was deposited into foreign banks, or used to purchase foreign property" (York 2012). Still, President Kiir has the distinction of being one of the very few political leaders on record to admit to corruption within his government. Whether he has the will or the power to do anything to prevent its continuation is another matter.

Final Thoughts

New, inexperienced governments do not become efficient, smooth-running machines overnight, especially in circumstances as difficult as those confronting South Sudan. Some allowances must accordingly be given to war-hardened political neophytes working in what all describe as vexing conditions. But it remains to be seen how far and for how long the international community will be prepared to tolerate both ineptitude and abuse of power before its patience is exhausted—and needless to say, South Sudan will need both economic and political assistance from the developed world for a long time to come, despite its considerable oil revenues.

"Donor fatigue" is a well-documented phenomenon. It is most likely to manifest itself when situations demand the commitment of resources over a long period of time, when assistance is seen to be swallowed up by corruption and/or inefficiency, or when some notable milestone is reached (or declared to have been reached), which provides an excuse to disengage and move on to pressing problems elsewhere. Western states have already on several occasions shown that their patience with the Kiir regime is not inexhaustible. For instance, according to information supplied to McLatchy News reporter Alan Boswell by unnamed White House sources, "the [US–South Sudan] relationship has soured ... all the way up to Obama" as a result of US officials' belief that "South Sudan's president personally lied to President Obama on several occasions," specifically in denying South Sudan's support for the SPLM-North, and in promising not to "send forces north to seize Heglig, a Sudanese-controlled oil field," which he in fact did eight days later (Boswell 2012). In a somewhat similar vein, Malcolm Bruce, the Chair of the British House of Commons International Development Committee, warned with respect to the South's stoppage of oil production: "The key priority now for the UK's aid programme in the country is to avert a humanitarian crisis.... However, the UK and other aid donors cannot be expected to bankroll the country while it struggles on without oil revenues. The Foreign Office must continue to press Khartoum and Juba to seek agreement on the export of oil through Sudan's pipelines" (quoted in Tran 2012). It should be noted, however, that Secretary of State Hillary Clinton visited Juba on 3 August 2012 (the first high-ranking US official to do so) and declared, "It is urgent that both sides, north and south, follow through and reach timely agreements on all outstanding issues, including oil revenue sharing, security, citizenship and border demarcation" (quoted in Revise and NcNeish 2012). Thus, however piqued Washington may have been with Juba, it had at this point not given up on trying to persuade it to better behaviour. Nor were its efforts in this case unproductive. Though Clinton's visit lasted only three hours, *The New York Times* reported only a day later that the two sides had reached agreement on the division of oil revenues. It was hoped that this might foretell "cooperation on other fronts and lead to a workable peace," though it was added that "the two sides have a history of making deals and never fully carrying them out, and many thorny issues—especially over disputed territory—remain unresolved" (Gettleman 2012).

Beginning in January 2013, efforts were made toward the resolution of some of those outstanding problems. Al-Bashir and Kiir met personally in Addis Ababa in an attempt to move the process forward, and it was announced on 6 January that, with the help of African Union negotiator Thabo Mbeki, an agreement had been reached "to demarcate those parts of the border which have been agreed" (quoted in AP 2013). CNN reported as well that "temporary administrative and security arrangements" had been agreed to for Abyei, and that the two presidents would "reconvene another summit to discuss the final disposition of the disputed region" (CNN 2013). Further reports toward the end of January, however, indicated that the two leaders had failed to reach additional agreements (AllAfrica 2013). It is of course unclear whether the leaders were, or are, sincere in wishing to settle the issues between them, or are merely playing to the international gallery. While comfort can be drawn from the fact that they are talking to each other at all, it must not be forgotten that since both are in weak positions, compromise is difficult.

In mid-April 2014, the situation became even more alarming when forces loyal to Mr. Machar took control of Bentiu, the capital of Unity State, and, spurred on by radio hate messages similar to those employed by the perpetrators of the Rwandan genocide in 1994, engaged in a flurry of rape and killing, including the massacre of those who had taken refuge in hospitals, mosques, and churches. Toby Lanzer, a UN official on the scene, claimed that the use of "hate speech via a public radio station to incite violence is a game-changer" (quoted in Smith 2014a). There seems to be little doubt that the conflict is essentially ethnic in character. As *Guardian* correspondent David Smith wrote, "what began as a political struggle in South Sudan quickly assumed an ethnic dimension, pitting President Salva Kiir's Dinka tribe against militia forces from the former vice-president Riek Machar's Nuer people. Peace talks have failed to stem the flow of atrocities on both sides" (2014a). His assessment was seconded by Amnesty International crisis advisor Donatella Rovera, who asserted that "whatever the reasons this conflict broke out on 15 December—and there were obviously political grievances—from the first day it has taken on markedly an ethnic dimension. We saw this clearly with the attack by opposition forces on Bentiu" (quoted in Smith 2014a).

US Ambassador to the UN Samantha Power was obviously concerned, commenting that "the world's newest state is clearly on a precipice." She cautioned the country's leaders that "failure to take bold action now very well could push South Sudan into a cycle of retaliatory killing, a deepening civil war, and an even more devastating humanitarian catastrophe" (quoted in AP 2014). US Secretary of State John Kerry also raised fears of a possible genocide. Speaking in Ethiopia, he said that "those who are responsible for targeted killings based on ethnicity or nationality have to be brought to justice, and we are actively considering sanctions against those who commit human rights abuses and obstruct humanitarian assistance" (quoted in Smith 2014b). The US did, in fact, impose travel restrictions and freeze the assets of one military leader on each side on 6 May 2014, but not on their political bosses (Gordon 2014). This may suggest that the latter have uncertain control over their followers, or that the US at least so far is prepared to assume this is the case.

Beyond question, however, the ongoing ethnic-political struggle within the south has troubled and frustrated all those who have worked for peace and security there, even more than long-standing north–south issues which, with the possible exception of the Nuba Mountains problem, are currently less actively violent. Adjoining African states, with the encouragement of Western governments, have tried assiduously to entice the rival South Sudan parties to cease hostilities and abide by ceasefire agreements, though it is also reported that Uganda has been supporting South Sudan's government forces, "including with air power" (Human Rights Watch 2014a), which is scarcely encouraging. There is also the fact that there is a 10,000-strong UN peacekeeping force in the country (UNMISS), composed of contributions from no fewer than 54 states. As in the DRC, such a force may be unable to protect civilians from deliberate attacks by armed vigilante groups, but it can provide refuge and humanitarian assistance for displaced persons, and, by its very existence, it demonstrates the continued determination of the world to promote non-violence and respect for human rights in the fledgling state.

It can only be hoped that that determination endures. To date it seems to have done so, despite, it must be said, grave temptation to do otherwise. On 19 May 2014, the Norwegian government convened an international conference in Oslo to urge increased assistance to South Sudan, and that resulted in the doubling of commitments to $1.2 billion (Lewis 2014). But in the final analysis, South Sudan's leaders must also be persuaded that they must take responsibility for their own salvation, and so far there is little indication that any of them are prepared to put the nation's needs above their personal ones. In recent days two new dangers have arisen. First, a cholera outbreak has taken eighteen lives and there is fear inadequate facilities will not be able to prevent its spread. Second, the clashes between rebels and government forces have meant that people have been forced off their land to the extent that the UN has warned of possible famine if crops cannot be planted and access to grazing land assured (Fouche 2014). One can only conclude that the business of preventing humanitarian disaster is not a simple matter.

NOTES

Notes to Chapter 1

1. For an extensive exposition on the slave trade in Sudan, see Collins 2005, 321–48.
2. Martin Meredith relates that, in 1951, King Farouk, in the year prior to his overthrow, "proclaimed himself 'King of Sudan'" in an effort to persuade Britain to accept Egyptian control over Sudan (2005, 35).
3. In July 2010, the ICC added three counts of genocide (against the Fur, the Masalit, and the Zughawa) to the earlier charges of war crimes filed against the Sudanese president (AP 2010).
4. Scopas Poggo explains that since the days of the British the Equatorial Corps in the Sudanese Army had been considered the south's army (2009, 30–31), and thus the north had an ulterior motive for moving the force. "The reality was that it wanted the soldiers removed from the South in order to permanently prevent the possibility of a Southern armed rebellion that might lead to secession" (41).
5. For a detailed analysis of the interwoven factors relating to the Accord, including international ones, see Johnson 2003, chapter 4; Poggo 2009, chapter 9; LeRiche and Arnold 2012, chapter 4.
6. Colonel John Garang (1945–2005) was perhaps the one person who could have made the CPA's "unity option" attractive to the south (see Fadl 2012). Born in the south to Christian Dinka parents, he went on the study in the US, receiving a B.A. in Economics from Grinell College and a Ph.D. in Agricultural Economics from Iowa State University. As a result of the Addis Ababa Accords, he was integrated into the Sudanese Army, where as an officer he received advanced military training at Fort Benning, Georgia. When the Addis Ababa Accords unravelled in 1983, he led the SPLM/SPLA both politically and militarily for twenty-two years. It was Garang who negotiated the 2005 CPA on behalf of the south. Always an advocate of a unified (but reformed) Sudan, following the signing of the CPA he was named First Vice-President of Sudan, only to die in a helicopter crash a few weeks later. Many believe that any hope for a united Sudan died with him (see Johnson 2003, 61–65, 92–101, 106–10, 112–22; Deng 2010, part 7, chapters 17 and 18; Natsios 2012, 61–69, 163–64, 174–76, 178–80). As phrased by LeRiche and Arnold, "barring a resurrected John Garang, there was little energy in the South for pursuing unity" (2012, 117). In fact, LeRiche and Arnold stressed the point that Garang's vision of the south as a part of a reformed Sudan was not shared by the majority of rank and file members of the SPLA/M (112–13, 117–19).

128   Notes to Chapter 1

7   Just prior to the start of the January 2011 referendum in the south, the Abyei referendum to decide whether the region would opt to join South Sudan or remain a part of Sudan was postponed until the actual status of the south was determined and agreement could be reached regarding voting eligibility. Citing an unnamed foreign observer, LeRiche and Arnold point out the difficulties involved in determining eligibility to vote: "There can't be a referendum because ... if the Misseriya aren't allowed to vote, they will fight. If they are, the [Ngok] Dinka will fight" (2012, 193).

8   In his discussion of the role of the Abyei region in the post-CPA period, Johnson points out the "failure to implement the referendum clause in Addis Ababa Agreement [ending the First Civil War] was a significant factor in the growing political alienation of Ngok [Dinka] in the 1970s and 1980s." Moreover, during the Second Civil War, "the Abyei Area became a testing ground for a new government strategy combining regular army forces with Arab militias to clear the Ngok Dinka population out of the oil fields and their traditional homes. This strategy was later applied to the Nuba Mountains, refined in Western Upper Nile oil fields, and transferred to Darfur" (2007, 7).

Notes to Chapter 2

1   With respect to strategies of conflict mitigation available to the international community, there is in fact considerable overlap between those applicable to conflict prevention and those used in post-conflict rebuilding. In light of Edward Azar's theory of "protracted social conflict" (1990), this should come as no surprise.

   In the case of South Sudan, for example, one can look at post-2005 CPA measures in terms of rebuilding, while in the pre-2011 independence period, these same measures fall into the category of prevention. With the exception of "Disarmament, Demobilization and Reintegration" (DDR) programs, which are obviously appropriate to the post-conflict rebuilding phase, all the long- and short-term strategies reviewed in the following chapter are, depending on timing, applicable to either the prevention or the rebuilding phases of long-term conflict.

2   Martha Finnemore and Kathryn Sikkink (1998) offered the seminal work on the process by which norms are adopted by the international community. And while the process has accelerated over time, we would describe the R2P norms as declaratory of what was seen to be a desired goal. With respect to implementation, Libya at first appeared to be major step forward. However, subsequent events there (as well as in Egypt) appear to have dampened any enthusiasm on the part of the international community to intervene militarily in Syria's chapter of the Arab Spring.

Notes to Chapter 3

1   Walter Soderlund began his graduate work at the University of Michigan in the fall of 1964—just in time to experience the academic reaction to Project Camelot first hand.

2   The data set and reports written by the Task Force (renamed the "Political Instability Task Force" in 2003) are available at http://globalpolicy.gmu.edu/pitf/.

3   In additional methodological critiques of the project, King and Zeng suggest that the addition of another three variables—*military population*, *population density*, and *legislative effectiveness*—significantly improve the forecasting ability of the model. *Military population* serves as an indicator of the number of weapons in the hands of those trained to use them; *population density* is based on the notion that "internal conflict requires people to be near others who might disagree"; while *legislative effectiveness* reflects the belief that "parliamentary institutions make a democracy more likely to endure" (2001,

637–40). The latest work of the Political Instability Task Force is reported in Goldstone et al. (2010).

4 Cato Institute foreign policy researchers Justin Logan and Christopher Preble reached a different conclusion: "The sheer diversity of the countries on the lists makes clear that few policy conclusions could be drawn for a country's designation as a failed state" (2011, 381). In fact they dismiss the validity of the failed state concept: "The obvious conclusion that should be drawn from the efforts to generate lists and rankings of failed states is that the category itself is not particularly useful and hopelessly broad" (384). They go on to argue that because failed states do not pose a threat to *national security*, the costs involved in the difficult process of attempting to "fix" them outweigh possible benefits. The researchers do not address the *human security* implications of violence associated with state failure that prompted the shift of intervention norms toward R2P.

Eric Berman and Katie Sams are similarly unimpressed with early warning research, which they characterize as "oversold." They recommend that "providing funding for peacekeeping missions to manage and resolve ongoing conflicts should take priority over providing funding for elaborate and expensive initiatives to collect and analyze data" (2000, 29).

5 In mid-December 2010, a Tunisian street vendor, Mohamed Bouazizi, burned himself to death following his mistreatment at the hands of public officials. Protests following his death led to the resignation of Tunisia's President Zine el Abidine Ben Ali less than a month later. This, in turn, prompted demonstrations leading to the swift overthrow of President Hosni Mubarak in Egypt and violent protests elsewhere in the Arab world, including Yemen, Libya, and Syria.

6 With respect to strategies of conflict reduction available to the international community, there is considerable overlap between conflict prevention and post-conflict rebuilding. In light of Edward Azar's theory of "protracted social conflict" (1990), this should come as no surprise. For example, in the case of South Sudan, we can look at post-2005 CPA measures in terms of *rebuilding*, while pre-2011 independence measures fall into the category of *prevention*. With the exception of "Disarmament, Demobilization and Reintegration" (DDR) programs, which are obviously appropriate to the post-conflict rebuilding phase, all the long- and short-term strategies examined in this chapter are applicable to either the prevention or rebuilding phases of long-term conflict, depending on timing.

7 The Canadian government appears to have reached the same conclusion with respect to its aid program for Haiti. In early 2013, International Co-operation Minister Julian Fantino froze aid to the island nation, claiming that "aid is not getting the results 'that Canadians have a right to expect'" (quoted in Clark 2013). In late summer 2013, the Department of Foreign Affairs, Trade and Development confirmed a significant reduction of Canadian aid to Haiti (from $205 million in 2012 to approximately $90 million per year thereafter). According to Professor François Audet, Director of the Canadian Research Institute on Humanitarian Crisis and Aid, "deciding to reduce the budget this much, for me it's a call to be out of this long term program" (quoted in Mackrael 2013). Audet also offered the assessment that "rebuilding Haiti will likely take generations."

8 Beer noted that "American sponsored programs generally followed generic plans of ICI-TAP that has been developed for and used in other countries within the US sphere of influence.... In the same vein, UN programs, administered by the French Command, were similarly selected and applied in accordance with the procedures of the 'Gendarmerie' of France" (2001, 43).

9 A decade later, in spite of massive international efforts, there is scant evidence that Haiti has made much forward progress, and indeed there is some pointing to regression. For example, Michel Martelly, who was elected president in 2011, has proposed

"to reconstitute the Haitian military as a kind of national guard or civil defense force *to supplement the weak national police*" (Archibald 2011; italics added).

Such outcomes are not uncommon. Jonathan Glennie cites a report from the European Court of Auditors that only "one third of [European Commission] projects have been, or are likely to be, successful in reaching their objectives" (as quoted in Glennie 2008, 57).

10 The problems faced by the International Security Assistance Force in Afghanistan, working in an environment far more difficult than the UN encountered in Haiti, dominate contemporary headlines and point out that "capacity building" is an uncertain strategy when a "post-conflict environment" exists in name only (see Suhrke 2006).

Matthew LeRiche and Matthew Arnold discuss the unique situation in Sudan during the period following the CPA when the international community was committed to capacity building in both north and south. This "balanced treatment" led to a situation where efforts to build the capacity of the Sudanese Sector contributed to its ability to destabilize the south, a policy which they argue "verges on the scandalous" (2012, 39).

11 Autessere's conception of "local conflict resolution" goes well beyond trust and confidence building. In fact, her major focus is on the need to settle land disputes. However, it is hard to imagine any long-term peaceful resolution of problems occurring in the absence of trust and confidence that the other side will live up to the agreements entered into.

She attributes the resistance to adopting local-level strategies in large part to organizational cultures. In the few organizations that employed micro-level strategies, "top managers recruited experts interested in or knowledgeable about local peacebuilding. At the same time, just as diplomatic missions and international organizations tend to attract people interested in macro-level approaches, these agencies attracted staff members attuned to micro-level action" (Autessere 2010, 211). Contrariwise, "the reform attempts threatened entrenched organizations interests. For diplomats and UN staffers, conceding that local peacebuilding was a priority would have ultimately required undergoing extensive training in bottom-up conflict resolution. Alternatively, they would have had to admit that their expertise was insufficient and that their superiors needed to hire new people who might eventually replace them" (216).

Autesserre also points to the fundamental contradiction that while the United Nations Mission in the Democratic Republic of Congo (MONUC) operated on the premise that "there was no military solution to the conflict … MONUC's main peacebuilding approach at the local level was military, rather than diplomatic, economic, or political" (2010: 201).

12 In addition to UNMEE, SHIRBRIG contributed to four other UN peacekeeping operations: UNOCI – 10 members; UNMIL – 24 members; UNAMIS – 17 members; and UNMIS – 308 members (Koops and Varwick 2008, 17–21).

13 It was noted that the "deployment of a military component within 14 days can only be performed by forces that are ready, assembled, fully equipped and exercised, with transport available on immediate call, with logistic supplies pre-packed and ready for delivery by air" (Cilliers 2008, 4).

14 The recent UN authorized, French-led intervention mission in Mali points to the continuing uncertainty of African funding. In citing the advantages of the transition to a UN-led peacekeeping force, Malian politician Ousmane Diara pointed that "until now, the African forces that have been in Mali have been financed by their countries.… This is a worry for us because it was not clear that the African countries could continue to finance their military mission in Mali" (quoted in Amed 2013).

15 Hamilton noted that while 7,731 troops had been authorized, "AMIS would not reach that number for another year, and even then, an even distribution of troops only equated

to one soldier per 25 square miles. It was the equivalent of having one police officer for all of Manhattan" (2011a, 74).
16 During the 1990s, insurgency-challenged governments in Angola and Sierra Leone retained the services of the South African–based "Executive Outcomes" for support (see LoBaido 1998; McGregor 1999; Shannon 2000).
17 Singer reports that in 1996 both the US National Security Council and the UNDPKO "discussed the idea that, in lieu of U.N. peacekeepers, a private firm be hired to create a secure human corridor" to deal with the Rwandan refugee crisis in eastern Congo. The stumbling block appeared to be "who would actually foot the bill" (2003b, 64). Two years earlier, Executive Options explored the possibilities of intervening in the Rwandan genocide.

Singer cites plans indicating "the company could have had armed troops on the ground within 14 days ... and been fully deployed with over 1,500 of its own soldiers, along with air and fire support ... within six weeks" (2003b, 65).
18 The UN "Intervention Brigade" deployed in eastern Congo in 2013 defeated the major rebel group (M23) in early November. The context, of course, was a much-needed response to nearly two decades of embarrassing failure. Will the Intervention Brigade provide a model for a much needed conflict-stabilization force? One would hope so, but it is simply too early to conclude that such a force would either be available or appropriate for conflict-prevention situations.

Notes to Chapter 4

1 The impact of the Internet on established patterns of media use is still in the process of unfolding. We discovered one such impact in doing the research for Chapter 7. Coverage of South Sudan's independence in *The Globe and Mail*, while available in its online edition, appeared only rarely (3 of 21 items of content) in its print edition (see Chapter 7, note 1). This said, while the Internet appears to be replacing hard-copy newspapers and television as sources of news (especially among young people), it appears that the majority of content most frequently accessed on the Internet is in fact generated by the same major media organizations that publish newspapers and produce television news programs.
2 There is an important difference here between the United States and Canada. Given the disparity in size of populations and economies (plus the percentage of Canadian exports going to the US), events in the US are followed very closely by both Canadian media and mass publics.
3 Beverley Hawk has argued that among the many sources of information available to Western audiences on Africa, none is more important than mass media (1992, 3–5). However, international news in general occupies a low position in news selection priorities, with Africa seeming to be particularly poorly covered (see Stewart 2002, 185; Sutcliffe et al. 2009, 131–46). An additional problem is that the reporting on Africa that does occur tends "to make events ... comprehensible to their viewers by drawing on a tradition that frames that part of the world through a lens of primitivism, backwardness, and irrationality" (Dunn 2003, 5; see also Keim 1999). For how media framing worked to discourage international intervention in the Congo Wars, see Soderlund et al. (2012).
4 In that the level of general political knowledge (at least on the part of the American mass public) is unfortunately low, press attention, in the form of agenda setting related to events in far-off lands, would appear essential for those events to become widely known and understood (see Althaus 2003).

132   Notes to Chapter 4

5   William Gamson and Andre Modigliani identify five textual elements involved in framing: metaphors, exemplars, catchphrases, descriptions, and visual images (1989, 3). With the exception of visuals, we examined the use of these elements in the narrative analysis of reportage on South Sudan's path to independence.
6   The analysis of visual images contained in television news stories was a major component of our study of US media coverage of the Darfur conflict. We of course would have liked to replicate that analysis with respect to the independence of South Sudan, but as mentioned, major television networks chose not to cover the key events in the process, including the actual declaration of independence in July 2011.
7   *Priming* relates to "the ability of news programs to affect the criteria by which political leaders are judged.… [It] is really an extension of agenda-setting and addresses the impact of news coverage on the weight assigned to specific issues" (Iyengar and Simon 1993, 368). While priming does not figure significantly in this research, in the case of the Gulf War, Iyengar and Simon conclude that the pattern of reporting that was episodic (event oriented) and focused heavily on military activities "altered the principal basic of President Bush's popularity from the state of the national economy to foreign policy matters" (377).
8   In studies of television coverage of Dafur and the Congo, NGO spokespersons were the primary sources used in story construction (Sidahmed, Soderlund, and Briggs 2010; Soderlund et al. 2012). In her account of reporting on the Rwandan genocide, Lindsey Hilsum (2007) discusses the impact of the reliance on NGOs as sources of news.
9   In their study of television news and newspaper coverage of the war in Darfur that began in 2003, Abdel Salam Sidahmed and colleagues found virtual consensus on the part of television and print news that the responsibility for the crisis rested with the Sudanese government and *Janjaweed* militias it sponsored (see 2010, chaps. 4 and 5).
10 From her study of citizen mobilization over Darfur, Rebecca Hamilton tells us not to expect too much from advocacy: "As the Darfur movement gained increasing media attention, many commentators fell into the trap of attributing any policy decision—good, bad, or otherwise—to advocates. But advocacy, even at its most influential, is just one of the many drivers of a system as complex as foreign policy formulation" (2011a, xviii).
11 Sherman goes on to offer an additional cautionary note that the importance of media influence "raises issues regarding the responsibility of a democratic citizenry to be critical rather than passive consumers of the media and its manipulation" (1998, 114). We see this as a very sound observation.
12 Study dates for each event will be presented at the beginning of chapters 5, 6, and 7.
13 An Internet ranking of 200 world newspapers in 2013 placed *The New York Times* 1st, *The Washington Post* 5th, and *The Globe and Mail* 31st (the highest rank for any Canadian newspaper). *The Ottawa Citizen* did not appear among the top 200 (4Internatonal Media and Newspapers 2013). While the criteria for these rankings were not disclosed, *The Globe and Mail* has in fact for many years enjoyed a very strong reputation, especially for its coverage of international news. Despite cutbacks that have affected the entire industry, *The Globe* maintains foreign bureaus in the US, Europe, China, South Asia, and, importantly for this study, Africa.
14 For all searches of electronic databases the key word "Sudan" was entered along with the appropriate start and stop dates. In cases where newspaper stories were available from more than one database, both were used. Interestingly, somewhat different results were obtained. "False positives" (those stories only minimally connected to Sudan) were easy to spot; however, some stories that dealt with the events in Sudan under study appeared on one database and not on the other. Thus for *The New York Times*, *The Washington Post*, and *The Globe and Mail* story-counts reflect a combination of relevant items appearing

on two databases. Readers are advised that the actual totals for *The Ottawa Citizen*, where only one database was available, may actually be somewhat higher than those presented. Our advice to researchers is that when they are available, to check all electronic databases to make sure that all relevant information has been included.

Notes to Chapter 5

1 Over the past twenty or so years, mass media have suffered financially and continue to suffer in terms of budget cuts and, as a consequence, a significant number of reporters have been lost (Pew Center 2010; see also Utley 1997). And, as Ginia Bellafante has argued, "shrinking budgets at news outlets across the country means that many atrocities in far corners of the globe receive diminished attention" (2008).

2 Given that Salva Kiir did not run against President al-Bashir nationally, Jeffrey Gettleman speculated that "a secret deal was cut between [the SPLM] ... and the ruling party in which the S.P.L.M. agreed to pave a clear path for Mr. Bashir to win the presidency without a runoff, in exchange for Mr. Bashir's guaranteeing that he would stick to the referendum deal" (Gettleman, 2010a).

Notes to Chapter 6

1 York reported that the government of the south had "studied Quebec's referendum" and that "there won't be any Quebec-style ambiguity over 'sovereignty-association' or shared passports" (York 2011b).

2 York contrasted current celebrity attention to south Sudan to that which was noticeably absent during the drawn out civil wars: "All of this activity is in stark contrast to the worldwide apathy that surrounded Sudan's civil war at its bloodiest moments. It was a conflict that killed civilians on a fantastic scale, yet few people outside Sudan seemed to care" (York 2011c).

3 Readers hardly need to be reminded that a very similar split between "Arab nomads" and "African farmers" was a key factor in the violence in Darfur (see Sidahmed, Soderlund, and Briggs 2010, chap. 2).

4 The difference between 50,000 and 143,000 returnees (reported in stories published two days apart) should alert us to the fragility of numbers reported in fluid situations in the developing world. Note also the million-person discrepancy in total numbers of possible returnees—1.5 million (cited by Jeffrey Fleishman 2011) versus 2.5 million (cited by Jennifer Pagliaro 2011). (For a discussion of the impact of uncertain numbers on interpretations of the death toll in Sudan's earlier conflicts, see Johnson 2003, 143).

5 Gettleman distanced himself from this assessment, commenting that "whether there is any truth to this theory may be immaterial, since many in Khartoum seem to firmly believe it" (2011a).

6 By mid-February the armistice had ended, reigniting a major security concern within the south (see Kron 2011c).

7 See the analysis of Abyei by Douglas Johnson discussed in Chapter 1.

8 In light of media fascination with "celebrity diplomacy," it is somewhat surprising that the "Satellite Sentinel Project," endorsed by Clooney and Project Enough, did not occasion much press interest. However, as might be expected, during our study period, it was the subject of the one in-depth US television news story on the referendum.

Notes to Chapter 7

1. We contacted the editors of *The Globe and Mail* regarding reasons for the unusually light coverage of South Sudan's independence and the period of conflict leading up to it. They checked their electronic files and kindly sent us copies of twenty-one items of content appearing over the time period, beginning with a story on the northern invasion and occupation of Abyei on 21 May 2011. However, when we checked these stories against the print version of the paper available at the University of Windsor's Leddy Library (the Ontario Edition), the only items that actually appeared in print were the three identified in the Factiva and ProQuest data bases. In light of the material sent to us, there is no doubt that online readers of *The Globe and Mail* would have had access to information on South Sudan and its problems comparable to that available in the print versions of the other newspapers. However, in that this material was not present in the print version of the paper, we felt that it would be inappropriate to include it in the analysis beyond calling attention to its availability online.
2. Abyei is the name of both the region and the key town within it.
3. It was noted that the air campaign missed destroying a strategic bridge that "could have crippled the southern army's ability to send reinforcements" (Gettleman and Kron 2011a).
4. To give an indication of the region's complexity, Governor Agar is from a northern Sudanese ethnic group. However, he is also "part of the Sudan People's Liberation Movement.… He, along with countless others from his area, personally battled as guerrilla fighters for the south against the north" (Gettleman and Kron 2011c).
5. Gettleman points to another connection to Darfur in that "Ahmed Haroun, indicted by the International Criminal Court on crimes against humanity for massacres in Darfur, was recently elected governor of Southern Kordofan." Gettleman also notes that "in the 1980s and 1990s, the Sudanese army and violent local militias swept across Kordofan, killing thousands of Nuban civilians and forcing many more into 'peace camps,' essentially concentration camps where many Nubans were forced to convert to Islam" (Gettleman 2011h).
6. By 23 June, the total number of displaced persons in South Kordofan had risen to 73,000, although it was reported that "some of these people have now returned to their homes" (UN Office for the Coordination of Humanitarian Affairs, quoted in Reuters 2011e).
7. Diehl's article ended with the suggestion that the president demonstrate the same level of commitment to "Syria, Bahrain, Libya or other Arab states where people are fighting for freedom.… It's not too late for him to show how concerted American diplomacy can make a difference elsewhere in the Arab Middle East" (Diehl 2011).

Notes to Chapter 8

1. Andrew Natsios, President Bush's Special Envoy to Sudan, differentiates between the National Congress Party, which he describes as having "a deserved reputation for making agreements they have no intention of honoring," and President al-Bashir, who in personal dealings "has been straightforward and [has] never misled me" (2012, 82).
2. Because our previous research dealing with the role of mass media and international intervention in Africa did not focus on key events, direct comparisons of South Sudan to coverage to other conflict situations is problematic. We did, however, re-examine our data on *New York Times* coverage of the 2006 election in the Democratic Republic of the Congo for a similar two-month period surrounding that election. There we found the newspaper printed sixteen stories, one more than it ran on the 2010 Sudanese election.

3 There is a complex relationship between mass media and influential citizens, first in creating public awareness and then building policy-influencing movements such as the "Save Darfur Coalition." Rebecca Hamilton explained that when Secretary of State Colin Powell used the word "genocide," he had, "in the minds of many Americans elevated Darfur from 'just another' crisis in Africa. The label pushed Darfur beyond elite advocacy circles and closed government doors to capture the attention of ordinary citizens" (2011a, 48). Amanda Grzyb focused on the ongoing role of citizen activism in maintaining momentum on the issue: "While the media has played a role in keeping Darfur in the public discourse, it is the NGO and Darfur activist organizations that have truly kept up the pressure for international intervention" (2009, 83).

Hamilton points out an important difference with respect to the effectiveness of citizen mobilization in Canada and the United States, claiming "that when congress was their target, the Darfur movement could affect the policy process." In parliamentary systems such as Canada's (especially in circumstances of a majority government), this avenue of grassroots advocacy is far less important and of course the executive branches of governments in both countries are far more isolated from citizen advocacy. On this point, Hamilton makes an important observation: "When pressuring congress, advocates could reach their representatives' offices directly. Reaching the president usually required indirect messengers. *For the most part advocates relied on the media as their means of communication*" (2011a, 101; italics added).

4 Interestingly, although the need for it was stressed, there was little discussion of the difficulties involved in carrying out long-term programs of assistance (see Chapter 3, this volume).

5 Nicholas Kristof was a leading critic of President al-Bashir and an advocate for a UN peacekeeping force to be sent to Darfur (see Sidahmed, Soderlund, and Briggs 2010), and one can only assume that the *New York Times* columnist would not have been pleased with the move toward even greater engagement with the Sudanese president that emerged as US policy following the 2010 election. In any event, the April 2010 article was Kristof's only contribution to reporting on South Sudan in coverage of the three key events included in our research.

6 With respect to the possible use of force by the US to depose al-Bashir or to intervene militarily in Sudan, from the time of the Clinton administration there appears to have been a serious misreading of US intentions on the part of the Sudanese government. For example, Andrew Natsios claims that in negotiations over the CPA during the Bush administration, "Khartoum most feared U.S. military action, a fear that surfaced repeatedly in conversations I had with NCP leadership" (Natsios 2012, 114–15, 165–66). However, Rebecca Hamilton's study of efforts to save Darfur during the same time period shows that "a U.S. deployment [of military forces] was never seriously mapped out. 'There was a resistance to even do planning for fear that if you planned you might be asked to implement the plan'" (presidential policy advisor, quoted in Hamilton 2011a, 75–77).

7 We reviewed the online material that *The Globe and Mail* sent us for evidence of R2P counter-framing of the type seen in the *The New York Times* and *The Washington Post* and found none. No stories were filed by the paper's Africa Bureau Chief Geoffrey York; most originated with the Associated Press and Reuters wire service reporters and dealt with ongoing developments.

8 An interesting feature in the coverage of pre-independence violence in Abyei and the Nuba Mountains was numerous references to the importance of celebrities (as well as grassroots evangelical Christian communities) in creating public awareness of what was happening in Sudan and in influencing US foreign policy. Though well short of proclaiming a "CNN effect," a number of officials engaged in foreign policy decision making

pointed to the importance of these groups in arriving at decisions that had been made (and by inference would be made) regarding US policy toward South Sudan (see Cooper 2008 for a discussion of the contributions of celebrity diplomacy).

9   Canadian Africa specialist John Young has a different view, describing the peace process as a failure because those promoting the 2005 CPA did not insist on a "democratic transformation" including all parties to the conflict, not just the SPLM and the Khartoum government. Moreover, he contends that once the CPA had been negotiated, the international community largely ignored warning signs that the agreement was flawed and disintegrating; for, example, he cites the 2010 elections (called for in the CPA), as giving the "ruling parties a veneer of undeserved democratic legitimacy" (Young 2012). Young is no doubt right on the last point (see Chapter 5, this volume), but we would argue that given the history of conflict between north and south any agreement ending the civil war, even if it did not solve all of Sudan's problems, was certainly a noteworthy diplomatic achievement.

We might add that democratic transformations are difficult to negotiate. For example, while leaders of revolts in Blue Nile and the Nuba Mountains were part of the SPLM team negotiating the CPA, Andrew Natsios maintains that in the case of Darfur SPLM leader John Garang would have welcomed Darfuri rebels as a part of a united delegation, but the latter "insisted on taking an independent negotiating position" (2012, 163).

REFERENCES

Abramowitz, Michael. 2011. "Will Sudan Explode on Obama's Watch?" *Washington Post*, 2 January, B1.
Aday, Sean. 2006. "The Framesetting Effects of News: An Experimental Test of Advocacy Versus Objectivist Frames." *Journalism and Mass Communication Quarterly* 83 (4): 767–84.
Adeleke, Ademola. 1995. "The Politics and Diplomacy of Peacekeeping in West Africa: The ECOWAS Operation in Liberia." *Journal of Modern African Studies* 33 (4): 569–93.
Agence France-Presse (AFP). 2011a. "Everything 'On Track' for Referendum: UN." *Ottawa Citizen*, 8 January, A8.
———. 2011b. "South Sudan Ratifies New Constitution; Public Consulted Minister Says." *Ottawa Citizen*, 8 July, A6.
———. 2014. "US, EU Threatens Sanctions for South Sudan Warring Parties." 19 March. http://www.eubusiness.com/news-eu/ssudan-unrest-us.uh5.
Alao, Abiodun, John Mackinlay, and Funmi Olonisakin. 1999. *Peacekeepers, Politicians, and Warlords: The Liberian Peace Process*. New York: United Nations Press.
Aliap, John. 2012. "Tribalism Most Dangerous Enemy to South Sudanese." *Sudan Tribune*, 9 July. http://www.sudantribune.com/spip.php?article43196.
AllAfrica. 2013. "Sudan: African Union Unable to Bring Peace to Warring Sudans." 29 January. http://allafrica.com/stories/201301290356.html.
Allison, Graham, and Philip Zelikow. 1999. *Essence of Decision: Explaining the Cuban Missile Crisis*. 2nd ed. New York: Longman.
Almond, Gabriel. 1950. *The American People and Foreign Policy*. New York: Harcourt, Brace.
Al-Monitor. 2013. "South Sudan's President Moves to Tighten Grip on Power." *Pulse of the Middle East*, 22 September. http://www.al-monitor.com/pulse/politics/2013/09/south-sudan-salva-kiir-moves-tighten-grip-power.html.
Alpert, Emily. 2012. "U.N.: South Sudan Failed to Stop Attacks That Killed Hundreds." *Los Angeles Times*, 26 June. http://latimesblogs.latimes.com/world_now/2012/06/south-sudan-violence-un-report-nuer-murle.html.
Althaus, Scott. 2003. *Collective Preferences in Democratic Politics: Opinion Surveys and the Will of the People*. New York: Cambridge University Press.

Amed, Baba. 2013. "France Vows to Keep Troops in Mali after Arrival of UN Force." *Globe and Mail*, 27 April.
An, Seon-Kyoung, and Karla Gower. 2009. "How do the News Media Frame Crises? A Content Analysis of News Coverage." *Public Relations Review* 35 (2): 107–12.
Archibald, Randal. 2011. "Haitians Train for a Future with a Military." *New York Times*, 25 October.
Associated Press (AP). 2010. "Omar al-Bashir Charged with Darfur Genocide." *Guardian*, 12 July. http://www.guardian.co.uk/world/2010/jul/12/bashir-charged-with-darfur-genocide.
———. 2011a. "Southern Sudan Makes Peace Deal." *New York Times*, 5 January, A8.
———. 2011b. "105 Killed in Fighting in Southern Sudan." *Washington Post*, 12 February, A6.
———. 2011c. "North Sudan Is Said to Have Taken Oil Town It and South Both Claim." *New York Times*, 22 May, A10.
———. 2011d. [No headline]. *Washington Post*, 22 May, A8.
———. 2011e. "Sudan: U.S. Voices Worry on North–South Disputes." *Washington Post*, 15 June, A8.
———. 2011f. "Sudan: Satellite Images Show Possible Mass Graves." *Washington Post*, 15 July, A8.
———. 2013. "Sudan, South Sudan Agree to Implement Oil Deal." *Wall Street Journal*, 6 January. http://pachodo.org/latest-news-articles/news-from-various-sources/5191-sudan-south-sudan-agree-to-implement-oil-deal-wall-street-journal.
———. 2014. "South Sudan Horror Sparks Fear of Deepening Civil War." *Windsor Star*, 25 April.
Auerbach, Yehudith, and Yaeli Bloch-Elkon. 2005. "Media Framing and Foreign Policy: The Elite Press vis-à-vis US Policy in Bosnia, 1992–95." *Journal of Peace Research* 42 (1): 83–99.
Autesserre, Séverine. 2010. *The Trouble with the Congo: Local Violence and the Failure of International Peacebuilding*. New York: Cambridge University Press.
Azar, Edward. 1990. *The Management of Protracted Social Conflict*. Aldershot, UK: Dartmouth.
Bariyo, Nicholas. 2012. "Full-scale War Fears for Sudan and Southern Neighbour." *Globe and Mail*, 24 April.
Bases, Daniel. 2010. "U.S. Might Support Brief Delay, but Sudan Says Elections Are Set to Go." *Washington Post*, 9 April, A9.
Beer, David. 2001. "The Partnership of Peacebuilding: A Case Study of Justice Development in Haiti." MA thesis, Department of Political Science, University of Windsor.
Bellafante, Ginia. 2008. "Congo's Horror, As Seen through a Personal Filter." Review of *The Greatest Silence: Rape in the Congo* (film), directed by Lisa F. Jackson. *New York Times*, 8 April. http://www.nytimes.com/2008/04/08/arts/television/08sile.html.
Berinsky, Adam, and Donald Kinder. 2006. "Making Sense of Issues through Media Frames: Understanding the Kosovo Crisis." *Journal of Politics* 68 (3): 640–56.
Berman, Eric, and Katie Sams. 2000. "Keeping the Peace in Africa." *Disarmament Forum* 3: 21–31. http://www.unidir.org/files/publications/pdfs/peacekeeping-evolution-or-extinction-en-362.pdf.
Boswell, Alan. 2011a. "Sudan, after the Split." *Ottawa Citizen*, 8 January, A11.
———. 2011b. "Southern Sudan Clashes Kill at Least 9." *Ottawa Citizen*, 5 February.
———. 2011c. "Troops Mutiny in Southern Sudan." *Washington Post*, 6 February, A18.

———. 2012. "Clinton Visit to South Sudan Colored by Accusations Its President Lied to Obama." *Miami Herald*, 2 August. http://www.miamiherald.com/2012/08/02/2927890/clinton-visit-to-south-sudan-colored.html.
Boutrous-Ghali, Boutros. 1992. "An Agenda for Peace: Preventive Diplomacy, Peacemaking, and Peacekeeping." *International Relations* 11 (3): 201–18.
Braestrup, Peter. 1977. *The Big Story: How the American Press and Television Reported and Interpreted the Crisis of Tet 1968 in Vietnam and Washington*. Boulder, CO: Westview Press.
Bräutigam, Deborah, and Stephen Knack. 2004. "Foreign Aid, Institutions, and Governance in Sub-Saharan Africa." *Economic Development and Cultural Change* 52 (2): 255–85.
Brown, Michael, and Chantal de Jonge Oudraat. 2001. "Internal Conflict and International Action: An Overview." In *Nationalism and Ethnic Conflict: An International Security Reader*, edited by M. Brown, O. Coté Jr, S. Lynn-Jones, and S. Miller, 163–92. Cambridge, MA: MIT Press.
Bunting, Madeleine. 2009. "The Road to Ruin." *Guardian*, 14 February. http://www.theguardian.com/books/2009/feb/14/aid-africa-dambisa-moyo.
Callaghan, Karen, and Frauke Schnell. 2001. "Assessing the Democratic Debate: How News Media Frame Elite Policy Discourse." *Political Communication* 18 (2): 183–212.
Canadian Media Research Consortium. 2004. "Report Card on Canadian News Media." Accessed 15 July 2010. http://www.cmrcccrm.ca/english/reportcard2004/01.html.
CanWest News Service. 2010. "Sudan: Problems Mar First Vote in 25 Years." *Ottawa Citizen*, 12 April, A6.
Caplan, Gerald, and Amanda Grzyb. 2012. "The Tragic Cost of the World's Inaction in Sudan." *Globe and Mail*, 5 September. http://theglobeandmail.com/news/politics/second-reading/the-tragic-cost-of-the-worlds-inaction-in-Sudan/article4520917.
Carment, David. 2003. "Assessing State Failure: Implications for Theory and Policy." *Third World Quarterly* 24 (3): 407–27.
Chalk, Frank, Roméo Dallaire, Kyle Matthews, Carla Barquerio, and Simon Doyle. 2010. *Mobilizing the Will to Intervene: Leadership and Action to Prevent Mass Atrocities*. Montreal: Montreal Institute for Genocide and Human Rights Studies. http://migs.concordia.ca/W2I/documents/ENG_MIGS_finalW2IAugust09.pdf.
Chapman Gates, Jana. 2011. "Dangers in Sudan." *New York Times*, 7 January, A20.
Chong, Dennis, and James Druckman. 2007. "A Theory of Framing and Opinion Formation in Competitive Elite Environments." *Journal of Communication* 57 (1): 99–118.
Cilliers, Jakkie. 2008. "The African Standby Force: An Update on Progress." ISS Paper 160. Pretoria: Institute for Security Studies. http://dspace.cigilibrary.org/jspui/bitstream/123456789/30855/1/PAPER160.pdf?1.
Clark, Campbell. 2013. "Haiti Stunned by Fantino Plan to Freeze New Aid." *Globe and Mail*, 5 January.
Clark, Jeffrey. 1993. "Debacle in Somalia: Failure of the Collective Response." In *Enforcing Restraint: Collective Intervention in International Conflicts*, edited by L. Damroach, 205–39. New York: Council on Foreign Relations.
Clinton, Hillary. 2011. "A Brighter Hope for All Sudanese." *Washington Post*, 10 July, A17.
Clooney, George, and John Prendergast. 2011. "Avoiding the Next Darfur." *Washington Post*, 28 May, A17.
CNN. 2013. "Leaders of 2 Sudans Agree to Temporary Administration of Disputed Oil-Rich Region." 6 January. http://www.cnn.com/2013/01/06/world/africa/sudans-leaders-meet/index.html.

Cohen, Bernard. 1963. *The Press and Foreign Policy.* Princeton, NJ: Princeton University Press.
———. 1994. "Introduction to Media and Foreign Policy: A View from the Academy." In *Taken by Storm: The Media, Public Opinion, and U.S. Foreign Policy in the Gulf War,* edited by W.L. Bennett and D. Paletz, 8–11. Chicago: University of Chicago Press.
Cole, Madeleine. 2011. "Sudan's Referendum." *Globe and Mail,* 18 January, A18.
Collins, Robert. 2005. *Civil Wars and Revolution in Sudan.* Hollywood, CA: Tsehai Publishers.
Commission on Global Governance. 1995. *Our Global Neighborhood.* New York: Oxford University Press.
Cooper, Andrew. 2008. *Celebrity Diplomacy.* Boulder, CO: Paradigm Publishers.
Dallaire, Roméo. 2003. *Shake Hands with the Devil: The Failure of Humanity in Rwanda.* Toronto: Random House.
Dallaire, Roméo, and Glen Pearson. 2010. "Birthing Pains of a New Nation? Canada Must Play a Lead Role Following January Referendums." *Globe and Mail,* 29 December, A17.
Deng, Francis. 2002. "Sudan: An African Dilemma." In *The Causes of War and the Consequences of Peacekeeping in Africa,* edited by R. Laremont, 61–89. Portsmouth, NH: Heinemann.
———. 2006. "Sudan: A Nation in Turbulent Search of Itself." *Annals of the American Academy of Political and Social Science* 603 (January): 155–62.
———. 2010. *New Sudan in the Making? Essays on a Nation in Painful Search of Itself.* Trenton, NJ: Red Sea Press.
Diehl, Jackson. 2011. "The Power of Leadership." *Washington Post,* 4 July, A15.
Donnelly, Jack. 2013. *Universal Human Rights in Theory and Practice.* 3rd ed. Ithaca, NY: Cornell University Press.
Druckman, James. 2001. "On the Limits of Framing Effects: Who Can Frame?" *Journal of Politics* 63 (4): 1041–66.
Dueck, Lorna. 2013. "Will We Respond to Sudan's Own Hell?" *Globe and Mail,* 28 January. http://www.theglobeandmail.com/commentary/will-we-respond-to-sudans-own-hell/article7874382.
Dunn, Kevin. 2003. *Imagining the Congo: The International Relations of Identity.* New York: Palgrave Macmillan.
Edwards, Steven. 2011. "Darfur Violence Being Ignored, Groups Warn." *Ottawa Citizen,* 7 January, A8.
Edy, Jill, and Patrick Meirick. 2007. "Wanted Dead or Alive: Media Frames, Frame Adoption, and Support for the War in Afghanistan. *Journal of Communication* 57 (1): 119–41.
Emery, Michael. 1989. "An Endangered Species: The International Newshole." *Gannett Center Journal* 3 (4): 151–64.
Entman, Robert. 2007. "Framing Bias: Media in the Distribution of Power." *Journal of Communication* 57 (1): 163–73.
Esty, Daniel, Jack Goldstone, Ted Robert Gurr, Barbara Harff, Pamela Surko, Alan Unger, and Robert Chen. 1998. "The State Failure Project: Early Warning Research for U.S. Foreign Policy Planning." Paper presented at the conference "Failed States and International Security: Causes, Prospects and Consequences," Purdue University.
Fadl, Abir. 2012. "(Un)attractive Unity: Critical Turning Points Leading to the Independence of South Sudan." MA Major Research Paper, Department of Political Science, University of Windsor.

Fenton, Anthony. 2005/2006. "'Legalized Imperialism': 'Responsibility to Protect' and the Dubious Case of Haiti." *Briarpatch Magazine*. 3 December. http://briarpatchmagazine.com/articles/view/legalized-imperialism-responsibility-to-protect-and-the-dubious-case-of-hai.

Fick, Maggie. 2011a. "North and South Sudan Agree to Establish Demilitarized Zone." *Washington Post*, 1 June, A8.

———. 2011b. "An Independent South Sudan Rejoices after Five-Decade Struggle." *Washington Post*, 10 July, A8.

Finnemore, Martha, and Kathryn Sikkink. 1998. "International Norm Dynamics and Political Change." *International Organization* 52 (4): 887–917.

Fitzsimmons, Scott. 2005. "Dogs of Peace: A Potential Role for Private Military Companies in Peace Implementation." *Journal of Military and Strategic Studies* 8 (1): 1–26. http://www.jmss.org/jmss/index.php/jmss/article/download/164/185.

Fleishman, Jeffrey. 2011. "'There Will Be a New Southern Sudan and I Will Have a Chance.'" *Ottawa Citizen*, 6 January, C7.

Foreign Policy. 2010. *The Failed States Index 2010*. Accessed 20 December 2011. http://www.foreignpolicy.com/articles/2010/06/21/2010_failed_states_index_interactive_map_and_rankings.

———. 2011. *The Failed States Index 2011*. Accessed 11 January 2012. http://www.foreignpolicy.com/articles/2011/06/17/2010_failed_states_index_interactive_map_and_rankings.

Fouche, Gwladys. 2014. "UN Warns of South Sudan Famine as Donors Pledge More Aid." Reuters, May 20. http://mobile.reuters.com/article/environmentNews/idUSKBN0E022J20140520.

4International Media and Newspapers. 2013. "2013 Newspaper Rankings: Top 200 Newspapers in the World." http://www.4imn.com/top200.

Frye, William. 1957. *A United Nations Peace Force*. New York: Oceana Publications.

Gamson, William, and Andre Modigliani. 1989. "Media Discourse and Public Opinion on Nuclear Power: A Constructivist Approach." *American Journal of Sociology* 95 (1): 1–37.

Gardner, Amy. 2011. "Palin Cancels Sudan Trip over Scheduling Conflicts." *Washington Post*, 23 June, A3.

Gershoni, Yeketiel. 1997. "War without End and an End to a War: The Prolonged Wars in Liberia and Sierra Leone." *African Studies Review* 40 (3): 55–76.

Gerson, Michael. 2010a. "Birth of a Nation? South Sudan Struggles toward Independence." *Washington Post*, 31 March, A17.

———. 2010b. "In Sudan, a Universal Fight for Freedom." *Washington Post*, 2 April, A19.

———. 2011a. "Born into War." *Washington Post*, 8 July, A15.

———. 2011b. "Can South Sudan's Liberators Become Founders?" *Washington Post*, 12 July, A17.

Gettleman, Jeffrey. 2010a. "Sudan Elections in Limbo after Parties Plan Boycott." *New York Times*, 2 April, A6.

———. 2010b. "With a Likely Outcome, Long-Awaited Sudanese Elections Begin." *New York Times*, 12 April, A4.

———. 2010c. "Prosperity in Sudan Wins Votes for a Leader Reviled Elsewhere." *New York Times*, 15 April, A4.

———. 2010d. "Sudan's President Wins Election as Country Nears Vote to Split." *New York Times*, 27 April, A12.

———. 2011a. "Peaceful Vote on Sudan Appears More Likely." *New York Times*, 2 January, A9.
———. 2011b. "In Sudan, a Colonial Curse Comes Up for a Vote." *New York Times*, 8 January, WK3.
———. 2011c. "Southern Sudan Feels Freedom Close at Hand." *New York Times*, 8 January, A1.
———. 2011d. "Roots of Bitterness in a Disputed Land Threatens Sudan's Future." *New York Times*, 16 January, A6.
———. 2011e. "Border Town Incursion Poses Big Risk for Sudan." *New York Times*, 24 May, A10.
———. 2011f. "Sudan: Leader Says He Won't Go to War over Abyei." *New York Times*, 27 May, A7.
———. 2011g. "Brinksmanship in Sudan as Deadline Nears." *New York Times*, 6 June, A4.
———. 2011h. "U.N. Officials Warn of a Growing 'Panic' in Central Sudan as Violence Spreads." *New York Times*, 16 June, A6.
———. 2011i. "Sudan Step Up Furious Drive to Stop Rebels." *New York Times*, 21 June, A1.
———. 2011j. "Sudan to Let Peacekeepers Patrol Area in Dispute." *New York Times*, 21 June, A12.
———. 2011k. "Sudan Signs Accord with Rebels." *New York Times*, 29 June, A11.
———. 2011m. "Another Area Girds for Revolt as Sudan Approaches a Split." *New York Times*, 1 July, A1.
———. 2011n. "Sudanese Struggle to Survive Endless Bombings Aimed to Quell Rebels." *New York Times*, 4 July, A4.
———. 2011o. "Newest Nation Is Full of Hope and Promise." *New York Times*, 8 July, A1.
———. 2011p. "Movement's Mission Is Secured: Statehood." *New York Times*, 9 July, A7.
———. 2011q. "Struggle Over, Independent South Sudan Rejoices." *New York Times*, 10 July, A6.
———. 2012. "Two Sudans Reach Deal on Fees for Oil Pipeline." *New York Times*, 5 August.
Gettleman, Jeffrey, and Josh Kron. 2011a. "Warnings of All-Out War in Fight over Sudan Town." *New York Times*, 23 May, A4.
———. 2011b. "UN Warns of Ethnic Cleansing in Sudan Town." *New York Times*, 26 May, A4.
———. 2011c. "Sudan Threatens to Occupy Two More Regions in Dispute with South." *New York Times*, 30 May, A4.
———. 2011d. "Ethiopian Peacekeepers May Be Brought in to Sudan Border." *New York Times*, 31 May, A8.
———. 2011e. "North and South Tentatively Agree to Demilitarize Disputed Border." *New York Times*, 1 June, A10.
———. 2011f. "Sudan: Abyei Officials Say 116 Were Killed Last Month." *New York Times*, 2 June, A13.
Glennie, Jonathan. 2008. *The Trouble with Aid: Why Less Could Mean More for Africa*. London: Zed Books.
Glickman, Dan. 2010. "Violence in Sudan." *New York Times*, 6 May.
Globe and Mail. 2011. "Uphill path." Editorial. 14 July, A16.

Goldstone, Jack, Robert Bates, David Epstein, Ted Robert Gurr, Michael Lustik, Monty Marshall, Jay Ulfelder, and Mark Woodward. 2010. "A Global Model for Forecasting Political Instability." *American Journal of Political Science* 54 (1): 190–208.

Goodhand, Jonathan, and David Hulme. 1999. "From Wars to Complex Political Emergencies: Understanding Conflict and Peace-Building in the New World Order." *Third World Quarterly* 20 (1): 13–26.

Gordon, Michael. 2014. "U.S. Imposes First Sanctions in South Sudan Conflict." *New York Times*. 6 May. http://www.nytimes.com.

Green Party of Canada. 2010. "A Canadian-First: Certification of Peace Professionals." 15 December. http://greenparty.ca/media-release/2010-12-15/canadian-first-certification-peace-professionals.

Greenwood, Christopher. 1993. "Is There a Right of Humanitarian Intervention?" *World Today* 49 (2): 34–40.

Grindle, Merilee, and Mary Hilderbrand. 1995. "Building Sustainable Capacity in the Public Sector: What Can Be Done?" *Public Administration and Development* 15 (5): 441–63.

Gross, Kimberly. 2008. "Framing Persuasive Appeals: Episodic and Thematic Framing, Emotional Response, and Policy Opinion." *Political Psychology* 29 (2): 160–92.

Grzyb, Amanda. 2009. "Media Coverage, Activism, and Creating Public Will for Intervention in Rwanda and Darfur." In *The World and Darfur: International Response to Crimes Against Humanity in Western Sudan*, edited by A. Grzyb, 61–91. Montreal: McGill-Queen's Press.

The Guardian. 2012. "Two Sudan's Oil Dispute Deepens as South Shuts Down Wells." 26 January. http://www.theguardian.com/world/2012/jan/26/south-sudan-shuts-oil-wells.

———. 2014. "South Sudan Rebel Offensive Threatens Oil Fields." 18 February. http://www.theguardian.com/world/2014/feb/18/south-sudan-rebel-assault-oilfields.

Hachten, William. 2004. "Reporting Africa's Problems." In *Development and Communication in Africa*, edited by C. Okigbo and F. Eribo, 79–87. Lanham, MD: Rowman and Littlefield.

Halton, Dan. 2001. "International News in the North American Media." *International Journal* 56 (3): 499–515.

Hamilton, Rebecca. 2011a. *Fighting for Darfur: Public Action and the Struggle to Stop Genocide*. New York: Palgrave Macmillan.

———. 2011b. "Abyei, Sudan's Potential Tinderbox." *Washington Post*, 24 January, A6.

———. 2011c. "For Nascent Nation, Oil Both Boon and Burden." *Washington Post*, 12 February, A6.

———. 2011d. "'Does This Mean the End of Our Peace?'" *Washington Post*, 28 May, A6.

———. 2011e. "Fighting in South Sudan Brings Chaos, Hunger." *Washington Post*, 31 May, A6.

———. 2011f. "Sudan Rejects U.N. Call to Pull Troops from Contested Town." *Washington Post*, 7 June, A6.

Hatcher, Jessica. 2014. "South Sudan Unrest Exacerbated by Conflict among Cattle Herders." *Guardian*, 11 March. http://www.theguardian.com/global-development/2014/mar/11/south-sudan-conflict-over-cows.

Hawk, Beverley. 1992. "Introduction: Metaphors of African Coverage." In *Africa's Media Image*, edited by B. Hawk, 3–14. New York: Praeger.

Helman, Gerald, and Steven Ratner. 1993. "Saving Failed States." *Foreign Policy* 89: 3–21.
Hendrickson, Dylan, and Andrzej Karkoszka. 2002. "The Challenges of Security Sector Reform." In *SIPRI Yearbook 2002: Armaments, Disarmament and International Security*: 75–201. Stockholm: Stockholm International Peace Research Institute.
Henry, Jehanne. 2014. "Justice Cannot Wait in South Sudan." Human Rights Watch. 31 January. http://www.thinkafricapress.com/south-sudan/justice-can't-wait-hrw-accountability.
Higgins, Andrew. 2011. "China Stands by Its Ally in Oil." *Washington Post*, 23 June, A10.
Hilsum, Lindsey. 2007. "Reporting Rwanda: The Media and Aid Agencies." In *Media and the Rwandan Genocide*, edited by A. Thompson, 167–87. Ottawa: International Research Centre.
Horowitz, Irving Leonard. 1967. *The Rise and Fall of Project Camelot: Studies in the Relationship between Social Science and Practical Politics*. Cambridge, MA: MIT Press.
Howard-Hassmann, Rhoda. 2010. "Mugabe's Zimbabwe: Massive Human Rights Violations and the Failure to Protect." *Human Rights Quarterly* 32 (4): 898–920.
Howe, Herbert. 1996/97. "Lessons of Liberia: ECOMOG and Regional Peacekeeping." *International Security* 21 (3): 145–76.
Human Rights Watch. 2014a. "South Sudan: Investigate New Cluster Bomb Use." 15 February. http://www.hrw.org/news/2014/02/14/south-sudan-investigate-new-cluster-bomb-use.
———. 2014b. "South Sudan: War Crimes by Both Sides." 27 February. http://www.hrw.org/news/2014/02/26/south-sudan-war-crimes-both-sides.
Innes, Michael. 2004. "Political Communication in Wartime Liberia: Themes and Concepts." *Centre D'Études des Politiques Étrangères et de Sécurité* 26: 1–34.
International Commission on Intervention and State Sovereignty (ICISS). 2001. *The Responsibility to Protect: Report of the International Commission on Intervention and State Sovereignty*. Ottawa: International Development Research Centre.
International Crisis Group. 2010. "Zimbabwe: Political and Security Challenges to the Transition." http://www.crisisgroup.org/en/regions/africa/southern-africa/Zimbabwe.aspx.
Iyengar, Shanto, and Adam Simon. 1993. "News Coverage of Gulf Crisis and Public Opinion: A Study of Agenda-Setting, Priming, and Framing." *Communication Research* 20 (3): 365–83.
Jacobs, Lawrence, and Robert Shapiro. 2000. *Politicians Don't Pander: Political Manipulation and the Loss of Democratic Responsiveness*. Chicago: University of Chicago Press.
Jacobsen, Peter. 1996. "National Interest, Humanitarianism or CNN: What Triggers UN Peace Enforcement after the Cold War?" *Journal of Peace Research* 33 (2): 205–15.
James, Alan. 1995. "Peacekeeping in the Post-Cold War Era." *International Journal* 50 (2): 241–65.
Johansen, Robert. 2006. *A United Nations Emergency Peace Service to Prevent Genocide and Crimes Against Humanity*. http://www.unitar.org/ny/sites/unitar.org.ny/files/UNEPS_proposal.pdf.
Johnson, Douglas. 2003. *The Root Causes of Sudan's Civil Wars*. Oxford: James Currey.
———. 2007. "Why Abyei Matters: The Breaking Point of Sudan's Comprehensive Peace Agreement." *African Affairs* 107 (426): 1–19.
———. 2011. "Sudan's Peaceful Partition, at Risk." *New York Times*, 31 May, A23.
Kasumba, Yvonne, and Charles Debrah. 2010. "An Overview of the African Standby Force." In *The Civilian Dimension of the African Standby Force*, edited by C. de Coning and Y. Kasumba, 10–19. Addis Ababa: African Union Commission.

Katz, Elihu, and Paul Lazarsfeld. 1955. *Personal Influence: The Part Played by People in the Flow of Mass Communication*. New York: Free Press.

Keim, Curtis. 1999. *Making Africa: Curiosities and Invention of the American Mind*. Boulder, CO: Westview Press.

Keller, Edmond. 2002. "Culture, Politics and the Transnationalization of Ethnic Conflict in Africa: New Research Imperatives." *Polis/ R.C.S.P./ C.P.S.R* Vol. 9, Numéro Spécial. http:///www.polis.sciencespobordeaux.fr/vol10ns/Keller.pdf.

Kent, Vanessa, and Mark Malan. 2003. "The African Standby Force: Progress and Prospects." *African Security Review* 12 (3): 71–81.

Khouri, Rami. 2011. "Three Paths to Change in the Arab World." *Globe and Mail*, 18 January, A17.

King, Gary, and Langche Zeng. 2001. "Improving Forecasts of State Failure." *World Politics* 53 (4): 623–58.

Kirby, Steve. 2011. "Envoy's Make a Last Push as South Sudan's Big Day Looms." *Ottawa Citizen*, 8 January, A11.

Koops, Joachim, and Johannes Varwick. 2008. *Ten Years of SHIRBRIG: Lessons Learned, Development Prospects and Strategic Opportunities for Germany*. GPPI Research Paper Series No. 11. Berlin: Global Public Policy Institute. http://www.academia.edu/449213/Ten_Years_of_SHIRBRIG_Lessons_Learned_Development_Prospects_and_Strategic_Opportunities_for_Germany.

Kosicki, Gerald. 1993. "Problems and Opportunities in Agenda-Setting Research." *Journal of Communication* 43 (2): 100–27.

Kristof, Nicholas. 2010. "Obama Backs Down on Sudan." *New York Times*, 22 April, A29.

Kron, Josh. 2010a. "Islamic Sudan Envisioned if South Secedes." *New York Times*, 19 December, A12.

———. 2010b. "Peace Hovers in Sudan, but Most Soldiers Stay Armed." *New York Times*, 30 December, A4.

———. 2011a. "Referendum Logos Accent Challenges Facing Sudan." *New York Times*, 14 January, A6.

———. 2011b. "Sudan Leader to Accept Secession of South." *New York Times*, 8 February, A7.

———. 2011c. "Southern Sudan Suffers a Blow as Fighting Ends a Truce." *New York Times*, 12 February, A10.

———. 2011d. "As It Emerges As a Nation, South Sudan Extends the Clout of Its Neighbor." *New York Times*, 7 July, A10.

Kron, Josh, and Jeffrey Gettleman. 2011a. "Broader Conflict Feared as Fighting Breaks Out on the Border." *New York Times*, 6 June, A9.

———. 2011b. "Thousands Flee in Sudan as North–South Clashes Grow, U.N. Says." *New York Times*, 11 June, A4.

Kushkush, Isama'il. 2011. "President Hints at Fresh Start for Sudan, but Many Are Skeptical." *New York Times*, 14 July, A8.

Lacey, Marc. 2006. "Sudan: African Union Lacks Darfur Funds." *New York Times*, 13 January.

Laessing, Ulf. 2011. "Looters in Sudan Set Fire to Part of Disputed Town." *Washington Post*, 24 May, A14.

Laessing, Ulf, and Alexander Dziadosz. 2012. "South Sudan Withdraws from Oil Area, Easing Border Crisis." *Euronews*, 21 April.

Laessing, Ulf, and Jeremy Clarke. 2011. "Dancing in South Sudan Streets; but in Khartoum, Emotions Vary Wildly." *Ottawa Citizen*, 10 July.

Lamb, Henry. 2001. *Global Governance*, 17 August. Accessed 6 July 2012. http://www.apfn/global_governance.htm.
Landler, Mark. 2010. "Sudan's Future Is Now, U.S. Envoy Says." *New York Times*, 28 April, A10.
———. 2013. "U.S. Pushes for Global Eye on South Sudan Conflict." *New York Times*, 29 July. http://www.nytimes.com/2013/07/30/us/us-pushes-for-global-eye-on-south-sudan-conflict.html.
Lavallee, Guilaume. 2010. "Sudanese Elections in Turmoil; Opposition Groups Boycott Some Polls." *Ottawa Citizen*, 3 April, A11.
LeRiche, Matthew, and Matthew Arnold. 2012. *South Sudan: From Revolution to Independence*. New York: Columbia University Press.
Levitt, Gabriel. 2010. "Rapid Deployment Requires a Permanent UN Force." *World Bulletin*. United Nations Associaton of the United States of America. Accessed 23 March 2012. http://www.unausa.org/worldbulletin/012010/levitt.
Lewis, Mark. 2014. "Nations Double South Sudan Refugee Aid to $1.2 Billion." Associated Press. 20 May. http://abcnews.go.com/International/wireStory/nations-double-south-sudan-refugee-aid-12-bln-23795506.
Lippmann, Walter. 1922. *Public Opinion*. New York: Macmillan.
Live 8. 2005. "Live 8: What's It All About." http:www.live8live.com/whatsitabout.
Livingston, Steven. 1997. *Clarifying the CNN Effect: An Examination of Media Effects According to Type of Military Intervention*. Research Paper R-18. Cambridge, MA: Joan Shorenstein Center, John F. Kennedy School of Government, Harvard University.
Livingston, Steven, and Todd Eachus. 1995. "Humanitarian Crises and U.S. Foreign Policy: Somalia and the CNN Effect Reconsidered." *Political Communication* 12 (4): 413–29.
LoBaido, Anthony. 1998. "Executive Outcomes: A New Kind of Army for Privatized Global Warfare." World Net Daily. 11 August. http://www.wnd.com/1998/08/3290.
Logan, Justin, and Christopher Preble. 2011. "Fixing Failed States: A Dissenting View." In *The Handbook on the Political Economy of War*, edited by C. Coin and R. Mathers, 379–96. Cheltenham, UK: Edward Elgar Publishing.
Lynch, Colum. 2011. "Obama Expresses 'Deep Concern' As Violence Surges in Sudan." *Washington Post*, 17 June, A7.
Maasho, Aaron. 2011a. "Sudan Border State Foes Agree to Talks; More Than 60,000 People Have Fled." *Ottawa Citizen*, 17 June, A11.
———. 2011b. "Abeyi Deal Signed by North and South Sudan; Disputed Region to Be Demilitarized." *Ottawa Citizen*, 21 June, A8.
MacFarquhar, Neil. 2011. "Sudan Strikes Could Be War Crimes, Report Says." *New York Times*, 15 July, A10.
Mackenzie, Lewis. 1993. *Peacekeeper: The Road to Sarajevo*. Vancouver: Douglas and McIntyre.
Mackinlay, John, and Jarat Chopra. 1992. "Second Generation Multilateral Operations." *Washington Quarterly* 15 (2): 113–31.
Mackrael, Kim. 2013. "Memos Show Cuts Planned for Aid to Haiti." *Globe and Mail*, 4 September.
Mallaby, Sebastian. 2002. "The Reluctant Imperialist: Terrorism, Failed States, and the Case for American Empire." *Foreign Policy* 8 (2): 2–7.

Marketing Charts. 2009. "Media Usage Study: Online and Radio Up; TV Still Most Credible." http://www.marketingcharts.com/wp/televison/media-usage-study-online-tv-still-most-credible-10516.

Matthes, Jörg. 2009. "What's in a Frame: A Content Analysis of Media Framing Studies in the World's Leading Communication Journals, 1990–2005." *Journalism and Mass Communication Quarterly* 86 (2): 349–67.

Matthews, Robert. 2005. "Sudan's Humanitarian Disaster: Will Canada Live Up to Its Responsibility to Protect?" *International Journal* 60 (4): 1049–64.

May, Roy, and Simon Massey. 1998. "The OAU Intervention in Chad: Mission Impossible or Mission Evaded?" *International Peacekeeping* 5 (1): 46–65.

Mays, Terry. 2002. *Africa's First Peacekeeping Operation: The OAU in Chad, 1981–1982*. Westport, CT: Praeger.

Mazen, Maram, and Nicole Gaouette. 2010. "Opponents Quit Sudanese Elections; U.S. Tries to Settle Vote-Rigging." *Ottawa Citizen*, 2 April, A7.

McChesney, Robert. 1999. *Rich Media, Poor Democracy: Communication Politics in Dubious Times*. Urbana: University of Illinois Press.

McCombs, Maxwell. 2005. "A Look at Agenda-Setting: Past, Present and Future." *Journalism Studies* 6 (4): 543–57.

McCombs, Maxwell, and Amy Reynolds. 2002. "News Influence on Our Pictures of the World." In *Media Effects: Advances in Theory and Research*, edited by J. Bryant and D. Zillmann, 1–18. 2nd ed. Mahwah, NJ: Lawrence Erlbaum Associates.

McCombs, Maxwell, and Donald Shaw. 1972. "The Agenda-Setting Function of Mass Media." *Public Opinion Quarterly* 36 (3): 176–87.

———. 1993. "The Evolution of Agenda-Setting Research: Twenty-Five Years in the Marketplace of Ideas." *Journal of Communication,* 43 (2): 58–67.

McCombs, Maxwell, Donald Shaw, and David Weaver. 1997. *Communication and Democracy: Exploring the Intellectual Frontiers in Agenda-Setting Theory*. Mahwah, NJ: Lawrence Erlbaum Associates.

McConnell, Tristan. 2013. "Hidden War: Scores Killed, Displaced in Sudan's Nuba Mountains." Global Post. 24 June. http://www.globalpost.com/dispatch/news/regions/africa/sudan/130620/sudan-war-nuba-mountains-khartoum-united-nations-yida-refugees.

McGregor, Andrew. 1999. "Quagmire in West Africa: Nigerian Peacekeeping in Sierra Leone." *International Journal* 54 (3): 482–501.

Mclean, Jim. 2010. "The Final Step to Freedom." *Ottawa Citizen*, 17 December, D6.

Melendez Olivera, Gabriela. 2010. "Clooney on 'Antigenocide' Watch." *Washington Post*, 29 December.

Meredith, Martin. 2005. *The Fate of Africa: From the Hopes of Freedom to the Heart of Despair. A History of Fifty Years of Independence*. New York: Public Affairs.

Mermin, Jonathan. 1997. "Television News and American Intervention in Somalia: The Myth of a Media-Driven Foreign Policy." *Political Science Quarterly* 12 (3): 385–403.

Messner, J.J. 2011. "States of Change." *Foreign Policy*, 20 June. http://www.foreignpolicy.com/articles/2011/06/20/states_of_change.

Minear, Larry, Colin Scott, and Thomas Weiss. 1996. *The News Media, Civil War, and Humanitarian Action*. Boulder, CO: Lynne Rienner.

Moyo, Dambisa. 2009. *Dead Aid: Why Aid Is Not Working and How There Is a Better Way for Africa*. New York: Farrar, Straus and Giroux.

Mueller, John. 1973. *War, Presidents, and Public Opinion*. New York: John Wiley.

Murithi, Tim. 2009. "The African Union's Transition from Non-Intervention to Non-Indifference: An Ad Hoc Approach to the Responsibility to Protect." *IPG* 1: 90–106. http://library.fes.de/pdf-files/ipg/ipg-2009-1/08_a_murithi_us.pdf.

Mutiga, Murithi. 2011. "A Civil Ending to a Civil War." *New York Times*, 8 January, WK12.

Natsios, Andrew. 2012. *Sudan, South Sudan, and Darfur: What Everyone Needs to Know*. New York: Oxford University Press.

Nelson, Thomas, Zoe Oxley, and Rosalee Clawson. 1997. "Toward a Psychology of Framing Effects." *Political Behaviour* 19 (3): 221–46.

New York Times. 2010. "Sudan's Other Crisis." Editorial. 3 May, A24.

———. 2011a. "Southern Sudan Votes." Editorial. 7 January, A20.

———. 2011b. "Another War in Sudan? A Dispute over the Region of Abeyi Must Not Spin Out of Control." Editorial. 28 May, A22.

———. 2011c. "The New State of South Sudan: After the Celebrations, the New Country and Its Supporters Cannot Relax." Editorial. 9 July, A18.

"The 1994 UN Human Development Report." 1994. *Refugee: Canada's Periodical on Refugees* 14 (2): 18–19.

Notter, James. 1995. "Trust and Conflict Transformation." Occasional Paper No. 5. Arlington, VA: Institute for Multi-Track Diplomacy. http://imtd.imtdeast.org/papers/OP-5.pdf.

Obama, Barack. 2011. "In Sudan, an Election and a Beginning." *New York Times*, 8 January, WK12.

OECD. 2008. *Guidance on Evaluating Conflict Prevention and Peacebuilding Activities*. Paris: OEDC Publishing. http://www.oecd.org/dac/evaluation/dcdndep/39774573.pdf.

Ottawa Citizen. 2011. "A New Start in South Sudan." Editorial. 9 July, B6.

Page, Benjamin. 1996. "Mass Media as Political Actors." *PS: Political Science and Politics* 29 (1): 20–24.

Page, Benjamin, and Robert Shapiro. 1992. *The Rational Public: Fifty Years of Trends in Americans' Policy Preferences*. Chicago: University of Chicago Press.

Pagliaro, Jennifer. 2011. "A Key Role for Canada: Ottawa Prepares to Provide Humanitarian Aid and Peacekeeping." *Globe and Mail*, 3 January, A9.

Parks, Michael. 2002. "Beyond Afghanistan: Foreign News: What's Next." *Columbia Journalism Review* 40 (5): 53–57.

Patey, Luke A. 2010. "Crude Days Ahead? Oil and the Resource Curse in Sudan." *African Affairs* 109 (437): 617–36. http://afraf.oxfordjournals.org/content/109/437/617.full.pdf+html.

Pew Center. 2010. "The State of the News Media 2010." http://stateofthemedia.org/2010.

Pflanz, Mike. 2011. "'Absurdly' High Hopes on Vote." *Ottawa Citizen*, 10 January, A6.

Podhur, Justin. 2005. "Is This What 'Responsibility to Protect' Looks Like?" *The Dominion*, 23 September. http://www.dominionpaper.ca/accounts/2005/09/23/is_this_wh.html.

Poggo, Scopas. 2009. *The First Sudanese Civil War: Africans, Arabs, and Israelis in the Southern Sudan, 1955–1972*. New York: Palgrave Macmillan.

Political Instability Task Force (PITF). 2010. "Internal Wars and Failures of Governance, 1955–Most Recent Year." 19 January. http://globalpolicy.gmu.edu.

Power, Samantha. 2002. *"A Problem from Hell": America and the Age of Genocide*. New York: Perennial.

Price, Vincent, David Tewksbury, and Elizabeth Powers. 1997. "Switching Trains of Thought: The Impact of News Frames on Readers' Cognitive Responses." *Communication Research* 24 (5): 481–506.

Prunier, Gérard. 2009. *Africa's World War: Congo and the Rwandan Genocide and the Making of a Continental Catastrophe*. New York: Oxford University Press.
Quinn, Andrew. 2012. "Clinton Urges South Sudan, Sudan to Settle Oil Dispute." Reuters. 3 August. http://www.reuters.com/article/2012/08/03/us-southsudan-clinton-idUSBRE8720G320120803.
Raghavan, Sudarsan. 2010. "Sudan: No Surprises in Vote: Bashir Retains Power." *Washington Post*, 27 April, A6.
———. 2011a. "South Sudan Revels as a Nation's Birth Nears." *Washington Post*, 8 January, A1.
———. 2011b. "'I Never Dreamed This Day Would Come.'" *Washington Post*, 10 January, A12.
Reeves, Eric. 2011. "Genocide Anew in Sudan?" *Washington Post*, 18 June, A15.
———. 2013. "Uprising in Sudan: What We Know Now." *Sudan Tribune*, 4 November. http://www.sudantribune.com/spip.php?mot705.
Reuters. 2010a. "Sudan." *Washington Post*, 21 March, A12.
———. 2010b. "Sudan: Monitors' Expulsion Threatened." *New York Times*, 23 March, A8.
———. 2010c. "Sudan: Critics Raise Pressure in Vote Fraud Charges." *Washington Post*, 21 April, A8.
———. 2010d. "Unity Efforts Have Failed: Presidential Aide." *Ottawa Citizen*, 17 December, D6.
———. 2011a. "Returnees Will Need More Aid, Groups Say." *Ottawa Citizen*, 6 January, C7.
———. 2011b. "Nearly 99% Vote for Sudan Split." *Ottawa Citizen*, 22 January, A6.
———. 2011c. "Sudan: South Acquires Helicopters." *New York Times*, 29 January, A8.
———. 2011d. "50 Left Dead after Mutiny by Army Unit in South Sudan." *New York Times*, 7 February, A6.
———. 2011e. "Sudan: U.N.: 73,000 Flee Border Fighting." *Washington Post*, 23 June, A8.
———. 2012. "S. Sudan Calls Market Attack Act of War." *Windsor Star*, 24 April.
Revise, Nicolas, and Hannah McNeish. 2012. "Sudan, South Sudan Must Strike 'Compromise' Deal: Clinton." Agence France-Presse. 3 August. http://www.unmiss.unmissions.org/LinkClick.aspx?fileticket=2cK4Jh6O2Os%3D&tabid=3540&language=en-US.
Riffe, Daniel, Charles Aust, Ted Jones, Barbara Shoemake, and Shyam Sundar. 1994. "The Shrinking Foreign Newshole for *The New York Times*." *Newspaper Research Journal* 15 (3): 74–88.
Roberts, Adam. 2008. "Proposals for UN Standing Forces: A Critical History." In *The United Nations Security Council and War: The Evolution of Thought and Practice since 1945*, edited by V. Lowe, A. Roberts, J. Welsh and D. Zaum, 99–130. New York: Oxford University Press.
Robinson, Piers. 2000. "The Policy-Interaction Model: Measuring Media Power during Humanitarian Crisis." *Journal of Peace Research* 37 (5): 613–33.
———. 2002. *The CNN Effect: The Myth of News, Foreign Policy and Intervention*. New York: Routledge.
Rogers, Everett, and James Dearing. 1988. "Agenda-Setting Research: Where Has It Been, Where Is It Going?" In *Communication Yearbook*, Vol. 11, edited by J. Anderson, 555–94. Beverley Hills, CA: Sage.
Rogers, Everett, James Dearing, and Dorine Bergman. 1993. "The Anatomy of Agenda-Setting Research." *Journal of Communication* 43 (2): 68–84.

Rogin, Josh. 2011. "Big Changes Coming to Obama's Asia Team." *Washington Post*, 6 January, A19.

Rotberg, Robert. 2002. "The New Nature of Nation-State Failure." *Washington Quarterly* 25 (3): 85–96.

Salwen, Michael. 1988. "Effects of Accumulation of Coverage on Issue Salience in Agenda-Setting." *Journalism Quarterly* 65 (2): 100–6, 130.

Schmitz, David. 2005. *The Tet Offensive: Politics, War, and Public Opinion*. New York: Roman and Littlefield.

Shannon, Ulric. 2000. "Human Security and the Rise of Private Armies." *New Political Science* 22 (1): 103–15.

Sheridan, Mary Beth. 2010a. "Sudan Accord in Peril, U.S. Envoy Says." *Washington Post*, 13 May, A8.

———. 2010b. "U.S. More Hopeful Sudan Will Hold Vote." *Washington Post*, 30 December, A6.

———. 2011. "Sudan Vote Nears after Rocky Effort." *Washington Post*, 7 January, A8.

Sheridan, Mary Beth, and Rebecca Hamilton. 2011. "For South Sudan, a Tense Independence Eve." *Washington Post*, 8 July, A6.

Sherman, Nancy. 1998. "Empathy, Respect, and Humanitarian Intervention." *Ethics and International Affairs* 12 (1): 103–19.

SHIRBRIG. 2009. *SHIRBRIG Lessons Learned Report*. Hovelte Barracks, Denmark: SHIRBRIG Headquarters. 1 June. http://www.operationspaix.net/DATA/DOCUMENT/566~v~Shirbrig_lessons_learned_report.pdf.

Smith, David. 2014a. "Bentiu Massacre Is a Game-Changer in South Sudan Conflict, says UN Official." *Guardian*, 22 April. http://www.theguardian.com/world/2014/apr/22/bentiu-massacre-south-sudan-united-nations.

———. 2014b. "John Kerry Warns of Possible Genocide in South Sudan." *Guardian*, 5 May. http://www.theguardian.com/world/2014/may/01/south-sudan-catastrophe-un-child-soldiers-famine.

Sidahmed, Abdel Salam. 2010. "Institutional Reform and Political Party Engagement: Challenges to Democratic Transformation in Post-CPA Sudan." *International Journal of African Renaissance Studies* 5 (1): 19–35.

Sidahmed, Abdel Salam, and Alsir Sidahmed. 2005. *Sudan*. London: RoutledgeCurzon.

Sidahmed, Abdel Salam, and Walter Soderlund. 2008. "Sudan, 1992: Humanitarian Relief Efforts Confront an Intractable Civil War." In *Humanitarian Crises and Intervention: Reassessing the Impact of Mass Media*, edited by W. Soderlund, E.D. Briggs, K. Hildebrandt, and A.S. Sidahmed, 73–94. Sterling, VA: Kumarian Press.

Sidahmed, Abdel Salam, Walter Soderlund, and E. Donald Briggs. 2010. *The Responsibility to Protect in Darfur: The Role of Mass Media*. Lanham, MD: Lexington Books.

Singer, P.W. 2003a. *Corporate Warriors: The Rise of the Privatized Military Industry*. Ithaca, NY: Cornell University Press.

———. 2003b. "Peacekeepers, Inc." *Policy Review* 119 (June–July): 59–70.

Soderlund, Walter, E. Donald Briggs, Kai Hildebrandt, and Abdel Salam Sidahmed. 2008. *Humanitarian Crises and Intervention: Reassessing the Impact of Mass Media*. Sterling, VA: Kumarian Press.

Soderlund, Walter, E. Donald Briggs, Tom Najem, and Blake Roberts. 2012. *Africa's Deadliest Conflict: Media Coverage of the Humanitarian Disaster in the Congo and the United Nations Response, 1997–2008*. Waterloo, ON: Wilfrid Laurier University Press.

Solovey, Mark. 2001. "Project Camelot and the 1960s Epistemological Revolution: Rethinking the Politics–Patronage–Social Science Nexus." *Social Studies of Science* 32 (2): 171–206.
Spearin, Christopher. 2001. "Private Security Companies and Humanitarians: A Corporate Solution to Securing Humanitarian Spaces." *International Peacekeeping* 18 (1): 20–43.
Statistics Canada. 2003. "Canada's Journey to an Information Society." http://www.statcan.gc.ca/pub/56-508-x/pdf/4200142-eng.pdf.
Stewart, Ian. 2002. *Ambushed: A War Reporter's Life on the Line*. Chapel Hill, NC: Algonquin Books of Chapel Hill.
Strobel, Warren. 1997. *Late-Breaking Foreign Policy: The News Media's Influence on Peace Operations*. Washington, DC: United States Institute of Peace.
Sudan Tribune. 2013. "Amnesty International Says More Than 200 Killed in Sudan Protests." 3 October. http://www.sudantribune.com/spip.php?article48306.
Suhrke, Astri. 2006. "The Limits of Statebuilding: The Role of International Assistance in Afghanistan." Paper presented to the Annual Meeting of the International Studies Association, San Diego, CA. 21–24 March. http://www.cmi.no/publications/2006/isapapermarch2006.pdf
Sutcliffe, John, Walter Soderlund, Kai Hildebrandt, and Martha Lee. 2009. "The Reporting of International News in Canada: Continuity and Change, 1988–2006." *American Review of Canadian Studies* 39 (2): 1–16.
Thompson, Allan. 2007. "The Responsibility to Report: A New Journalistic Paradigm." In *The Media and the Rwanda Genocide*, edited by A. Thompson, 433–45. Ottawa: International Development Research Centre.
Tran, Mark. 2012. "British MPs Issue Bleak Report on South Sudan's Prospects." *Guardian*, 12 April. http://www.guardian.co.uk/global-development/2012/apr/12/british-mps-bleak-report-south-sudan.
UN. 1945. *Charter of the United Nations*. http://www.un.org/en/documents/charter.
———. 2000. *Report of the Secretary-General on the Work of the Organization*. http://www.un.org/documents/sg/report00/a551e.pdf
UNDP. 2009. "Supporting Capacity Development: The UNDP Approach." http://content.undp.org/CDS_Brochure_2009.pdf.
———. 2011. *Human Development Index 2011 Rankings*. http://hdr.undp.org/en/statistics.
USAID. 2009. "Security Sector Reform." http://pdf.usaid.gov/pdf_docs/pnadn788.pdf.
Utley, Garrick. 1997. "The Shrinking of Foreign News: From Broadcast to Narrowcast." *Foreign Affairs* 76 (2): 2–10.
Verjee, Aly. 2011. "Two Nations, Two Messes." *Globe and Mail*, 6 July, A15.
Von Einsiedel, Sebastian. 2005. "Policy Responses to State Failure." In *Making States Work: State Failure and the Crisis of Governance*, edited by S. Chesterman, M. Ignatieff, and R. Thakur, 13–35. New York: United Nations University Press.
Warren, David. 2011. "Reason for Hope in a New Country." *Ottawa Citizen*, 9 July, B6.
Washington Post. 2010. "A Wager on Sudan; Omar Al-Bashir, Reelected by Fraud, Says He'll Allow a Fair Vote on Dividing the Country." Editorial. 2 May, A16.
———. 2011. "Crisis in Sudan." Editorial. 25 May, A18.
Weaver, David. 2007. "Thoughts on Agenda Setting, Framing, and Priming." *Journal of Communication* 57 (1): 142–47.

Western, Jon. 2005. *Selling Intervention and War: The Presidency, the Media, and the American Public*. Baltimore, MD: Johns Hopkins University Press.

Williams, Rocklyn. 2000. "Africa and the Challenges of Security Sector Reform." In *Building Stability in Africa: Challenges for the New Millennium*, edited by Jakkie Cilliers and Annika Hilding-Norberg. Monograph 46. Pretoria: Institute for Security Studies. http://www.issafrica.org/Pubs/Monographs/No46/Africa.html.

Wire Services. 2011a. "Sudan; Northern Army Takes Control of Oil-Rich Region." *Ottawa Citizen*, 23 May, A7.

———. 2011b. "Sudan; Bashir Says Abyei Belongs to North." *Ottawa Citizen*, 25 May, A9.

———. 2011c. United Nations; Officials Propose Sudan Peacekeeping Force." *Ottawa Citizen*, 26 May, C6.

———. 2011d. "U.N. Report Warns of Ethnic Cleansing." *Washington Post*, 4 June, A5.

———. 2011e. "Sudan; 'Huge Suffering' Caused by Airstrikes, UN Says." *Ottawa Citizen*, 15 June, 12.

———. 2011f. "United Nations; Security Council Orders Force to Sudan." *Ottawa Citizen*, 28 June, A8.

———. 2011g. "Sudan's Warring Parties Sign South Kordofan Accord." *Ottawa Citizen*, 29 June, A8.

———. 2011h. "Birth of a Nation; After a Half-Century Struggle, the Republic of South Sudan Marks Its Independence Day." *Globe and Mail*, 9 July, A23.

———. 2011i. "United Nations; South Sudan Acclaimed As Member." *Ottawa Citizen*, 15 July, A6.

Wolfsfeld, Gadi. 1997. *Media and Political Conflict: News From the Middle East*. Cambridge: Cambridge University Press.

———. 2004. *Media and the Path to Peace*. Cambridge: Cambridge University Press.

World Bank. 2011. *Data: Poverty*. http://data.worldbank.org/topic/poverty.

Wu, Haoming. 1998. "Investigating the Determinants of International News Flow: A Meta-Analysis." *Gazette* 60 (3): 493–512.

Wyatt, Clarence. 1993. *Paper Soldiers: The American Press and the Vietnam War*. New York: Norton.

York, Geoffrey. 2010a. "As Vote Nears, Hope for Change Fades in Sudan." *Globe and Mail*, 7 April, A14.

———. 2010b. "Sudanese Prepare to Vote, but Keep the Guns Handy." *Globe and Mail*, 10 April, A17.

———. 2010c. "Peace Prevails as Sudan Goes to the Polls." *Globe and Mail*, 12 April, A11.

———. 2010d. "For Sudanese Activists, Path to Peace Is Online." *Globe and Mail*, 14 April, A16.

———. 2010e. "Sudanese President's Re-Election Pushes Country toward Breakup." *Globe and Mail*, 27 April, A12.

———. 2011a. "Sudanese Son Returns Home for the Birth of a New Nation." *Globe and Mail*, 6 January, A1.

———. 2011b. "To Divide but Not to Conquer." *Globe and Mail*, 7 January, A13.

———. 2011c. "Countdown to the World's Unlikeliest State." *Globe and Mail*, 8 January, F5.

———. 2011d. "The Great Divide." *Globe and Mail*, 8 January, A18.

———. 2011e. "Clooney's Cameo in a National Drama." *Globe and Mail*, 10 January, A11.

———. 2011f. "Queues Long, Emotions High as Sudan Votes." *Globe and Mail*, 10 January, A11.

———. 2011g. "Violence Erupts in Disputed Area of Sudan." *Globe and Mail*, 11 January, A13.

———. 2011h. "Calm Prevails as Southern Sudanese Vote." *Globe and Mail*, 14 January, A14.

———. 2011i. "New Law/New Order/Old Values." *Globe and Mail*, 17 January, A1.

———. 2011j. "Sudan Split Likely—But Hurdles Still Remain." *Globe and Mail*, 22 January, A22.

———. 2011k. "Darfuri Refugees Take Hope in Southern Sudan." *Globe and Mail*, 25 January, A16.

———. 2012. "South Sudan's Riches Lost in Black Hole of Corruption." *Globe and Mail*, 6 June.

Young, John. 2012. "Sudan and the Failure of Liberal Peacemaking." Canadian International Council. 17 May. http://opencanada.org/features/the-think-tank/sudan-and-the-failure-of-liberal-peacemaking.

Zartman, I. William. 1995. *Collapsed States: The Disintegration and Restoration of Legitimate Authority*. Boulder, CO: Lynne Rienner.

Zayan, Jailan. 2010. "Arrest Warrant an Insult." *Ottawa Citizen*, 10 April, A13.

THE AUTHORS

E. Donald Briggs (Ph.D., University of London, 1961) is Professor Emeritus of Political Science at the University of Windsor, where he taught international relations and African politics from 1963 until his retirement in 1999. His interest in intervention and mass media dates back to his Ph.D. dissertation, *The Anglo-French Incursion into Suez, 1956*, which analyzed press opinion regarding the legality of the 1956 Suez invasion. Among his publications are *Media and Elections in Canada* (1984), "The Zapatista Rebellion in Chiapas, 1994" (2003), *Humanitarian Crises and International Intervention: Reassessing the Role of Mass Media* (2008), *The Responsibility to Protect in Darfur: The Role of Mass Media* (2010), and *Africa's Deadliest Conflict: Media Coverage of the Congo and the United Nations Response, 1997–2008* (Wilfrid Laurier University Press, 2012). For many years he was the coordinator of the WUSC (World University Service of Canada) program at the University of Windsor, in which capacity he was responsible for sponsoring fifteen refugee students from conflict-ridden countries in Africa to Canada.

Walter C. Soderlund (Ph.D., University of Michigan, 1970) is Professor Emeritus in the Department of Political Science at the University of Windsor. He has a long-standing interest in intervention, beginning in the late 1960s with research for his Ph.D. dissertation, *The Functional Roles of Intervention in International Politics*. He has also worked extensively in the area of international communication, where his focus has been on the Caribbean, especially the way in which events in Cuba and Haiti have been portrayed in North American media and the possible impact of this coverage on US foreign policy. He is the author of *Media Definitions of Cold War Reality* (2001) and *Mass Media and Foreign Policy* (2003), and the co-author of *Humanitarian Crises and Intervention: Reassessing the Role of Mass Media* (2008), *The Responsibility to Protect in Darfur: The Role of Mass Media* (2010), *Cross-Media Ownership and Democratic Practice in Canada: Content-Sharing and the Impact of New Media* (2012), and *Africa's Deadliest Conflict: Media Coverage of the Congo and the United Nations Response, 1997–2008* (Wilfrid Laurier University Press, 2012).

INDEX

Abboud, Ibrahim, President of Sudan, 7
Abramowitz, Michael, 78–79, 113
Abyei crisis: accusations of ethnic cleansing during, 99, 105; air strikes, 90, 134n3; efforts to resolve, 99–100; international reaction to, 91–92, 98–99; Khartoum tactics in, 93–94; media coverage, 90; refugees, 99. *See also* South Sudan, Republic of
Abyei region: capital town, 134n2 (chap. 7); characteristics, 11–12; Ethiopian peacekeeping forces in, 42, 88, 92, 114; ethnic groups and violence, 68, 77, 128n8; militia, 73–74; oil production and revenue, 67, 128n8; post-referendum situation in, 80–81; referendum on territorial status in, 128n7; Sudanese army invasion in, 85, 86, 87–88. *See also* Sudan
Aday, Sean, 49, 50–51
Addis Ababa Accord (1972), 7–8, 127n5, 127n6, 128n8
Afghanistan, 49, 130n10
African Standby Force (ASF), 32, 33, 35–37, 130n13
African Union (AU), 32, 35, 37
African Union Mission in Sudan (AMIS), 37–38, 130n15
African Union Peace and Security Council (PSC), 35
Agar, Malik, 92, 94, 134n4
Agence France-Presse, 55, 56, 70, 71, 87, 88

Agenda for Peace (Boutros-Ghali), 16
Ajang, John, 77
al-Bashir, Omar. *See* Bashir, Omar al-, President of Sudan
Allison, Graham, 27
Amnesty International, 120
An, Seon-Kyoung, 47
Anglo-Egyptian Condominium, 3–4
Anglo-Egyptian Treaty (1899), 4
Angola, 131n16
Annan, Kofi A., 17, 30
Anya Nya movement, 7, 8
Arab Spring, 120, 129n5
Aristide, Jean-Bertrand, 26
Arman, Yasser, 56
Arnold, Matthew, 2, 121, 127n6, 128n7, 130n10
Associated Press, 74, 81, 90, 97, 100
Athor, George, 74, 78, 81
Audet, François, 129n7
Australia, 31
Autesserre, Séverine, 23, 28, 130n11
Azar, Edward E., 128n1 (chap. 2), 129n6

Ban, Ki-moon, 86, 118
Bashir, Omar al-, President of Sudan: accusations of genocide, 6, 75, 78, 107, 115, 127n3; anti-Western policy, 73; character, 134n1 (chap. 8); control over militia, 118; meeting with Salva Kiir, 124; policy toward South Sudan, 58, 77, 103, 105; position on Abyei crisis, 87, 93;

role in Sudanese referendum, 67, 107; SLMP's opposition to, 59, 62; Sudanese elections and, 53–54, 55, 57, 61, 133n2 (chap. 5); threats to political regime of, 71, 73, 120; trip to China, 100; US negotiations with, 29, 61, 115
Battalion 105, mutiny of, 8
Beer, David, 26–27, 129n8
Bellafante, Ginia, 133n1 (chap. 5)
Ben Ali, Zine El Abidine, 129n5
Benjamin, Barnaba Marial, 70, 88, 90
Bentiu region, 100, 118, 124, 125
Berinsky, Adam, 49, 51
Berman, Eric, 129n4
Bin Laden, Osama, 10
Blair, Dennis, 61, 111
Bloomberg, 55
Blue Nile, State, 92, 93, 120, 136n9
Boswell, Alan, 71, 72, 81, 123
Bouazizi, Mohamed, 129n5
Boutros-Ghali, Boutros, 16
Bräutigam, Deborah, 24
Brennan, John, 92
Britain: Equatorial Corps, 127n4; policy toward Sudan, 4, 6; "Southern Policy," 3; in Suez Crisis, 14
Brown, Michael, 22
Bruce, Malcolm, 123
Bush, George, 43
Bush, George W., 29, 79, 96, 102

Cable News Network (CNN), 44, 124
Callaghan, Karen, 44, 47
Canada: foreign aid, 66, 86, 129n7; mass media, 52; policy toward Sudan, 54, 66–67, 113–14
Canadian International Development Agency, 89
Canadian Media Research Consortium, 109
Canwest Global, 55
capacity building, 25, 26–27, 130n10
Caplan, Gerald, 119
Carment, David, 41
Carter Center, 69, 88
celebrity diplomacy, 68, 96, 104, 133n2 (chap. 6), 133n8, 135–36n8
Central Intelligence Agency (CIA), 20

Chad, 33–34
Chalk, Frank, 43, 52
Cheney, Dick, 73
China's economic interests in Sudan, 92, 100
Chrétien, Jean, 17
Christian missionaries in Sudan, 3, 7
Cilliers, Jakkie, 39
Civilian Peace Service Canada (CPSC), 38
Clark, Jeffrey, 43
Clarke, Jeremy, 89
Clinton, Hillary, 61, 73, 97, 101, 102, 105, 123–24
Clooney, George, 68, 78, 96, 97, 98–99, 101, 104, 112, 114, 133n8
Cohen, Bernard, 43, 44, 45
Cold War, 14, 16, 35, 43
Cole, Madeleine, 69
collective security, 13
Comprehensive Peace Agreement (CPA), 11–12, 107, 127n6, 136n9
Conference on Environment and Development (UNCED), 15
conflict mitigation, 128n1 (chap. 2)
conflict prevention, 19, 22–23, 41–42, 117
conflict prevention strategies: capacity building, 25–27; development aid, 22–25; preventive diplomacy, 29–30; rapid deployment of peacekeeping missions, 30–31; trust and confidence building, 27–29
conflict resolution, concept of local, 130n11
conflicts, nature of modern, 16, 20
Congo, Democratic Republic of the, 14, 28, 51, 121, 131n18
Corporate Warriors: The Rise of the Privatized Military Industry (Singer), 39
Côte d'Ivoire, 32
Cuban Missile Crisis, 27
Cyprus, 14, 28

Daily Telegraph, The, 70, 71
Dallaire, Roméo, 43, 52, 66, 113
Darfur crisis: al-Bashir's role in, 6, 105; comparison to Nuba Mountains crisis, 94, 95; efforts to resolve, 37, 75; media coverage, 45–46, 51, 71, 132n6, 132n9,

135n3; origin of, 133n3; potential consequences for Sudan, 120; public reaction to, 115
Darfur region: genocide in, 75, 135n3; Khartoum's policy toward, 70, 91; poverty in, 57; UN mission in, 30. *See also* Sudan
Debrah, Charles, 34, 35, 36
Deng, Francis Mading, 1–2, 6, 11
Deng, William Deng, 73
development aid, 23, 24–25
Diara, Ousmane, 130n14
Diehl, Jackson, 101, 134n7
Dinka. *See* Ngok Dinka people
Doctors Without Borders, 119
Donnelly, Jack, 29
donor fatigue, 123
Druckman, James, 49, 50
Dueck, Lorna, 119

Eachus, Todd, 44
Eagleburger, Lawrence, 43
Eastern Africa Standby Force (EASBRIG), 32
Economic Community of West Africa Cease-fire Monitoring Group (ECOMOG), 35
Economic Community of West African States (ECOWAS), 32, 34–35
Edwards, Steven, 71
Edy, Jill, 49
Egypt: during Arab Spring, 97, 98, 120, 129n5; links to Sudan, 2–4, 5, 127n1; in Suez Crisis, 14
Einsiedel, Sebastian von, 19, 21, 22
Enough Project, 57, 90, 133n8
Entman, Robert, 46
Equatorial Corps' mutiny, 7
Eritrea, 9, 32, 86
Ethiopia: peacekeeping mission in Abyei region, 42, 88, 92, 114; policy toward Sudan, 8–9, 10; Standby High Readiness Brigade's mission to, 31–32; US criticism of, 76
Ethiopian Standby Force, 42
ethnic cleansing, 91, 100, 104, 105, 113, 114
European Union, 69, 122

failed state, 20, 21, 128n3, 129n4
Failed State Index, 21
Fantino, Julian, 129n7
Farouk I, King of Egypt, 127n2
Finnemore, Martha, 128n2 (chap. 2)
Fitzsimmons, Scott, 40
Fleishman, Jeffrey, 70
Flint, Julie, 94
Foreign Policy (journal), 21
foreign policy decision making, 43–44, 135n3
France, 14, 26, 31, 34

Gamson, William, 132n5
Gaouette, Nicole, 55
Garang, John, 8, 127n6, 136n9
Gates, Jana Chapman, 74
genocide: accusations of al-Bashir in, 107, 127n3; in Darfur, 75, 135n3; in media language, 100, 101, 104, 114; in Rwanda, 21, 124, 131n17, 132n8; in Sudan, fears of, 61, 79, 105, 111, 113, 119
Gershoni, Yekutiel, 35
Gerson, Michael, 60, 101, 102, 112
Gettleman, Jeffrey, 56, 57, 58, 62, 72–76, 90, 92–93, 95, 96, 97, 133n2 (chap. 5), 134n5
Gieng, William Garjang, 81
Glennie, Jonathan, 23, 24, 130n9
Glickman, Dan, 59, 62, 112
Global Centre for the Responsibility to Protect, 71
Globe and Mail, The: on Canada's role in Sudan, 114; on conflicts in Abyei and Nuba Mountains regions, 108; on independence of South Sudan, 85–87, 104, 134n1 (chap. 7); online editions, 52, 131n1; ranking, 132n13; on Sudanese election, 53–55; on Sudanese referendum, 65–70; type of content, 82
Goldstone, Jack, 129n3
Gower, Clara, 47
Graham, Franklin, 101
Gration, Scott, 72, 80, 107, 112
Gration, Scott, Special Envoy to Sudan, 58, 61
Grindle, Merilee, 25

Griswold, Eliza, 73, 91
Grzyb, Amanda, 119, 135n3
Gulf War (1990–1991), 48–49

Haiti, 16, 26–27, 129–30n9, 129n7
Hamad, Mohammed, 73, 77
Hamilton, Rebecca, 22, 37–38, 42, 78, 80–81, 98–99, 102, 107–9, 130n15, 132n10, 135n3, 136n6
Haroun, Ahmed, 134n5
Hawk, Beverley, 131n3
Heglig oil field, 118, 123
Helman, Gerald, 23, 41
Henry, Jehanne, 122
Hikmat, Fouad, 98
Hilderbrand, Mary, 25
Hilsum, Lindsey, 132n8
Hogendoorn, E.J., 57
Howe, Herbert, 34
Hua Jiang, 94
humanitarian intervention, 16
human rights violations, 11, 17, 20, 69, 95, 98, 99, 122
Human Rights Watch, 122
human security, 14, 31, 66, 114, 129n4

Innes, Michael, 35
International Commission on Intervention and State Sovereignty (ICISS), 17–18, 19, 41
International Country Risk Guide, 24
International Criminal Court (ICC), 6, 127n3
International Criminal Investigative Training Assistance Program (ICITAP), 26, 129n8
International Crisis Group, 57, 71
International Monetary Fund, 120
International Relief and Development, 71
International Security Assistance Force in Afghanistan, 130n10
Internet, 109, 131n1. *See also* mass media
Islam: in Africa, expansion of, 4; in Egypt, 2; in Sudan, spread and consolidation of, 9–10
Iyengar, Shanto, 48, 132n7

Johansen, Robert, 38
Johnson, Douglas, 3, 7, 8, 11, 83, 91, 104, 114, 128n8
Jonge Oudraat, Chantal de, 22
Jonglei State, 74, 121
Juba, 54, 58, 96, 119, 122, 123. *See also* South Sudan, Republic of
Juma'a, Izdihar, 97
Justice Africa-Sudan, 71
Just Peace movement, 89

Kadugli, 93
Kasumba, Yvonne, 34, 35, 36
Keefe, Tania, 32
Keller, Edmond, 33, 41
Kent, Vanessa, 37
Kenya, 3, 5, 30
Kerry, John, 72, 79, 80, 112, 121, 125
Khartoum, 2, 6, 7, 9, 10, 66, 71, 89, 120. *See also* Sudan
Khouri, Rami, 69
Kiir, Salva: corruption allegations admitted by, 122–23; meeting with al-Bashir, 124; political rivals, 121, 122; position on Abyei crisis, 91; President of South Sudan, 102, 118; Sudanese elections and, 54, 55, 62, 133n2 (chap. 5); US policy toward, 123
Kinder, Donald, 49, 51
King, Gary, 21, 128n3 (chap. 3)
Kirby, Steve, 72
Knack, Stephen, 24
Koka Dam Declaration (1986), 10
Koops, Joachim, 31, 32
Kosovo Crisis, 30, 49–50
Kristof, Nicholas, 58, 62, 112, 114, 135n5
Kron, Josh, 72–73, 76, 78, 90, 92, 93
Kuol, Kuol Deng, 80
Kushkush, Isma'il, 97

Lacey, Marc, 37
Lacher, Wolfram, 67
Laessing, Ulf, 89, 98
Lagu, Joseph, 7
Landler, Mark, 58
Langille, Peter, 32
Lanzer, Toby, 124

Lavallee, Guillaume, 56
Lebanon, 14
LeRiche, Matthew, 2, 121, 127n6, 128n7, 130n10
Liberia, 34–35, 41, 96
Libya, 10, 116, 128n2 (chap. 2)
Lie, Trygve, 31
Lippmann, Walter, 45
Livingston, Steven, 44
Logan, Justin, 129n4
Lord's Resistance Army (Uganda), 76
Lueth, Michael Makuei, 67
Lyman, Princeton, 90, 98, 101

Maasho, Aaron, 88
Machar, Riek, 121–22, 124
Mahdi, Sadiq al-, 9, 76
Mahdiyya (Mahdist regime), 4
Malan, Mark, 37
Malek, Nyandeng, 99
Mali, 130n14
Mallaby, Sebastian, 23, 41
Martelly, Michel, 129n9
Massey, Simon, 34
mass media: agenda setting, 45–46; on Canada's role in Sudan, 114–15; comparison of US and Canadian, 61–62, 61–82, 103–5, 131n2; criticism of US policy in Sudan by, 112–13; Darfur conflict coverage by, 132n6, 132n9, 135n3; events in Sudan covered by, 51–52, 82; foreign policy decision making and, 43; framing, 47–51, 62–63, 82–83, 104–5, 110–15, 132n5; international news coverage, 131n3; language of, 113–14; newspaper content study, 109–10; online archives, 52, 132n14; power and influence, 44, 45, 110, 132n11; priming, 132n7; research methods, 51–52, 53; role of printed, 109; shrinking budgets, 133n1 (chap. 5); sources of information, 132n8, 132n10; South Sudan coverage by, 108, 109–10; Sudanese election coverage by, 53–62; Sudanese referendum coverage by, 65–81; television and Internet, 109, 131n1; type of content, 110. *See also* news; individual newspapers and news agencies

Matthes, Jörg, 48
Matthews, Robert, 10
May, Roy, 34
Mays, Terry, 34
Mazen, Maram, 55
Mbeki, Thabo, 87–88, 103, 124
McClatchey-Tribune News, 70, 71
McCombs, Maxwell, 45, 46
McDonald, Alun, 72
Mclean, Jim, 70
Meirick, Patrick, 49
Meredith, Martin, 127n2
Mermin, Jonathan, 44
Misseriya people, 68, 77, 81, 90, 118
Modigliani, Andre, 132n5
Mohammed, Hafiz, 71
Moyo, Dambisa, 24
Mubarak, Hosni, 129n5
Mudawi Ibrahim Adam, 58
Mugabe, Robert, 30
Muhammad Ali, Governor of Egypt, 3
Muritihi, Tim, 36
Murle tribes, 121
Musa, Nagi, 55
Mustafa, El-Tayyib, 89
Mutiga, Murithi, 74, 75

Nafie, Nafie Ali, 70
National Congress Party (NCP), 71, 134n1 (chap. 8)
Natsios, Andrew, 3, 7, 29, 59, 62, 80, 115, 120, 134n1 (chap. 8), 135n6, 136n9
Nelson, Thomas, 46, 47
news: factual content and presentation, 46–47; low attention to international, 108; sources of, 109. *See also* mass media
New York Times, The: on Abyei crisis, 90; on Clinton's visit to Juba, 124; on Congo election, 134n2 (chap. 8); crisis news stories in, 47; online archive, 52; ranking, 132n13; on Sudanese election, 53, 56–59; on Sudanese independence, 89–97; on Sudanese referendum, 72–78; type fo content, 82, 109
Ngok Dinka people, 11, 77, 81, 87, 96, 99, 102, 118, 122, 124, 128n8
Nigeria, 34

Nimeiri, Jaafar, President of Sudan, 7, 8
Notter, James, 27–28
Nuba Mountains region, 93, 94, 95, 118–19
Nuba Mountains revolt, 136n9
Nuba people, 87, 94, 95, 103, 105
Nubia, 2
Nuer people, 96, 121, 122, 124
Nuland, Victoria, 118

Obama, Barack: on Abyei crisis, 92, 100; criticism of foreign policy, 112; diplomacy, 78; policy toward Sudan, 62, 74–75, 77, 79–80, 101, 102, 103, 107, 134n7; President Kiir and, 123; on Sudanese election, 58. *See also* United States
oil industry, 113, 118, 123
Organization for Economic Cooperation and Development (OECD), 19
Organization of African Unity (OAU), 33–34, 76
Ottawa Citizen, 53, 61, 81; on Canada's role in Sudan, 114; on independence of South Sudan, 87–89, 104; online archive, 52; ranking, 132n11; on Sudanese election, 55–56; on Sudanese referendum, 70–72
Owens, Richard, 71

Pagliaro, Jennifer, 66, 113
Palin, Sarah, 101
Patey, Luke, 12
peace enforcement, 16
peacekeeping: concept of, 14; contradiction to principle of state sovereignty, 16; missions in Africa, 33–38; private military contractors and, 39–41
peacekeeping forces in Africa, 30–31, 87, 88, 92
Pearson, Glen, 66, 113
Pflanz, Mike, 72
Poggo, Scopas Sekwat, 127n4
Political Instability Task Force reports, 128n2 (chap. 3)
Postmedia Network Canada Corporation, 71
Postmedia News, 70, 71
Powell, Colin, 46, 135n3

Power, Samantha, 78, 80, 112, 125
Preble, Christopher, 129n4
Prendergast, John, 57, 90, 97, 98–99, 104, 114
press. *See* mass media
preventive diplomacy, 30, 107–8
Price, Vincent, 47
private military contractors, 39–41
project Camelot, 19–20, 128n1 (chap. 3)
Project Enough. *See* Enough Project
public opinion, 43–44, 135n3

Raghavan, Sudarsan, 78, 80
Ratner, Steven, 23, 41
Reeves, Eric, 92–93, 94, 97, 100, 104, 114
refugees, 6, 70, 81, 99, 119, 131n17
Refugees International, 59
Reno, William, 76
responsibility to prevent, 17–18
responsibility to protect (R2P), 17–18, 19, 114, 128n2 (chap. 2)
responsibility to react, 62, 113
Reuters, 56, 70, 71, 72, 77–78, 87
Revolutionary Front (Sierra Leone), 40
Reynolds, Amy, 46
Rice, Susan, 60, 61, 94, 95, 101, 102, 107, 112
Rio Conference. *See* Conference on Environment and Development (UNCED)
Robinson, Piers, 44, 45, 115
Rovera, Donatella, 124
Rwanda, 16, 17, 30; genocide in, 21, 124, 131n17, 137n8

Sams, Katie, 129n4
Sankoh, Foday Saybana, 40
Satellite Sentinel Project, 68, 78, 103, 133n8
Savimbi, Jonas Malheiro, 40
Scheufele, Dietram, 49
Schnell, Frauke, 44, 47
Semetko, Holli, 47
Serrano, Monica, 71
Shaw, Donald, 45
Sheridan, Mary Beth, 61, 78, 79–80, 102
Sherman, Nancy, 51, 132n11
Sidahmed, Abdel Salam, 5, 11, 132n9
Sidahmed, Alsir, 5
Sierra Leone, 40, 131n16

Sikkink, Kathryn, 128n2 (chap. 2)
Simon, Adam, 48, 132n7
Singer, P. W. (Peter Warren), 39, 40, 131n17
slave trade, 2–3, 7
Smith, David, 124
Soderlund, Walter, 43, 128n1 (chap. 3), 131n3
Somalia, 16, 43
Southern Africa Development Community (SADC), 34
Southern Sudan (region): autonomy, 7–8; British policy toward, 5, 88–89; cholera outbreak, 125–26; hostility to Arabs, 80; humanitarian crisis, 60; impact of secession on wider Africa, 76; international aid to, 71; islamization of, 7, 9; land abandonment, 126; literacy rate, 67, 69; media coverage of situation in, 132n6; parallels between Congo and, 29; politics, 74; post-war reconstruction, 76–77; poverty, 54; pre-referendum situation, 75–76; prospects of independence, 6, 54, 58, 69, 70; public attention to, 46, 131n4; public health and living conditions, 67, 69; representation in federal government, 6; returnees, 71, 133n4; slave trade in, 3; UN peacekeeping forces in, 79; victims of armed conflict, 12; violence in, 67, 68, 78; water contamination, 81
Southern Sudan Disarmament, Demobilization and Reintegration Commission, 73
Southern Sudan Liberation Movement (SSLM), 7–8
South Kordofan: fears of genocide in, 105; human rights violations in, 95; mass graves in, 103; Mbeki's efforts to resolve conflict in, 87–88; media coverage, 87, 88, 90, 92, 93; refugees, 100, 134n6; territorial integrity of Sudan and, 120; UN policy in, 94, 96; violence in, 85, 86, 134n5
South Sudan, Republic of: Christians in, 101; corruption, 122–23; declaration of independence, 85; domestic policy, 86–87, 103, 121–22, 125–26; ethnic conflicts, 122, 124, 125; international aid to, 86, 125; international conference on, 125; Khartoum's embargo, 99; media coverage of situation in, 85–103, 108t, 109–11; oil revenue division agreement, 124; post-independence development, 97, 101–3; poverty rate, 86; prospects of survival, 63, 88–89; relations with the north, 101–2; social conditions after independence, 86, 89, 102; ties with Uganda, 95–96; violence in, 121, 122. *See also* Abyei crisis; Juba
Spearin, Christopher, 41
Standby High Readiness Brigade (SHIRBRIG), 31–33, 37, 42
State Failure Task Force, 20
Strobel, Warren, 44
sub-Saharan Africa, 23, 24–25, 117
Sudan: Addis Ababa Accord, 7–8; African Union mission in, 37–38; al-Qaeda links to, 10–11; Arab Spring and, 69, 120; army, 73, 127n4; Bentiu bombing, 118; British policy in, 4; Canada's policy in, 54, 66–67, 113–14; city riots, 120; civil war casualties, 57, 79; economy, 57, 120; elections (2010), 53–62; fears of genocide in, 61, 79, 105, 111, 113, 119; First Civil War, 6–7, 8; foreign policy, 9–10; independence, 5; indigenous values and institutions, 5–6; mass media on situation in, 45–46, 52, 113–14; National Congress Party (NCP), 54; nation building, 1–2; north–south divide, 3–4, 71–72, 89, 101–2, 118; north–south peace agreement (2005), 96; oil industry, 67, 113, 118; opposition parties, 71–72; political regimes, 4, 6; post-conflict rebuilding in, 128n1 (chap. 2), 129n6, 130n10; poverty, 57; preventive diplomacy in, 29–30; referendum (2011), 65–81, 133n1 (chap. 6); Second Civil War, 9, 128n8; Turkiyya (Turco-Egyptian rule), 3; US policy toward, 10–11, 78–79, 107–8, 125, 135n6. *See also* Abyei region; Darfur region
Sudan People's Liberation Army (SPLA), 8–9, 72, 87, 127n6

Sudan People's Liberation Movement (SPLM), 54, 55, 56, 60, 88, 119, 120, 133n2 (chap. 5)
Suez Crisis, 14
Syria, 30, 116

television, 109. *See also* mass media
Temin, Jon, 78, 81
terrorism, 10–11
Times, The, 70
trust-building strategies, 27–28
Tunisia, 69, 97, 98, 129n5
Turabi, Hassan al-, 10

Uganda, 76, 89, 95–96
UN Commission on Global Governance, 15–16
UN Emergency Peace Service (UNEPS), 38–39
Union for the Total Independence of Angola (UNITA), 40
United Nations: Abyei crisis and, 91; Brahimi Report, 35; conferences and summits, 15; Department of Peacekeeping Operations (DPKO), 31, 32, 131n17; diplomacy, 29; Intervention Brigade, 131n18; Millennium Assembly (2000), 17; Mission in the Democratic Republic of Congo (MONUC), 130n11; missions to Darfur, 30; origin and goals, 13; peacekeeping forces, 16, 17, 30–31, 87; peacekeeping operations, 14, 16, 31, 130n12, 130n14, 131n17; programs and commissions, 15–16, 17; report on violence in Sudan, 71; support of South Sudan independence, 86; use of private contractors, 39
United Nations–African Union Mission in Darfur (UNAMID), 38
United Nations Development Programme (UNDP), 25–26
United Nations Mission for South Sudan (UNMISS), 87
United Nations Mission in Liberia (UNMIL), 130n12
United Nations Missions in Sudan (UNMIS), 130n12
United Nations Operation in Côte d'Ivoire (UNOCI), 130n12

United States: Abyei crisis and, 90, 91–92, 98; Darfur conflict and, 96; intervention to Somalia, 43; mass media, 52; negotiations with al-Bashir, 29, 61, 115; policy toward Sudan, 10–11, 78–79, 107–8, 125, 135n6; position on Sudanese referendum, 60–61; response to violence in Sudan, 58–59; Suez Crisis and, 14
United States Agency for International Development, 76
United Nations: Disarmament, Demobilization and Reintegration (DDR), 128n1 (chap. 2), 129n6
US Army's Special Operations Research Office (SORO), 19–20
USA Today, 47
US International Criminal Investigative Training Assistance Program (ICITAP), 26

Valkenburg, Peter, 47
Varwick, Johannes, 31, 32
Verjee, Aly, 86
Vertin, Zach, 71, 80, 90
violence: in Abyei region, 77; Bentiu bombing, 118; Christmas Day rampage, 68, 113; in Darfur, 70; failed states and, 21; in Nuba Mountains, 95, 118–19; prediction of, 22; in Southern Kordofan, 85, 86, 134n5; in Southern Sudan, 67, 68–70, 81, 96; during Sudanese election, 54

Waal, Alex de, 99
Walkley, R. Barrie, 96
Warrap State, 99
Warren, David, 88
Washington Post, The: criticism of Obama's policy, 113; online archives, 52; ranking, 132n13; on Sudanese election, 59–61, 62; on Sudanese independence, 97–103; on Sudanese referendum, 78–81
West African Standby Force (ECOBRIG), 32
Western, Jon, 47
Williams, Rocklyn, 26
Williams, Rowan, 94
Winter, Roger, 94

Wolf, Frank, 101
Wolfsfeld, Gadi, 46, 51, 108, 110
World Summit of Children (1990), 15

Yin Gang, 100
York, Geoffrey, 53, 54, 65, 66–69, 112, 113, 123, 133n1 (chap. 6), 133n2 (chap. 6), 135n7

Young, John, 136n9
Yugoslavia, disintegration of, 16

Zartman, William, 21
Zayan, Jailan, 56
Zelikow, Philip, 27
Zeng, Langche, 21, 128n3 (chap. 3)
Zuber, Robert, 38

**Books in the Studies in International Governance Series
Published by Wilfrid Laurier University Press**

Irrelevant or Indispensable? The United Nations in the 21st Century edited by Paul Heinbecker and Patricia Goff | 2005 | xii + 196 pp. | ISBN 978-0-88920-493-5

Haiti: Hope for a Fragile State edited by Yasmine Shamsie and Andrew S. Thompson | 2006 | xvi + 131 pp. | ISBN 978-0-88920-510-9

Canada and the Middle East: In Theory and Practice edited by Paul Heinbecker and Bessma Momani | 2007 | ix + 232 pp. | ISBN 978-1-55458-024-8

Exporting Good Governance: Temptations and Challenges in Canada's Aid Program edited by Jennifer Welsh and Ngaire Woods | 2007 | xx + 343 pp. | ISBN 978-1-55458-029-3

Critical Mass: The Emergence of Global Civil Society edited by James W. St.G. Walker and Andrew S. Thompson | 2008 | xxviii + 302 pp. | ISBN 978-1-55458-022-4

Afghanistan: Transition under Threat edited by Geoffrey Hayes and Mark Sedra | 2008 | xxxiv + 314 pp. | ISBN 978-1-55458-011-8

Emerging Powers in Global Governance: Lessons from the Heiligendamm Process edited by Andrew F. Cooper and Agata Antkiewicz | 2008 | xxii + 370 pp. | ISBN 978-1-55458-057-6

Can the World Be Governed? Possibilities for Effective Multilateralism edited by Alan S. Alexandroff | 2008 | vi + 438 pp. | ISBN 978-1-55458-041-5

From Civil Strife to Peace Building: Examining Private Sector Involvement in West African Reconstruction edited by Hany Besada | 2009 | xxiii + 287 pp. | ISBN 978-1-55458-052-1

The Global Food Crisis: Governance Challenges and Opportunities edited by Jennifer Clapp and Marc J. Cohen | 2009 | xviii + 270 pp. | ISBN 978-1-55458-192-4

Implementing WIPO's Development Agenda edited by Jeremy de Beer | 2009 | xvi + 188 pp. | ISBN 978-1-55458-154-2

Redesigning the World Trade Organization for the Twenty-first Century edited by Debra P. Steger | 2009 | xx + 478 pp. | ISBN 978-1-55458-156-6

Backpacks Full of Hope: The UN Mission in Haiti by Eduardo Aldunate, translated by Alma Flores | 2010 | xx + 232 pp. | ISBN 978-1-55458-155-9

From Desolation to Reconstruction: Iraq's Troubled Journey edited by Mokhtar Lamani and Bessma Momani | 2010 | xi + 246 pp. | ISBN 978-1-55458-229-7

Africa's Deadliest Conflict: Media Coverage of the Humanitarian Disaster in the Congo and the United Nations Response, 1997–2008 by Walter C. Soderlund, E. Donald Briggs, Tom Pierre Najem, and Blake C. Roberts | 2012 | xix + 237 pp. | ISBN 978-1-55458-835-0

The Independence of South Sudan: The Role of Mass Media in the Responsibility to Prevent by Walter C. Soderlund and E. Donald Briggs | 2014 | xvi + 166 pp. | ISBN 978-1-77112-117-0

www.ingramcontent.com/pod-product-compliance
Lightning Source LLC
Chambersburg PA
CBHW070859080526
44589CB00013B/1125